MANAGEMENT OF INNOVATION STRATEGY IN JAPANESE COMPANIES

Japanese Management and International Studies
(ISSN: 2010-4448)

Editor-in-Chief: Yasuhiro Monden *(University of Tsukuba, Japan)*

Published

For the complete list of titles in this series, please go to
http://www.worldscientific.com/series/jmis

Japanese Management and International Studies – Vol. 13

MANAGEMENT OF INNOVATION STRATEGY IN JAPANESE COMPANIES

editors

Kazuki Hamada

Kwansei Gakuin University, Japan

Shufuku Hiraoka

Soka University, Japan

W **World Scientific**

EW JERSEY · LONDON · SINGAPORE · BEIJING · SHANGHAI · HONG KONG · TAIPEI · CHENNAI · TOKYO

Published by

World Scientific Publishing Co. Pte. Ltd.

5 Toh Tuck Link, Singapore 596224

USA office: 27 Warren Street, Suite 401-402, Hackensack, NJ 07601

UK office: 57 Shelton Street, Covent Garden, London WC2H 9HE

Library of Congress Cataloging-in-Publication Data
Names: Hamada, Kazuki, editor. | Hiraoka, Shufuku, editor.
Title: Management of innovation strategy in Japanese companies / Kazuki Hamada
    (Kwansei Gakuin University, Japan) & Shufuku Hiraoka (Soka University, Japan).
Description: New Jersey : World Scientific, [2016] | Series: Japanese management and
    international studies ; volume 13
Identifiers: LCCN 2015050085 | ISBN 9789814759625 (hc : alk. paper)
Subjects: LCSH: Management--Japan. | Technological innovations--Management--Japan. |
    New products--Japan. | Strategic planning--Japan.
Classification: LCC HD70.J3 M27184 2016 | DDC 658.4/0630952--dc23
LC record available at http://lccn.loc.gov/2015050085

British Library Cataloguing-in-Publication Data
A catalogue record for this book is available from the British Library.

Desk Editors: Herbert Moses/Lum Pui Yee

Typeset by Stallion Press
Email: enquiries@stallionpress.com

Printed in Singapore

Japan Society of Organization and Accounting (JSOA)

Mission of JSOA and Editorial Information

For the purpose of making a contribution to the business and academic communities, the Japan Society of Organization and Accounting (JSOA) is committed to publishing *Japanese Management and International Studies* (*JMIS*), which is a refereed annual publication with a specific theme for each volume.

Focusing on Japan and Japan-related issues, the series is designed to inform the world about research outcomes of the new "Japanese-style management system" developed in Japan. However, as the series title suggests, it also promotes "International Studies" on the interface of managerial competencies between Japan and other countries that include Asian countries as well as Western countries under the globalized business activities of Japanese companies.

Research topics included in this series are management of organizations in a broad sense (including the business group or inter-firm network) and the accounting for managing the organizations. More specifically, topics include business strategy, business models, organizational restoration, corporate finance, M&A, environmental management, operations management, managerial and financial accounting, manager performance evaluation, and reward systems. The research approach is interdisciplinary, which includes case studies, theoretical studies, normative studies, and empirical studies, but emphasizes real world business.

Our JSOA's board of directors have established an editorial board of international standing. In each volume, guest editors who are experts on the volume's special theme serve as the volume editors. The details of JSOA is shown in its by-laws contained in the homepage: http://jsoa.sakura.ne.jp/english/index.html

Japanese Management and International Studies (JMIS)

Rolf G Larsson, Lund University, Sweden
Jose Antonio Dominguez Machuca, University of Sevilla, Spain
Luis E. Carretero Diaz, Universidad Complutense, Spain
John Y. Lee, Pace University, USA
Kenneth A. Merchant, University of Southern California, USA
Jimmy Y.T. Tsay, National Taiwan University, Taiwan
Stephen DunHou Tsai, National Sun Yat-Sen University, Taiwan
Yanghon Chung, KAIST, Korea
Mohammad Aghdassi, Tarbiat Modarres University, Iran
Mahfuzul Hoque, University of Dhaka, Bangladesh
Walid Zaramdini, Al Akhawayn University, Morocco

Contents

Japanese Management and International Studies Vol. 13:
Management of Innovation Strategy in Japanese Companies
World Scientific Publishing Company, September 2016

Preface

In this volume, we will explore how innovation management for industrial revitalization and activation is conducted in Japanese companies. "Innovation" has diverse definitions, but we have adopted the one proposed by J. A. Schumpeter. Schumpeter notes that the purpose of innovation is to create new combinations, which involves the following: (1) introduction of a new, high-quality good, (2) introduction of a new method of production, (3) opening of a new market, (4) development of a new source of supply for raw materials or half-manufactured goods, and (5) reorganization of an industry.

Traditionally, innovation has been considered difficult to manage, as it occurs through contingent discoveries and inventions. However, effective innovation management is required for strategic management. For innovation management, it is necessary to determine what provides new value to customers and to achieve this new value efficiently while solving the technical problems. It is especially important to consider the following: (1) how we should place innovation in strategic management, (2) how the information required for encouraging the development of ideas is acquired and used, (3) what type of planning and control is used to encourage efficient innovation, and (4) how organizational culture affects innovations. Moreover, we need to consider the evaluation and resource allocation criteria for creating innovations.

This volume will cover all of these important themes in the context of Japanese companies and from the standpoint of management accounting and business administration. The book consists of three parts. The first part covers theoretical researches on the innovation management strategy and positive analyses using questionnaires. The second part discusses how innovation management strategy is being implemented specifically in individual industries and companies (i.e. case-based studies). The third part discusses the management philosophy and features underlying innovation management in Japanese companies, although innovation management is not exclusively considered here. Each paper is as follows.

PART 1. Management of Innovation Strategy and Management Control

Strategic Management and Profit Creation in the Context of Innovation: The Management of Innovation Value Chains

Japanese companies are required to gain competitive advantages through innovation and development of new products and businesses. This paper covers management methods that facilitate innovation strategies. In particular, the author divides innovation activities into three stages: (1) development of ideas, (2) selection of ideas and resources allocations, and (3) obtaining results from the products and services that have been selected. Next, he considers the appropriate management methods at each stage. In the development stage of ideas, management methods such as the promotion of innovation emergence and organizational learning are important. In the stage of idea selection and resource allocation, the establishment of appropriate evaluation criteria and allocation criteria is important. In the stage of obtaining results, it is important to create mechanisms for earning profits.

Idea Decision-Making for Innovation: How Can Good Ideas be Discovered Organizationally?

In the management control process in new business development, the author first creates and lists the ideas for new R&D projects, businesses, actions, and capital expenditures. After reviewing the list, managers have to evaluate, justify, prioritize, allocate expenses and capital budget, execute, review, and conduct an ex-post evaluation. In this paper, which reviews prior studies and company practices, the author first analyzes the current situation of this new business development. Based on the analyses, he presents several problems concerning this process and recommends better ways of handling these problems. The mission or purpose of the company, which are customer value and financial performance, plays a very important role in managing this process and solving the problems inherent in it.

Management Control System to Promote Innovation and Corporate Venturing

In this paper, by focusing on a strategy emergence model and examining if management control system (MCS) plays any role in the model to promote innovation and corporate venturing, the author proposes the possibility that an MCS may be related to strategy emergence and involve resource allocation. He adopts the Burgelman model as a strategy emergence model to examine from a broader perspective the role MCS plays in facilitating innovation and corporate venturing. The significance of Burgelman's model is that it seems to be consistent with the facts surrounding strategic changes in actual corporate organizations (particularly large corporations). The model focuses on analyzing resource allocation through vertical interactions between top and middle managements and, in particular, the role played by middle management. What is important is that a strategy has no particular meaning when it is simply formulated, and it first gains substantial meaning only when it survives competition within a company (discussion stage) and resources are allocated for it. The design of the MCS has considerable influence on the process of corporate venturing. By considering the actual examples of a leading company, the function of MCS to promote innovation and corporate venturing is examined.

Do Management Control Systems Really Contribute to Product Innovation?

The purpose of this paper is to reveal what kind of elements are requisites for MCS that affect product innovation. Recently, many articles have discussed the effects of MCS in product innovation. However, none of the articles shows definite relationships between MCS and product innovation. This paper explores organizational capabilities for exploiting management control, and monitors if these capabilities moderate the relationship between management control and product innovation. The author conducts empirical researches to determine these relationships.

Solving the Wage Differentials Throughout the Supply Chain by Collaborative Innovations for Changing the Parts Prices and Costs

The theme of this paper is to investigate how the profit differences among the companies could be resolved through changing the transaction price and costs of the parts in the supply chain, thereby reducing the wage differentials among companies. Here, the transaction price of the parts has the function to allocate the profit to be jointly attained by the ordering company (i.e. the buyer) of the parts and the ordered company (i.e. seller who will manufacture and supply the parts). For allocating the joint profit, both companies must have the collaborative activities in determining the transaction price or reducing the parts costs. Such collaboration is also required by the laws or government. The collaboration between the buyer and the seller of the parts implies that both companies will mutually provide the ideas for reducing the manufacturing cost of the parts. Depending on how each company has contributed to reduce the parts costs by applying the various ideas of each party, the total reduced amount of costs will be allocated as benefits to each partner, based on the contributing grade of each company, and thus the transaction price of the part will finally be determined. In the case of Japanese automobile industry, through the "innovation" in the parts development phase and through the "continuous improvement" in the parts manufacturing phase, both the carmaker and the parts maker have tried to reduce costs and improve quality in the longer-term transaction relations. They have actually encouraged each other to make efforts for their many times of evolutions. Such process has contributed to enhance the competitive power of the technology, productivity, and quality of both parties.

The Inherent Roles of Management Accounting for Promoting Innovation: The Case of Material Flow Cost Accounting

The purpose of this paper is to consider the inherent roles of management accounting for promoting innovation. The understanding of the relationship between innovation and management accounting has changed from negative to positive since Simons presented the concept of "interactive control systems." Studies on Simons' concept have shown the positive role of management accounting towards innovation. However, the understanding of the roles of management accounting has been limited, because Simons' concept focuses only on the ways of using information. Thus, this paper focuses on the inherent roles of management accounting to deepen our understanding of management accounting roles in promoting innovation. Through the case that material flow cost accounting (MFCA) is one of the management accounting tools that promotes innovation, this paper considers the inherent roles of management accounting for promoting innovation.

PART 2. Considerations of Innovation Management From the Perspective of Individual Industries and Companies

Innovation Strategies and Segment Reporting: A Case Study of Corporate Electronics Groups in Japan

Japan's electronics corporate groups have faced numerous challenges in the last decade. Therefore, these corporate groups have executed innovation strategies and re-structured their business portfolios to improve their financial performance. It is said that a key to success is to resolve environmental and social problems within businesses. In this paper, the author analyzes the innovation strategies of six major corporate groups involved in the business of electric goods. The impact of these strategies and consolidated financial statements on the performance of the business segments is analyzed. He then analyzes the impact of these strategies on the performance within geographical segments.

Front Loading: Key Concept of Strategy for Business Innovation in Japanese Automobile Industry

For more than half a century, the Japanese automobile industry has promoted strategic innovations and strengthened its competitiveness mainly from the viewpoints of cost competitiveness, economies of scale, and productivity. The important common trend among these innovations has been "front loading". Under these circumstances, the strategies in the Japanese automobile industry have changed to reduce the imitability of such innovations by shifting them from the visible stage of mass production/selling to the invisible stage of R&D and to raise profitability of these innovations by implementing them at the beginning of the product life cycle. In this paper, these are conceptualized as the "invisible competitive strategy".

Changes in Product Development Approaches and Target Costing

Because target costing is regarded as the management technique for the simultaneous achievement of various targets in the product development stage, and its function is extendable, its approach depends significantly on a product development approach. Regarding this point, the movements toward changes in the product development approach are observed in automakers that have, to date, made advanced efforts in target costing. This paper clarifies the changes in the product development approaches of automakers and suggests a fundamental framework for determining how the target costing approach is modified as a result of such changes. The following three features can be listed as part of the target costing approaches called for under new product development approaches: (1) Importance of target costing in the preceding development phase of common elements, (2) Importance of the development interface between the common element development and the individual product development, and (3) Importance of cost reductions from economies of scale.

Organizational Learning via Strategy Formulation and the Role of MCS in That Process: The Case of Kikkoman Corporation

In this paper, the author illustrates the process through which corporate international strategy has emerged from a strategic initiative implemented by local production of a Japanese company in the U.S. The initiative was implemented by a lower-level manager who noticed the market change. In this emerging process, for the discussion and the exchange of opinions, a task force provided the company with "ba" which means places, and the board of directors played an important role in the evaluation and selection of a strategic proposal. Local production was put off at the beginning and the process of bottling was outsourced to a local firm. This decision created an opportunity for the company to postpone the decision about local production until the local market extension was confirmed.

Management Control Systems and Innovation: The Case of Micro-Profit Centers

This qualitative study explores the relationships between MCS and innovation processes. MCS could play an important role in accumulating and using intangibles, and may encourage creativity and innovation. An MCS package potentially creates change and effectively motivates organizational members to take up challenges. The author investigates the micro-profit center system and the belief system (corporate spirit or management philosophy) at a Japanese company, and finds that using MCS in a specific manner can help manage the tension between creativity and stability, and stimulate innovation.

PART 3. Related Topics in Business Administration and Management Accounting

Intrinsic and Extrinsic Motivation Viewed from HRM: Based on a Questionnaire Survey of Regular Employees in Middle-Ranking Companies in the Tokyo Area

The purpose of this research is to question: (1) what regular employees working at middle-ranking companies think about working at their current workplaces (work awareness) and (2) what issues management faces in personnel today's companies. This is based on the actual state of the workplaces. Therefore, this research (1) identifies the types of intrinsic motivation of employees by conducting a pilot survey and (2) conducts factor analysis on the actual state of the intrinsic motivation of employees. The study data are collected through a questionnaire survey meant to identify the latent variables which cannot be measured through measurable variables, thus clarifying the role of the organization.

Japanese Multinational Enterprises' Preventive Actions Against Transfer Pricing Taxation

This paper analyzes the actions taken by Japanese multinational enterprises (JMNEs) against transfer pricing taxation (TPT) using empirical data. TPT is legislation requiring companies to determine their corporate income tax under the assumption that they trade with their foreign affiliates at a theoretical transfer price, the "arm's length price," for tax purposes. This legislation was not intended to interfere with international transfer pricing practices or MCS in multinational enterprise groups. However, the results of this study show that, first, JMNEs resolve their income transfer overseas by adjusting the international transfer price, not through tax adjustments, and that, second, JMNEs applying the transactional net margin method make decisions about the sales and manufacturing functions of their foreign affiliates. Thus, JMNEs' actions against the TPT are intended to prevent its application.

Economic Analysis of Strategy Risk and Transaction Cost: The Case of an Air Transportation Company

The three main reasons for innovation failure have been given as (1) unrealistic expectations from top management regarding the opportunity of direct cross-Taiwan Strait flights, (2) the decisions to expand fleet by leveraged financing, and (3) far too much focus on investments and ignoring other options for innovation. After resumed operations, this company makes the following reviving innovation: (1) it provides regular flights to Angkor in Cambodia, (2) the chairman combines aviation business know-how with cross-industry experience, and (3) has drawn up a "model flight attendants" service strategy, and "one-stop shop" for tours.

I am very grateful to Ms. Lum Pui Yee and Mr. Herbert Moses, in-house editors, World Scientific Publishing Company, for their invaluable efforts in making this volume a reality. Furthermore, I would like to express my special thanks to Prof. Yasuhiro Monden, Japan Society of Organization and Accounting, who made it possible for me to publish this Vol. 13 of the Institute.

Kazuki Hamada
October 20, 2015

About the Volume Editors

Kazuki Hamada
Professor, School of Business Administration,
Kwansei Gakuin University, Japan
Vice President, Japan Society of Organization and Accounting
Executive Director, The Japanese Association of Management Accounting
Councilor, Japan Accounting Association
B.A and MBA from Kwansei Gakuin University,
Ph.D. in Management Science and Engineering from University of Tsukuba

Current main research theme
Studies of innovation, inter-company supply chain management, and group management from the view of management Accounting

Main publications
"Management Accounting Information for Consolidated Group Management," in Hamada, K., ed., *Business Group Management in Japan*, World Scientific Publishing Co. Pte. Ltd., 2010.

"Total Productivity Management and the Theory of Constraints: An Integrated Application of Supply Chain Management Methods," in Monden, Y. *et al.*, eds., *Japanese Management Accounting Today*, World Scientific Publishing Co. Pte. Ltd., 2007.

"Managerial Roles of Financial and Non- Financial Measures in Supply Chain and Engineering Chain Management," in Monden, Y. *et al.*, eds., *Value-Based Management of Rising Sun*, World Scientific Publishing Co. Pte. Ltd., 2006.

"A Method for Simultaneously Achieving Cost Reduction and Quality Improvement," "A Management System for the Simultaneous Attainment of Customer Satisfaction and Employee Satisfaction," in Monden, Y., ed., *Japanese Cost Management*, Imperial College Press, 2000.

"Target Costing and Kaizen Costing in the Japanese Automobile Companies," *Journal of Management Accounting Research*, Vol. 3, 1992 (co-authored with Monden, Y.).

Shufuku Hiraoka
Professor, Faculty of Business Administration,
Director, Accounting & Tax Education Center,
Soka University, Japan
Director, Japan Society of Organization and Accounting
Executive Director, The Japanese Association of Management Accounting
B.A from Soka University, Master of Economics from Tsukuba University
Ph.D. in Business Administration from Meiji University

Current main research theme
Studies of innovation, segment reporting, economic profit and group management from the view of management Accounting

Main publications:
"Challenge to the Business Crisis by Applying Capital Cost Management: The Case Study of Panasonic Group." in Monden, Y., ed., *Management of Enterprise Crisis in Japan*, World Scientific Publishing Co. Pte. Ltd., 2013.

"Business Valuation of a Company Group in Japan: A Case Study of Segment Reporting by Panasonic Electric Works." in Hamada, K., ed., *Business Group Management in Japan*, World Scientific Publishing Co. Pte. Ltd., 2010.

"Changes in the Concept of Capital and Their Effects on Economic Profit in Japan" in Monden, Y. *et al.*, eds., *Japanese Management Accounting Today*, World Scientific Publishing Co. Pte. Ltd., 2007.

"Valuation of Business Based on EVA-Type Metrics in Japanese Companies," in Monden, Y. *et al.*, eds., *Value-Based Management of Rising Sun*, World Scientific Publishing Co. Pte. Ltd., 2006.

The Study of Financial Metrics for Corporate and Business Valuation., Tokyo, Soseisya (in Japanese). This book was awarded the 2011 Book Prize from Business Analysis Association.

List of Contributors

Junji Fukuda
Professor, Faculty of Business Administration,
Hosei University, Japan

Kazunori Fukushima
Associate Professor, Department of Commerce,
Seinan Gakuin University, Japan

Kazuki Hamada
Professor, School of Business Administration,
Kwansei Gakuin University, Japan

Shufuku Hiraoka
Professor, Faculty of Business Administration,
Soka University, Japan

Noriyuki Imai
Part-time Professor, Graduate School of Business,
Meijo University, Japan

Katsuhiro Ito
Professor, Faculty of Economics,
Seikei University, Japan

Takeshi Ito
President, Value Co-Creation, Inc., Tokyo

Chiungfeng Ko
Associate Professor, Department of Accounting, Business School,
Soochow University, Taiwan

Yuichi Kubota
Professor, Graduate School of Business Administration,
Nanzan University, Japan

Yasuhiro Monden
Professor Emeritus,
The University of Tsukuba, Japan

Eiji Okamoto
Former Professor, Faculty of Business Administration,
Mejiro University, Japan

Tatsumasa Tennojiya
Associate Professor, Faculty of Economics,
Hiroshima University of Economics, Japan

Koji Umeda
Reseacher, Graduate School of Economics,
Nagoya City University, Japan

Naoya Yamaguchi
Associate Professor, Graduate School of Professional Accountancy,
Aoyama Gakuin University, Japan

Part 1
Management of Innovation Strategy and Management Control

Strategic Management and Profit Creation in the Context of Innovation: The Management of Innovation Value Chains

Kazuki Hamada

Professor, School of Business Administration,
Kwansei Gakuin University, Japan

1. Introduction: The Present Conditions of the Innovation in Japan

Recently, Japanese companies have been compelled to improve competitive advantage strategically through innovation by developing new products and businesses. Schumpeter (1934) mentions that the purpose of innovation is "to produce new things or to produce existing things by new methods"; in other words, "to combine things and power in the forms that are different from before". Further, innovation must realize profitable results in markets. Schumpeter (1934) goes on to explain five types of the new combination: (1) new products and services, and the introduction of new qualities in them; (2) the introduction of new production methods; (3) the development of new markets; (4) the acquisition of new sources of raw materials and half-finished goods; and (5) the realization of new organizations. (1) is related to product innovation and (2)–(5) are related to process innovation.

Some investigations of innovation in Japan focus only on product innovation and some consider both types of innovation. A report of the National Institute of Science and Technology Policy, Ministry of Education, Culture,

Japanese Management and International Studies Vol. 13:
Management of Innovation Strategy in Japanese Companies
World Scientific Publishing Company, September 2016

Sports and Technology (2014) investigates Web- and mail-based research conducted among 20,405 companies. Of these companies, 7,034 provided useful answers. In the investigation, innovation refers to the introduction of something new for a company; further, innovation does not limit anything new to the market (in other words, a perfect new product or service). According to the findings, the realization ratio of product innovation and process innovation in Japan is low in comparison with America and European countries. Among the factors responsible are the lack of certain abilities among employees, the lack of information about technologies and markets, the uncertainty of demand for new products and services, and the high costs of innovation.

A report of Deloitte Tohmatsu Consulting Co. Ltd. and Deloitte Tohmatsu Financial Advisory Co. Ltd. (2013) examines innovation by using Web- and mail-based research conducted among 2,309 listed companies and 726 non-public companies. Of these companies, 335 provided useful answers. According to the findings, the ratio (by consolidation) of the sales of new businesses, products, and services that Japanese companies introduced into the markets within the most recent three years to the total sales is half that of American companies. In addition, the findings show that the ratio of the sales volume of products/services that are new for the companies to those that are not new to the markets is high; and the ratio of the sales volume of products/services that are new for the companies to those that are new to the markets is low. Further, the following problems in the enforcement of innovation are highlighted.

(1) There are few innovative top and middle managers.
(2) Activities to create new ideas are an "extension of existing strategies".
(3) The method of investment judgment and organizational continuous processes of knowledge are weak.
(4) There are no mechanisms that repeatedly produce new business.
(5) Actions regarding intellectual property utilization are weak.

The investigation that the Japanese Ministry of Economy, Trade and Industry assigned to the Techno Research Institute (2012) considered 2,093 listed companies and 2,543 non-public companies. Of these, 996 provided useful answers. The investigation's highlights are as follows.

(1) Innovations that occur because of needs are 64%; those that occur because of seeds are 36%.

(2) If we divide innovations into those produced strategically and those produced accidentally, the former amounts to more than 75% of all cases of technology, products/services, and related businesses.

(3) Consecutive innovations (innovations whose performance and sales are continually and progressively improved by technologies on conventional production lines) are more numerous than non-consecutive innovations (innovations developed from just a few areas of the production line) with a ratio of almost 3:1.

(4) With regard to (3), many companies want to increase the ratios of non-consecutive innovations because the impact of such innovations on superior performance and competitiveness is significant.

These investigations show that the realization ratio of innovation, especially non-consecutive (radical) innovation is low. In addition, they show that strategic management is necessary for innovation. Managers must collect information about intellectual assets, technologies, and demand. They must also build learning and administration systems in order to generate new business and encourage employees to become innovative. Further, the research shows that appropriate investment judgment and cost management (profit management) are necessary because innovation costs are high.

When we consider the situation of Japanese companies, there are not only products whose product performance has a significant influence on customer satisfaction, but there are also many products that reach a level at which their performance provides sufficient customer satisfaction. If customers are satisfied with product performance, technological improvements do not lead to competitive advantages. Thus, although innovation has so far focused on improvements in technological performance, innovation must be considered from the viewpoint of customer value. However, it is important to think about technological aspects because these affect the durability of competitive advantages. In addition, the development of new business structures (business models) is important for the profitability of products.

I only consider product innovation in this paper, because the focus becomes blurred if I examine innovation too widely. However, I consider process innovation in its widest sense, because the sales process of products must be given due consideration in terms of profit acquisition.

2. Relations Between Corporate Strategies and Innovation Strategies

Innovation is an issue related to all sections of a company because it is important for innovation to encompass all processes from research and development to sales. Thus, innovation must be managed alongside corporate strategies and considered as one of the key activities in a company's operations.

Corporate strategies have intentional and emerging strategies. Intentional strategy is a strategy formulated on purpose and is based on data analysis about market growth rates, market sizes, customer needs, and the situations of competing companies and technologies. Emerging strategy wells up within an organization and is a strategy that comes from the accumulation of daily job-related decisions. The appropriate management of such intentional and emerging strategic processes is important. However, these two processes complement each other. Further, managers and on-site employees must deal with problems and opportunities that emerge, and that were not foreseen in the intentional strategic process. They must then adapt their intentional strategy and pursue it if the process of emergence is to be strategically effective.

With regard to innovation strategy, there are cases where it is first conducted intentionally with a clear design, and cases where it is first conducted emergently because it has no clear design. Managers need to use these strategies properly. However, even if innovation is conducted intentionally, it must correspond flexibly to environmental changes in terms of emergence because of the uncertainties that accompany innovation. In contrast, even if innovation is conducted for reasons of emergence, managers must not wait for emergence to occur but must create a system to bring about emergence intentionally.

3. Innovation Strategies and Management Control

3.1. *Types of innovation and innovation strategy*

Types of innovation can be classified in various ways. For example, innovation can be divided into gradual innovation (continuous innovation) and radical innovation (discontinuous innovation). The former is innovation based on abilities that can be developed and learned relatively easily in an organization and often has a low-risk low return. The latter is innovation that may change an industrial structure dramatically and often has a high-risk high return.

Gradual innovation can often anticipate a future situation to some extent although it is accompanied by uncertainty. In this case, an intentional process occurs. Managers hypothesize on the basis of market and technical information, and it is important how they formulate achievable aims and implement them. However, even with gradual innovation, the environment is uncertain, and if there is environmental change, it is necessary to change hypotheses, revise aims, and cope with emergence flexibly. In contrast, radical innovation that is not realized on the production line has rarely a development design. Thus, market needs and technological possibilities must be considered in order to produce a development design and sufficiently utilize the emergence processes. In addition, it is rare for a development design to be put into practice as it was originally formulated; indeed, it is usually revised many times if market and technological requirements change.

With regard to both gradual and radical innovation, using feedback to check on progress is an effective means of management as is feedforward. Feedforward management is a method whereby managers predict outputs using input information that is available in a system. Such managers recognize the differences between predicted outputs and goals and manage on the basis of predictions so that goals are accomplished through information. The practice of this approach is difficult because comparisons developed from predictions play a key role in feedforward management. Timeliness is also significant because managers can find problems by themselves immediately and introduce measures to resolve such problems.

Feedforward management is important for product innovation because managers change hypotheses on the basis of information about environmental change and adjust predicted results. They also change the development of products if there is a difference between goals and forecasts. In addition, the number of hypotheses increases in terms of predictions because product innovation is conducted in an environment where the degree of uncertainty is extremely high. Such hypotheses change depending on environmental changes; consequently modified actions are often necessary. Information must be acquired quickly to change hypotheses, predict results, and engage promptly in modified actions in order to conduct feedforward management effectively. Such a cycle becomes faster as organizational learning accumulate, because the discovery of areas in which management must be careful becomes faster as does the consequent standardization of predictive work. In this regard, a system can easily cause an overreaction if managers strengthen feedforward; thus, attention must be paid because the system can become significantly unstable.

After a development design is provided in one way or another, managers progress through organizational learning while coordinating intentional and emergence processes based on the design. Thus, the management of innovation in order to give a more concrete form to a development design becomes particularly important. Development designs change many times through the processes of realization and hypotheses. At this stage, feedforward management is effective and conducted using concrete accounting values for profit evaluation.

3.2. *Innovation strategies and management control*

According to the conventional way of thinking, management control (MC) is intended to support and adjust decision-making processes in order to conduct strategies effectively and efficiently, and to motivate organizational members to achieve strategies. Recently, MC has emphasized the usefulness of strategic formulation as well as strategic execution management.

Figure 1 shows the relations between corporate strategies and MC. As the figure illustrates, with the strategies of existing businesses and the intentional innovation strategies of new businesses, managers decide strategic goals and conduct MC to achieve such goals. In the figure, this is the relation shown by (1). There is also feedback from MC to strategies. In contrast, with emerging innovation, managers do not have clear strategies from the start; indeed, the relations between strategies and MC are not clear at an early stage even if managers have strategies. In the MC enforcement process, organizational learning accumulates through information obtained from the execution processes of existing businesses and intentional strategies; emerging innovation then arises. In the figure, this is the relation shown by (2). The strategies that drive these relations are emerging innovation strategies.

In this context, the question arises whether MC is effective for the emergence of innovation. Conventionally, with regard to the emergence of

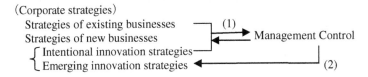

Fig. 1. Relations between corporate strategies and MC

innovation and the development of new products, many studies suggest that employing accounting information to help MC is not a useful practice. However, studies that suggest MC is useful for innovation have increased in recent years. The common ground of these studies is that the conventional usage of MC must be significantly changed. The type of MC must be non-impositional and must support the duties of employees by giving them enforcement authority and providing information for strategic emergence. In other words, MC must promote learning through experiences, discoveries, and knowledge creation. Thus, MC must help the systematization of on-site knowledge and offer information that employees can use to search for new solutions and monitor innovation processes. A profitable result using round numbers must also be computed if possible.

4. Innovation Value Chains and Management Systems

I have considered innovation strategies and MC in the prior section; however, innovation strategies cannot be immediately decided based on information but can be formulated by trial and error. Porter explains business processes through the concept known as a value chain. Hansen and Birkinshaw (2007) explain innovation formulation processes as an innovation value chain (IVC). Thus, innovation strategies must be devised while being aware of IVC. Figure 2 illustrates the IVC.

Next, three obstacles must be overcome in the IVC so that innovation leads to profit acquisition (Konnou and Takai, 2012).

(1) The Devil's River

Although many resources are used, superior technologies cannot be introduced. Superior new technologies are hoarded without being tied to product designs.

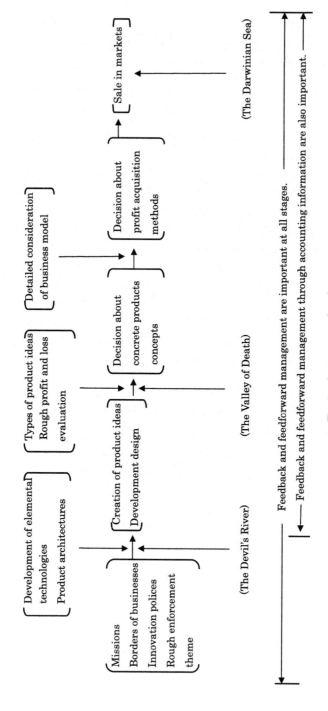

Fig. 2.   Innovation value chain

(2) The Valley of Death

Concrete products accepted in markets cannot be produced because of the difficulty of developing a product through technological advancement, complexity, and the diversification of customer demand.

(3) The Darwinian Sea

Products cannot win against the competition and cannot achieve stable profits. With highly profitable products, conflicting products appear sequentially.

To overcome "The Devil's River," missions, policies, and the borders of businesses must be stated clearly, enforcement theme frameworks must be shown, and management must promote the creation of product ideas. The major issues for management are the development management of elemental technologies that constitute products and the decision to create architectures that produce products by linking these with the elemental technologies.

A technology road map that illustrates a future image of technology and the route technology that must take to achieve the image is effective for the development management of elemental technologies. With regard to the decision about product architecture, managers must decide whether they adopt a modular or integral type. The former is a method whereby managers decide only about rules of pairs of parts beforehand and progress independently of them. The latter is a design method that managers use to make adjustments among parts while they consider total optimization at a development practice stage without deciding about the rules of combination among parts beforehand and ensuring completeness.

Accounting information is not effective at "The Devil's River" stage. Instead, managers set technological goals and conducted management effectively through feedback and feedforward, which I explained in a prior section, without using accounting information. Moreover, managers must predict the effects of the development of elemental technologies, even if they simply make rough estimates, because they must determine how many resources they must distribute into such development. In this regard, managers have risk of falling behind in the development of elemental technologies if they make decisions that are too conservative.

In order to calculate a development design in accordance with customer needs, namely to decide how to put elemental technologies together, ideas from inside and outside a company must be collected. It is important that such ideas come from not only a technological viewpoint but also a company-wide viewpoint. Thus, it is effective to consider technological evaluations that involve most of the concerned persons inside and outside the company. The creation of networks inside and outside the company to counteract a lack of ideas is also effective. In Japan, brainstorming for ideas is a technique that is commonly used. In addition, managers contact customers to discover their needs, produce trial products for technical evaluation, and devise means to improve communications between customers and executives.

In order to complete a development design in the form of a concrete product, "The Valley of Death" must be overcome. At this stage, the development of the product concept with the participation of various departments and related companies, and a profit and loss evaluation for commercialization, are conducted. In the development of the product concept, managers determine the market segment on which they intend to focus, and research and manage the product idea.

In addition, because large-scale resources mobilization is necessary for commercialization, managers must persuade those involved with the product plan that the product in development is profitable. In other words, managers must justify resource mobilization. A profit and loss evaluation conducted by accountants helps with a logical and objective management evaluation and assists resource mobilization. The profit and loss evaluation can be more effective if it uses subjective information such as the opinions and expertize of company staff appropriately, together with objective information such as market, investment, and competition data. However, a means of achieving profit acquisition must be planned to some extent in order to conduct the profit and loss evaluation.

Further, managers must devise a way of enforcing the product plan that differs from prior plans because new product evaluation is accompanied by significant uncertainty. In this regard, discovery-driven planning (DDP) that managers conduct while changing possible hypotheses in the context of environmental, time, and other possible changes is effective. I consider DDP further in the following section.

Managers must not only demand significant results but must also consider the commercial viability of minor results from the study processes and how to achieve continuous profit to ensure innovation success. If successful results are not produced, innovation technology development is canceled. An example of successful development is the carbon fiber that Toray Industries, Inc. currently uses for planes and satellites, but initially employed in the manufacture of fishing rods, golf club shafts, and tennis rackets.

The construction of a superior business model is important in order to overcome "The Darwinian Sea." Such a business model provides the structure for a series of activities that are required before offering products to customers and achieving profitability. It is easy to retain competitive advantage when a company can build a suitable business model even if competitors imitate a part of it. The business model consists of a business system and a profit model. The former is a series of structured duties that occur before delivering products to customers. These duties include research/technology development, product development, manufacturing, sales, and after-sales services. The latter profit model is a structure whereby profit is achieved by offering customers' value. It is important for a company to build a business system and a profit model that are hard to copy because imitators can produce highly profitable products immediately.

5. DDP to Promote Development Ideas and Product Development

I mentioned in the prior section that feedforward management is particularly important because managers must repeatedly change hypotheses regarding innovation strategy development processes. One planning method that uses feedforward management is DDP. The DDP concept was first developed and named by McGrath and MacMillan (2000). They state that plans must be formulated using hypotheses in situations of uncertainty such as new businesses. Planning methods similar to this have been introduced under various names such as hypothesis planning and theory focused planning by many researchers.

DDP's main feature is the way it adopts the possibility of real options, an approach that is effective after a rough development design is formulated. This planning technique differs from conventional methods. A goal of a target profit (the profit necessary for approval of the innovation plan) is first decided. Plans are then formulated while engaging in trial and error proposals starting at a future point and going back to the present in order to achieve the goal.

The DDP procedures are as follows.

(1) Determination of target profit

Managers decide on the target profit that is necessary for the approval of strategic plans. When they decide on a business framework to achieve the target profit, they must identify, to some extent the business model. I will consider this later.

(2) Formulating reverse financial statements and making a list of problems

Managers start with the target profit and clarify those factors that can achieve it from the perspective of revenue and costs. The results are summarized in reverse financial statement, a name that refers to the consideration of revenue and costs to achieve the target profit under adverse conditions. Managers clarify any problems in achieving the target profit when they create a reverse income statement. A reverse balance sheet is also formulated when needed.

(3) Determination of problem solution activities based on hypotheses

Managers decide on the operational activities that must be conducted while taking account of uncertainty about the solutions to a list of problems. They must make decisions while hypothesizing in order to deal with uncertainty. Uncertainty includes factors that managers can mitigate by acting by themselves and factors that they cannot control. Managers must address the former positively. The hypotheses are often estimated; for example, from optimistic and pessimistic perspectives. Managers create a checklist of hypotheses and establish confirmation points. It is also effective to decide which hypotheses and which confirmation points managers should inspect.

(4) Examination of hypotheses and the accumulation of organizational learning

The processes needed to deploy the target profit into various factors while examining hypotheses at checkpoints are processes of organizational learning. Managers repeat the examination of hypotheses many times and change a plan if necessary. In this process, managers can accumulate organizational learning.

(5) Full-scale practice of the plan and the practice of equipment investment

Managers conduct their plan in earnest when the hypotheses are finally inspected and the accomplishment of the target profit can be forecasted.

Then, they engage in the necessary capital expenditure. It is important that managers conduct their economic intentions thoroughly until they accomplish their goal.

The Kao Corporation previously adopted DDP (McGrath and MacMillan, 2000). The company manufactures soap and toiletry products, but in the late 1970s it began supplying surfactant to the floppy disk (FD) industry. Using the knowledge it gained, the company employed DDP to examine whether it could enter magnetic media industries such as the FD industry with the surfactant business acting as its main prop. Consequently, the Kao Corporation entered the FD industry in 1986. Managers revised hypotheses, calculated effects, and elaborated revenues and costs to attain a target profit based on the reverse income statement and the balance sheet, and used DDP whenever environmental conditions changed and new measures were devised. When they considered any measures, the managers created detailed lists of problems and used hypotheses. Organizational learning was accumulated as a part of the processes in order to elaborate the target profit and seemed to help when managers considered any measures.

To begin with, the Kao Corporation's new business grew; however, FD profitability then fell significantly because of an intensification of competition. The result was a business deficit of ¥10 billion in 1997; consequently, Kao withdrew from the business. Although the business was planned using DDP and ultimately failed, this is a significant example that indicates a way of elaborating profit when managers consider an innovation strategy.

6. Profit Acquisition Management with Regard to Product Innovation

The profit acquisition method with regard to product innovation should be examined when formulating strategy and before marketing. Even if an epoch-making product is developed based on a superior idea, such an examination should occur because a great product alone does not guarantee profit acquisition.

First, when considering the introduction of a new product, managers must decide whether all of the design, production, and sales stages of the product should be conducted in-house. The type of company where this method is suitable is one that has significant design capability and production technology, and a suitable sales force. In addition, if this method is adopted, new large-scale capital expenditure is necessary; thus, only a company with financial power can engage in new product development. Further, product development must have a long life cycle and requires future stable demand because the period of payback for capital expenditure is longer with a large-scale investment. In addition, a company with a new product must ensure exclusive possession of any profit, prevent technologies from being generalized and adopt measures to maintain a high earnings structure.

For example, Canon Inc. unified part of the function necessary to copy images with toner containers and cleaner, both of which are expendable supplies, thereby adapting built-in cartridge technology to change the toner's function. This allowed anyone to change the toner easily; further, the adjusted technologies were imitated by built-in cartridge technology (Herstatt *et al.*, 2006). This example shows that the power of profit acquisition can be managed through the choice of product architecture.

If a company cannot retain control of the entire design, production, and sales processes of a new product, it must assign these parts that it cannot retain to other companies. This approach is desirable when the technological capability of a supplier and the level of cooperation between the client company and the supplier are high; indeed, many companies can become partners. In addition, this approach is effective when the processes that a company retains have a high level of technology and such technology is hard to imitate, even if the partner companies that handle other processes are in intense competition and highly competitive products exist. It is a precondition of success to be able to cooperate with other companies and to have a high level of ability in managing the entire process, including those elements handled by other companies. However, by using this approach, costs and risks increase significantly with regard to any adjustments and unifications with other companies. Further, investment is necessary in those processes for which the company retains control.

In addition, a company may adopt an approach whereby it only designs a product and licenses production and sales to other companies. This approach is suitable for a company whose financial power is weak because the company receives fees for use of the licenses and other companies bear all the costs of production and sales. Thus, the company only needs funds for development. With regard to this approach, a management system must maintain skills that include arranging contracts, developing new products, and regulating intellectual property.

7. Summary and Conclusion

The findings of many studies show that the realization ratio of innovation is low in Japan; thus, I considered how companies should address this problem. First, I did not regard the innovation as a problem limited to technology development field; instead, I considered it as a problem that is concerned with all sections of a company. I also pointed out that it is necessary to consider innovation relating to corporate strategies. Such innovation includes gradual and radical innovation, and I emphasized the importance of management promoting innovation in both instances.

With regard to innovation management, I suggested that managers should grasp innovation and that appropriate sequential processes should be developed. I proposed that innovation development processes should be included as a part of the IVC. Specifically, I pointed out that managers formulate plans based on hypotheses because innovation is accompanied by a significant degree of uncertainty; further, managers must revise hypotheses and plans many times if the environment changes and new information is acquired. Organizational learning is accumulated by correcting such plans and examining process measures repeatedly, thereby providing positive effects for innovation. In addition, with regard to innovation strategy development, many studies show that information provided by interactive MC affects strategic emergence.

"The Devil's River," "The Valley of Death," and "The Darwinian Sea" are major obstacles to IVC progress; thus, I considered what kinds of management a company should adopt to overcome them at every stage. I explained in detail feedforward management, and DDP that is based on it, as management methods that are used in company processes to conduct IVC. When managers consider a problem such as innovation that has significant future uncertainties, a decision is first made to use a method such as DDP that targets profitability; then, the kinds of condition or measure that are needed to achieve profitability effectively are examined. In addition, DDP can prevent problems that arise because of the tendency of innovation strategies not to be connected with profit acquisition. In this regard, DDP definitely helps with the achievement of a target profit.

Recently, innovation has become increasingly important to corporate management. Thus, many studies have been conducted from many viewpoints. Numerous points must still be examined in detail; however, this study shows an important direction in which it addresses innovation management.

References

Andrew, J. P. and H. L. Sirkin (2003). Innovating for cash. *Harvard Business Review* 81(9): 76–83.

Deloitte Tohmatsu Consulting Co. Ltd., Deloitte Tohmatsu Financial Advisory Co. Ltd. (2013). *Innovation Fact-finding of Japanese Companies,* Deloitte Tohmatsu (in Japanese).

Hansen, M. T. and J. Birkinshaw (2007). The innovation value chain. *Harvard Business Review* 85: 121–130.

Herstatt, C., C. Stokstorm, H. Tschirk and A. Nagahira (2006). *Management of Technology and Innovation in Japan.* Berlin and Heidelberg: Springer-Verlag.

Konnou, Y. and A. Takai (2012). *Core-Text: Innovation Management.* Tokyo: Shinseisha (in Japanese).

Maruta, O. (2005). *Feedforward Control and Management Accounting.* Japan: Dobunkan (in Japanese).

McGrath, R. G. and I. MacMillan (2000). *The Entrepreneurial Mindset: Strategies for Continuously Creating Opportunity in an Age of Uncertainty.* Boston: Harvard Business School Press.

National Institute of Science and Technology Policy, Ministry of Education, Culture, Sports and Technology (2014). *A Report on the Japanese National Innovation Survey 2012,* Ministry of Education, Culture, Sports and Technology (in Japanese).

Nonaka, I., R. Toyama and T. Hirata (2012). *Managing Flow: The Dynamic Theory of Knowledge-based Firms.* Toyo Toyokeizai-Shinposha (in Japanese).

Schumpeter, J. R. (1934). *The Theory of Economic Development: An Inquiry into Profits, Capital, Credit, Interest, and the Business Cycle.* Cambridge: Harvard University Press.

Takeishi, A., Y. Aoshima and M. Karube (2012). *Reasons for Innovation: Creating Legitimacy for Resource Mobilization.* Tokyo: Yuhikaku (in Japanese).

Techno Research Institute (2012). *Industrial Technology Investigation in the 2011 Fiscal Year: Fact-finding Report about Medium-and-Long-term Research and Development of Japanese Companies Contributing to Innovation Creation,* Techno Research Institute (in Japanese).

Idea Decision-Making for Innovation: How Can Good Ideas be Discovered Organizationally?

Takeshi Ito

President,
Value Co-Creation, Inc., Tokyo

1. Introduction

A company employee makes a visit to a corporate client and, during conversations with customer representatives, comes up with a business idea. Excited about the possibilities, the employee heads back to the company office and tells his supervisor and colleagues. They might respond by asking whether the idea would be profitable or even feasible. Having just dawned on the employee, however, the idea is still only starting to hatch — it seems like it might have business potential, but it is not ready for close examination yet. The employee might have to tell his supervisor and fellow employees that he simply does not know if the idea has any profitability or feasibility, let alone how many customers there might be or how many units the product could sell. The chances of that idea eventually generating sales, profits, and other business-related benefits, especially in the short-term, are uncertain at this point in time.

Spontaneous "bright ideas" rarely produce results in the real world. That is why the employee's supervisor and coworkers might lose interest in the idea and shy away from supporting it. They might even tell the employee that it would be a waste to spend time on an idea that is going nowhere or that he

Japanese Management and International Studies Vol. 13:
Management of Innovation Strategy in Japanese Companies
World Scientific Publishing Company, September 2016

or she would be better off focusing on his or her personal performance goals for the year. These sorts of situations are routine at companies of all kinds.

Some companies handle new ideas well, though. Nobeoka (2008) has demonstrated how the process works at Keyence, factory automation solution provider, where employees continue to take ideas that come out of dealings with customers, develop them into businesses and products, and reap considerable revenue from the results. Nonaka *et al.* (2010, pp. 185–195) state that each employee at Eisai devotes around 1% of his or her yearly working hours toward meeting and relating with customers, in this case, patients. That interaction apparently produces approximately 500 proposals for new product development and similar projects every year.

What separates the type of company in the first scenario from the companies in the third paragraph? What factors stand in the way of developing ideas into good proposals, businesses, and products? How can companies eliminate those obstacles? These are the questions and issues at the core of this paper.

My main goal for this paper is to discuss and propose a decision-making process that companies can use to take ideas for new product development and other innovations, break down the barriers to successful idea incubation, and bring the ideas to fruition. Although the specifics of my discussion center on product development, the approach covers and applies to ideas across the board.

2. Previous Research

In this section, previous research on decision-making process for creating innovative ideas is reviewed. The research addresses decision-making process, criteria of choice, idea, or innovation creation.

2.1. *Decision-making process and its criteria of choice*

Aristotle (350 BC, p. 1112b) said that "they take some end for granted, and consider how and by what means it can be achieved. If they find that there are several means of achieving it, they proceed to consider which of these will attain it most easily and best." This shows one criterion of choice which will best attain the "result". The "result" is a purpose or an objective. The other criterion is how the choice is attained most easily. This is viability. Ulrich *et al.* (2002, pp. 136–137) stated that the same criteria of choice are used in a problem-solving method, the WorkOut of General Electric (GE). GE WorkOut uses a payoff matrix to prioritize and choose better ideas to execute with the same two criteria, results and viability.

Mintzberg *et al.* (1976) analyzed 25 cases of the decision-making process. The process consists of three central phases: identification, development, and selection. The identification phase consists of two routines: decision recognition and diagnosis. The development phase consists of two routines: search and design. And the selection phase consists of screen, evaluation-choice, and authorization.

Simon (1977, pp. 39–41) developed a decision-making model. The model has three steps: intelligence, design, and choice. The latter two steps have feedback to the previous steps.

2.2. *Idea creation method and process*

Young (1940) defined five steps for creating ideas. They are (1) gathering raw materials (inputs), (2) digesting the materials, (3) unconscious processing, (4) the actual birth of the idea, and (5) Idea meets reality. The first four steps are for creating ideas by combining inputs, and the last step is to evaluate ideas as to whether to execute the ideas or not.

The Hasso Plattner Institute of Design at Stanford (d.school) (2011) suggested a process model for designing new products and services, "the design thinking process." The process consists of five steps such as (1) empathize, (2) define, (3) ideate, (4) prototype, and (5) test. The first three steps are the ways of creating ideas. The prototype step is for improving ideas, and the final test step is for evaluating ideas. This process is not linear and has a feedback loop.

2.3. *Product development process*

Monden and Hamada (1991) showed steps of Target Costing, cost reduction process for product development of a new model: (1) corporate planning, (2) developing the specific new product project, (3) determining the basic plan for a specific new product, (4) product design, (5) the production transfer plan, and (6) production. The second step in this process includes (a) building a product planning proposal or a business case, (b) selection of a proposal in product planning, and (c) building a basic product plan.

Cooper (2011, pp. 101–102, first edition 1983) suggested a Stage-Gate process for product development that has one pre-stage and five stages. The pre-stage is Discovery stage and the five stages are Scoping, Build the Business Case, Development, Testing and Validation, and Launch. In the Discovery stage, customer focus is needed. Cooper stated that Discovery is prework designed to discover and uncover opportunities and generate ideas. Scoping is a quick, preliminary investigation, and sizing of the project which is largely desk research. The Build the Business Case stage is a more detailed investigation involving primary research, both market and technical, leading to a Business Case, including product and project definition, project justification, and a project plan.

3. The Decision-Making Process in Innovation and its Problem Points

3.1. *Scope and definition of idea development process*

This paper focuses on the early stage of the product development process of Monden and Hamada, and Cooper, i.e. the second step of Monden and Hamada, and the prestage and first stage of Cooper. The process of Young and d.school focus on idea creation. This paper will focus more on idea development of product development. Therefore, the scope of the process in this paper takes place after idea creation and follows through idea selection. We can call this process the idea development process.

Previous research has shown that the decision-making process has one or more decision makings and also one or more feedback (Mintzberg *et al.*, 1976). Not only the whole product development process has this feature, but the idea development process focused in this paper also does.

This idea development process has the features of decision-making process defined by Mintzberg *et al.* (1976) and Simon (1977). Mintzberg *et al.'* phases are (1) identification, (2) development, and (3) selection and Simon's phases are (1) intelligence, (2) design, and (3) choice. The process suggested by Young focuses on idea creation, but the d.school design thinking process focuses more on idea development, particularly on the steps of prototype and test.

This paper defines the idea development process that includes four steps: (1) identification of a purpose, (2) creation, (3) development, and (4) selection. The process has one or more decision makings and one or more feedback.

3.2. *New product development process examples*

The process defined here will be introduced through the examples given in this paper focusing, in particular, on the idea development and improvement stage.

A sales manager has been requested by an enterprise customer to create a new product for that company. The manager takes the idea for that product back to his company. At this time, (1) goal and target awareness takes place, that is, to make money by providing a new product to the customer. At the same time, (2) the act of creation is also being performed. As it was an idea that arose from a proposal made by the customer, it can be said to be an idea gained from activities Mintzberg and others refer to as the development phase search.

However, it is at this early time still difficult to judge whether an idea is good enough to be made into a product and be successful. For this reason, they (3) enter the improvement phase. This is the information gathering and fleshing out that will lead to the execution of the idea.

In the (3) idea improvement stage, "the customer needs"; "the viability of development, manufacturing, and sales"; and "the profitability" are to be clarified. If this much information is understood, it may be possible to make a decision whether or not to put the product on the market. Here, for the first time we can enter into (4) the final selection phase.

3.3. *A new product development decision-making process plagued by incomplete information and forecast uncertainty*

The information that was obtained in the improvement phase and is on hand in the final selection phase was not available at the point when the sales manager returned to the company with requests for a new product from the customer. If the sales manager is highly competent with experience in marketing, development, and manufacturing divisions, he or she may be able to forecast a certain amount of information about the product even if it is not exact. However, there are not many managers like this. A manager who only has experience in sales or who has comparatively little experience would not be capable of making such a forecast.

Regardless of whether the idea for the product was raised by a specific customer or a sales manager, at the point that the idea arises, it lacks sufficient concreteness and is not ready for a final decision. This is to say, it is not in a state in which a decision can be made whether or not to make a product. However, if the idea that arose at that time is not carried through to the final decision stage, it goes without saying that no decision will be made, nor will the product be put on the market. When that happens, no new product will be created. As a result, current products will continue to be sold.

In actuality, there are many places from which ideas arise. Of course, ideas may arise in marketing and product development, but as seen in the example, ideas can also arise among customers, in sales, research, or manufacturing, or at the company's head office. Are there any ideas among these that are wasted, without ever being turned into products? What are the differences between instances in which it is easy to convert a new idea into a product, and when it is difficult to convert?

3.4. A factor obstructing the supply and improvement of ideas: the tendency to seek the perfect idea

When selecting between alternative measures, Aristotle chose that which is best to attain results and that which is easiest to attain. Anyone would be pleased when many ideas are brought before them, polished like diamonds, attractive and profitable in terms of being the best and easiest to attain the goal. If it is easy to attain, then everyone would be rich. However, in a competitive world, that sort of situation does not occur easily.

However, there are likely to be some superiors that tell their subordinates to bring ideas that are likely to be viable, that ensure profitability and are clear on customer needs. Naturally, if the submitted idea is not attractive to customers, or if it lacks profitability or viability, the superior will say that it cannot be carried out.

Let's say that the new idea is a good-quality rough diamond. Being a rough diamond, if the idea is improved through appropriate information gathering or other means, it should be possible to prove that it will meet customer needs and is viable as well as profitable. However, when the collection of information is inadequate, managers can only say that it is impossible to state whether it is sufficiently attractive, viable, and profitable.

When it is assumed that only ideas that have attractiveness, profitability, and viability are worth proposing, ideas are immediately rejected if they cannot be said to have attractiveness, profitability, and viability due to a lack of information. As a result, subordinates will only be able to submit perfect ideas to their superiors. If a superior adheres to that kind of policy, his or her colleagues will eventually also come to demand as such.

Once this kind of message is transmitted, all of the subordinates will only be able to submit ideas with sufficient information. Without receiving support from the superiors, good quality ideas will then disappear without ever getting polished. As an organization, this creates a problem as well. All of the employees will imitate the superiors who submit polished diamonds, will begin to criticize one another's ideas, and will crush ideas without polishing them. The common practice among Japanese businesses to have a single idea passed around for approval promotes this error. Each one of the people to whom the approval request is circulated will evaluate whether the idea is 100% in its perfection. If this is the case, the person proposing the idea can only circulate a polished diamond, any ideas that are not polished will disappear. This practice which appears natural obstructs the supply and improvement of ideas.

3.5. Analyze and solve the problem obstructing the supply of ideas

At the point of *final selection*, making a selection on an idea that adequately fulfills the conditions is a logically correct action. However, as we examine up to this point, one understands that what makes the problem difficult is this correctness in and of itself.

The problem is not the decision-making action itself of the decision-maker but the message implicitly demanding the certain actions of the organization and the subordinates. If the only demand is to make a final selection when all of the conditions are adequately fulfilled, it is tantamount to saying that ideas that do not adequately fulfill the conditions are not needed.

The reason for this is because the statement *"selections should be made on ideas that adequately fulfill the conditions ≪at the point of final selection≫"*

omits the phrase *"at the point of final selection."* Furthermore, the message *"selections should be made on ideas that adequately fulfill the conditions"* is conveyed throughout the organization with the words *"whether in the creation, improvement, selection or any other phase"* implicitly attached. Although, in actuality, the concept of *conditions being adequately fulfilled* is demanded of ideas in the final selection phase, that condition is mistakenly conveyed as being applied to all other ideas as well.

As a means for resolving this problem of demanding that all ideas *adequately fulfill the conditions*, first one can consider sharing the following policy. (1) At the final selection phase, ideas that adequately fulfill the conditions are desirable. However, (2) it is natural that ideas in the creation and improvement stages do not fulfill the final selection requirements. For this reason, it is encouraged to (3) express underdeveloped ideas, and (4) work on ideas in the creation or improvement phases so that they make it to the final selection phase.

This policy is useful in getting ideas to the final selection. However, this will entail a side effect that cannot be overlooked. The ideas that occur are a jumble of gems and rocks. Even though not all of the ideas are mere stones, it is impossible to spend adequate capital and time to improve every idea that arises. This is because it is assumed that there are constraints on resource investment.

4. Constraints on Resource Investment in Improving Ideas and Measures for Their Maximum Utilization

In this section, we will examine resource investment constraints, and with those constraints as a precondition, we will give consideration towards making the process of decision-making on ideas effective and fruitful by selecting and refining promising ideas while sifting the raw diamonds out of the stones to the greatest extent possible.

4.1. *Results require wasteful resource investment*

It is a fact that many new ideas are rejected. Additionally, there are some instances in which the idea is selected and makes it to implementation but fails as a business. If ideas that in the end did not bear fruit are only viewed as a failure, the resources invested in those ideas will be seen as a waste.

Whether in research and development (R&D) or market research, results show that not everything is useful. Even if R&D is carried out, there are many instances in which the technology cannot be developed well, and even when the technology is created, in many instances it does not result in an actual product. As a result, most instances of R&D and market examination when viewed as an individual case can be said to have been wasteful in terms of capital, expense, and time. However, from these many cases, there are some that bore fruit, and it can therefore be said that many wasteful instances were necessary to produce the successful instances.

4.2. Constraints on resource investment that can allow necessary waste

Unless one takes an action even if that means being resigned to the occurrence of waste most of the times, nothing new will be created. Even if this is understood and shared, it still will not do to randomly throw around money and waste time. This is to say that there is a limit to the capital and profits created by an extant enterprise or business over a fixed period of time.

At the company or business level and at the level of individual organizational constituents, the resources that can be used to give consideration to an idea are limited. However, these resources cannot be allowed to be zero. In pharmaceutical companies, most R&D for medicines disappear without any direct results. Similarly, if an organizational constituent puts forth an idea for a new product or work reform measure, in the majority of instances these will be fruitless and not adopted. Conversely, if a pharmaceutical company halts its R&D, its expenses will drop considerably, its short-term profits will rise, and it will be possible to reduce idea consideration and working time spent for idea considered by organizational constituents as well. If one wishes to create this kind of short-term profit, it is unnecessary to come up with new ideas. However, new products and reforms will not be created. Patience is necessary to continue the consideration of things that do not promise results. It is also difficult to maintain motivation.

Upon considering that there are constraints to the necessity of wastefulness and the resources invested into wastefulness, there is a need to effectively utilize that necessary wastefulness. From here, we will examine methods to operate the process from idea creation to the final selection with effective utilization of resources.

4.3. *Idea selection standards for effective resource investment*

If it is true that there is almost no need for lead time or resource investment within the process from idea creation to final selection for individual ideas, then there is no need to worry about resources. However, in actuality, getting sufficient information about an idea takes time. Having said that, if there were a method in which resources could be saved, that would be more efficient. Additionally, if it was possible to make a decision on an idea before the final selection and halt its consideration, it would be possible to save on resource investment. If a consideration process including midway selections is appropriate, then there is a possibility of increasing success overall by keeping relatively good ideas and improving those ideas.

If it is possible to select from the pool of ideas that could be relatively good rough diamonds and disposed of the other stones, the amount of resources invested in stones is reduced and the chance of acquiring a diamond increases. Here, we will examine this midway decision.

Decisions require criteria of choice. We can utilize *"results"* and *"viability"* as criteria shown in the examples of Aristotle (350 BC) and GE (Ulrich *et al.,* 2002). Here, the definition of viability can be thought of as, *"the extent to which the idea in question can be implemented."* For example, can the product that results from the idea actually be put on the market? However, the results of putting the product on the market and the extent of the profits that are likely to be had are not included in viability; these are thought to be included in results.

In contrast, one can consider that results in business can be broadly divided into two categories. The first are those concepts that can be expressed as profitability, expense vs. benefit, or investment vs. benefit. If it is a product idea, the question is whether that product will be profitable in the short-, medium- or long-term, and for equipment investments, the question is the ratio of investment to benefit. The second is customer needs, that is the evaluation of benefit only, disregarding the expenses and investments such as the ratios of expense to benefit and investment to benefit. For example, for product or equipment investments, the questions are how great a number can be sold or manufactured and how much will the amounts be for sales or manufacturing.

(1) Viability

The viability of development and manufacturing is easy to judge. Viability can be expressed as whether something can be realized 100%, 50%, or 0%. However, this changes based on the scope. Viability depends on whether it is to be realized individually, as a department, as a company, or with an existing partner, and whether worldwide resources can be utilized. If the scope is widened, viability increases.

(2) Profitability

It is thought that profitability is the next easily judged aspect following viability. The idea can be abandoned if profitability does not exceed a certain amount or ratio of profits in excess of capital costs. Profitability can be calculated relatively easily if certain manufacturing and sales volumes as well as price are set as preconditions. However, profitability changes considerably based upon the preconditions. In particular, if the volume of products or services manufactured and sold increases, there is the possibility of cost reductions through the workings of economies of scale. If the price remains unaltered when costs decrease, profitability rises. Additionally, when costs decrease, the price can be lowered while maintaining profitability. When the price decreases, there is a possibility that the demand will increase. There is also a possibility of improving price competitiveness and increasing sales volumes.

(3) Customer Needs

Customer needs create market demand. Demand is the number of customers with needs and the volume they purchase. The price of the product and comparative advantage are determined by the competitive environment. Based on these, market share and sales volume are determined. Customers and competitors exist outside of the enterprise, so forecasting their reaction is difficult especially when it comes to new products. The scale of demand, be it from zero to a vast sum, relies in part to conditions and ingenuity employed.

Customer needs determine the scale of demand, and as they determine the sales amount, they serve as preconditions to the profitability of that business. A certain scale to the sales amount is necessary in consideration of the time investment as well as the capital and expenses involved in product development and manufacturing. For this reason, the scale of the sales amount being in excess of a certain level should be a judgment criterion.

If these three criteria are to be made decision criteria for ending the consideration of an idea, then (1) *viability is not 100%*, (2) *profitability is not in excess of a certain level*, and (3) *customer needs are not in excess of a certain scale*.

4.4. Customer needs as the evaluation criterion: take the viewpoint of the customer and measure the attractiveness of the idea

We will further examine customer needs. Benefits within customer needs are not only those of sales volumes and sales amounts, but also include benefits that take the viewpoint of the customer. Customer needs is not an enterprise-centered viewpoint of taking the market from someone, but rather it is a customer-centered viewpoint of creating new products and services that currently do not exist in the market. The reason customers purchase a product or service is not because the enterprise will get profits. In actuality, both the enterprise-centered position based on profits and the customer-centered position based on needs are important.

Thinking from this viewpoint, the value within Value Engineering (VE) is calculated by dividing utility by costs (meaning the amount or price paid by customers). In other words, this value is the ratio of cost (expense) to utility for the customers, and if this utility is considered as a benefit, it becomes the ratio of expense to benefit for the customers. As with the case of the criterion mentioned earlier, in doing this it is possible to think of the benefit with the expense removed, which is to say the utility exclusively as the criterion. This utility has no relation to how much the price is for the customers. It indicates unadulterated customer needs in terms of what kind of utility or benefit is desired. Simply put, it shows what the customers want.

4.5. Describing a process that increases the attractiveness of ideas

Now, we will draw up a process for idea consideration and examine how the evaluation criteria for an idea comes into play. Here, we can introduce the following scenario on B to B to C manufacturer. This company provides a certain component to business customers for several applications. The applications are not limited to those initially identified. If sales can be expanded to other applications, the amount of demand will rise further. If there are similar products for the newly expanded application, it is acceptable to forecast demand based on the same price as those similar products. Through this, both the amount of sales and profit will become larger. If by expanding applications, the demand volume, sales volume, and sales amount increase, while manufacturing costs will decrease based on economies of scale. If manufacturing costs decrease, even if there was an initial gap with the market price this will shrink, and profitability at viable manufacturing costs will increase. If it is forecast that applications will increase and a certain level of profitability will also be ensured, then it will be easier to obtain organizational cooperation, and the amount of capital, expenses, and time that can be invested will increase, as well as the viability.

Conversely, if consideration is given with only the application as a precondition, problems such as the following arise. As this is originally the sole application, demand volume, sales volume, and sales amount are small. Also, calculating viable manufacturing costs with this small amount of sales as the precondition and setting the price based on those costs might result in the price being too high, and demand volume diminishing or decreasing to zero. If that happens, the business cannot be sustained. Profitability will decrease if the price is lowered. Additionally, if an attempt is made to achieve profitability while supplying the new product at the same price as similar products, the gap with viable manufacturing costs will be large, it will become more difficult to decrease costs, and viability decreases.

Based on this example, any attempt to enhance the possibility of an idea must follow the following process. (1) First, the extent of customer needs and the demand volume are clarified. Efforts are made to expand customer needs and demand volumes. This should be done based on the utility of the products or services. In other words, demand volumes are assessed based on the same price as similar products, not manufacturing costs or prices that are assumed to be viable. (2) Next, profitability is considered. If customer needs are expanded, then profitability should increase. (3) Finally, viability is considered. If profitability increases, then the amount of resources that can be invested also increases. By considering ideas in this manner, it is possible to expand their possibilities of success.

Here, the focus has been on demand volume, and the logic and importance of expanding ideas have been discussed. However, applications and demand volumes are not the only approaches to expanding ideas. The goals in selling new products include becoming a pioneer in a certain area, building a brand, expanding a product lineup, testing a product on the market, and other important considerations besides acquiring sales amounts and profitability. There are also businesses that cannot ensure profitability with income from beneficiaries alone.

What we have been observing here is that, in actuality, criteria of choice that we have considered are not only to be used for making decisions, but are also viewpoints that need to be emphasized within the considerations made at every stage of the idea consideration process. In other words, the process is to first consider and expand customer needs, and then to work out the profitability and viability concerns.

5. Designing Idea Screening Process

Idea screening process depicted in this paper has six idea screening gates to decide "go" or "no-go" for proceeding to the next step. Scope of this process is Cooper's pre-stage and first stage of Stage-Gate system. That means this process has the most upstream steps of a product development process.

Cooper's pre-stage, Discovery, corresponds to the first two steps of this process. In these two steps of Discovery, customer needs including number of customers and sales volume are used as evaluation criteria. Differences between two screenings of the two steps are the levels of accuracy. First screening uses low level of accuracy, and the second screening is done with a high level of accuracy. The ideas that are evaluated at high level of customer needs and go through the second screening of customer needs should systematically be added to the list of candidates for future opportunity, even if the ideas have low profitability and viability forecast at that point. The reason is such forecasts may change and be improved as social trend changes and technology innovation happens.

Cooper's "Scoping" stage corresponds to the remaining four steps. In these Scoping screenings, the first screening evaluates ideas by profitability, and the remaining three use viability as the evaluation criterion. Second screening

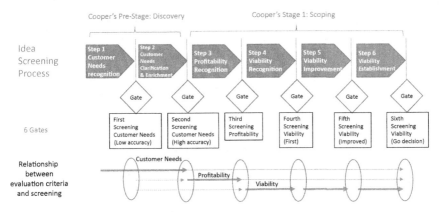

Fig. 1. The idea screening process design
Source: Adapted from R. G. Cooper, 2011, *Winning at New Products: Accelerating the Process From Idea to Launch*, New York: Basic Books. Figure 2.4, p. 40.

evaluates current and forecasted status of viability, the third one evaluates improvement of viability status, and in the last screening viability is 100% and an idea is proposed to proceed to the next stage of product development.

In this manner, the evaluation criterion are fixed in each screening. At the same time, information on two criteria other than the evaluation criterion should be collected naturally and reasonably (Fig. 1 Lower side arrow).

Any resource put into these six screenings is human resources and is limited to a small percentage of working hours. The lead time from idea creation through the sixth screening depends on the individual circumstance of each idea. If levels of customer needs, profitability, and viability are satisfactory, then one or two meetings is enough to make a decision and lead time is almost none. On the other hand, initially, even though the idea has sufficient customer needs, if the levels of profitability and viability are not enough, it may take a long time to make a final decision.

6. Discussion on Requirements for Operating the Process

For making the process work, it is assumed that several prerequisites are needed as organization infrastructure.

(1) Sharing mission, vision, and value toward creating business

Eisai Co. Ltd do not look at their diethylcarbamazine (DEC) tablet grant to the WHO (World Health Organization) for preventing tropical filarial as corporate philanthropy.[1] For Eisai, this activity for patients or future patients is a part of their Mission. Company and society have to satisfy their customer needs and make enough profits to be sustainable. If sustainability is the premise, then everyone has to contribute to make ideas for current and future business.

(2) Securing certain percentages of resources for creating and nurturing ideas

3M states that "we have encouraged our employees to spend 15% of their working time on their own projects".[2] Google has a 30% rule (Schmidt *et al.*, 2014). Eisai's employees use 1% of their working hours with patients, their ultimate customers (Ito, 2013). A company should ideally have a rule to reserve a certain amount of working time of its employees for their own project or customer touchpoint. By squeezing and securing resources to idea creation and development, employees will be able to use time to not only work on their short-term roles and responsibilities, but also to work on a long-term goal and go beyond their current responsibilities and collaborate with others for the future.

(3) Preparing and utilizing a value-based personal evaluation system

Personal evaluation system is also needed. Asahi Kasei sets Corporate Group Values, "Sincerity, Challenge, Creation" and uses the values as criteria to evaluate individual activity in their management by objective (MBO) system (Ito, 2013). By using criteria based on missions and values to evaluate individual activity, an employee has an incentive to work on such an activity.

Employees in organizational functions of development, production, and sales and marketing (1) recognize missions and values that

---

[1] WHO website:

"WHO to receive more than 2 billion tablets as contribution to help eliminate lymphatic filariasis", http://www.who.int/neglected_diseases/eisai_co/en/ (access date: 30-9-2015).

[2] 3M website:

"A culture of innovation3M innovation", https://solutions.3m.com/3MContentRetrievalAPI/BlobServlet?lmd=1349327166000&locale=en_WW&assetType=MMM_Image&assetId=1319209959040&blobAttribute=ImageFile (access date: 30-9-2015).

pursue sustainability, (2) use secured human resources to create and develop ideas, and (3) will be evaluated by mission and values criteria to have internal and external incentives to create and develop ideas. They are the people who practice the idea screening process effectively and ideally.

7. Conclusion

The purpose of this paper is to design design a decision-making process and mechanism for supporting the process, which enables to identify, nurture, and choose good ideas to execute. This paper first defined the decision-making process, then clarified problems such as disincentives to propose immature ideas and nurture them, and limitations of management resources for early phase of product development.

This paper makes a contribution to studies of the decision-making process. A decision-making process model is suggested in this paper, which can solve the problem many managers confront. This model uses three evaluation criteria and applies proper criteria for proper timing. This paper also describes a detailed design of the process so that managers can easily practice the process.

Remaining issues are how to fine-tune the process to fit particular business in a particular environment are discussed in Section 5 of this paper and the evaluation of requirements is discussed in Section 6. These issues are to be solved by studying business case, action research, and quantitative study.

References

Aristotle (350 BC). Nicomachean Ethics (Translated by W.D. Ross). The Internet Classics Archive of MIT.

Cooper, R. G. (1983, 2011). *Winning at New Products: Accelerating the Process from Idea to Launch*. New York: Basic Books.

Ito, T. (2013). Customer value makes people happy. *The Journal of Cost Accounting Research* 38(1): 11–20.

Monden, Y. and K. Hamada (1991). Target costing and Kaizen costing in Japanese automobile companies. *Journal of Management Accounting Research* 3: 16–34.

Mintzberg, H., D. Raisinghani and A. Théorêt (1976). The structure of unstructured decision processes. *Administrative Science Quarterly* 21: 246–275.

Nobeoka, K. (2008). Kachizukuri no Gijutukeiei (Technology Management for Creating Value) (in Japanese)

Nonaka, I., R. Toyama and T. Hirata (2010). *Managing Flow — The Dynamic Theory of Knowledge-Based Firm*, Tokyo: Toyokeizaishinbosha (in Japanese).

Schmidt, E., J. Rosenberg and A. Eagle (2014). *How Google Works.* New York: Grand Central Publishing.

Schumpeter, J. A. (1983, English originally in 1934, originally in 1911, 1926). *The Theory of Economic Development*, Transaction Publisher (Original Title: Theorie Der Wirtschaftlichen Entwicklung).

Simon, H. A. (1977, first printed in 1960). *The New Science of Management Decision, revised edition.* Englewood Cliffs: Prertice-Hall.

The Hasso Plattner Institute of Design at Stanford (2011). *The d.School Bootcamp Bootleg.* The Hasso Plattner Institute of Design at Stanford.

Ulrich, D., S. Kerr and R. Ashkenas (2002). *The GE Workout.* New York: McGraw-Hill.

Young, J. W. (1940). *A Technique for Producing Ideas.* New York: McGraw-Hill.

Management Control System to Promote Innovation and Corporate Venturing

Katsuhiro Ito

Professor, Faculty of Economics,
Seikei University, Japan

1. Introduction

According to Anthony (1965), who is well known to have pioneered the systematic discussion of management control systems (MCS), MCS had been expected to efficiently put the goals set by strategic planning into action.[1] In other words, an MCS would function within the scope defined by strategic planning and was not assumed to influence strategic planning. Such a conventional view, namely, that an MCS passively follows strategic change has been explicitly or implicitly supported by a large number of researchers. However, with the increasing importance attached to strategy emergence, some have come to think that an MCS plays a definite role in strategic change,[2] a prime example being the concept of interactive control systems (ICS) proposed by Simons (1995).

---

[1] In this paper, the scope of an MCS is broad, as defined in Malmi and Brown (2008), and is assumed to include not only ordinary cybernetic control but also cultural controls, corporate missions, remuneration systems, and organizational structures and rules.

[2] The relationships between strategic change and an MCS were organized by Davila (2005), who provides an excellent review that triggered this study. For emergent strategies, refer to Mintzberg (1978).

Japanese Management and International Studies Vol. 13:
Management of Innovation Strategy in Japanese Companies
World Scientific Publishing Company, September 2016

In this paper, we investigate the relationship between strategic change made by trial and error (strategy emergence) and an MCS. More specifically, based on Burgelman's strategy formation model (Burgelman, 1983, 1991, 2002, etc.), we attempt to reevaluate from a broader perspective the role an MCS plays in strategy emergence by examining mechanisms by which strategy emergence occurs. Our conclusion is that an ICS acts mainly on the front end processes (promotion of autonomous initiatives) of strategy emergence. We also confirmed the importance of discussing the function of an MCS in the backend processes (approval and resource allocation in an organization) should also be discussed and suggested some possibilities. These models of MCS explain the reality of Japanese large company's practice much better than traditional ones.

2. Strategy Emergence Model of Simons

An ICS promotes strategy emergence by the following process. Subordinates are motivated to direct their attention to something that their superiors are focusing on (strategic uncertainties). Superiors repeatedly seek information via official meetings or informal dialogues, and subordinates start to conscientiously collect data or engage in trial and error on the matter in question.

As a result of this, new information is collected and previously untried experiments, projects, or action plans are proposed in and around the strategic uncertainties specified by the superiors. Many of the various trial and error efforts fail to produce good results and are ignored, but some lead to desirable results (tactical learning). The experience of a successful experiment having brought about good results spreads within an organization and is shared (learning from a successful case). Through such a process, a new strategy that was not initially intended is adopted (emergent strategy is formulated).

Simons' pioneering research, which related strategy emergence to MCS, has served as the basis for a large number of subsequent researches. However, the following issues remain prominent:

(a) Can any other MCS, except ICS, that affects autonomous action be devised?
(b) Does "learning from a successful case" always lead to "strategic change?"
(c) Is it always appropriate to consider top management as the starting point for strategy emergence?

Simons model cannot be applied to the Japanese context. In order to clarify the essence and limitations of ICS, we examine the role an MCS plays in the strategy emergence process based on Burgelman's strategy formation model, which also incorporates strategy emergence.

3. Burgelman's Strategy Formation Process Model

3.1. *Structure of Burgelman's model*

To construct his model, Burgelman applied the concepts of ecology to the strategy emergence process. The evolutionary process in ecology follows the pattern of *variation, selection,* and *retention.* Similarly, variation occurs first in Burgelman's depiction of the strategy emergence process. The origin of new strategies (mutation) are autonomous strategic behaviors (trial and error or proposals by managers) outside the scope of an intended strategy (concept of corporate strategy). The same is true in that not all variations are necessarily allowed to survive in an organization. The next process in line is selection. Even if they begin to develop, most new strategies are eliminated as a result of screening under existing concept of corporate strategies or management control mechanisms (structural context). Some variations impressively survive the selection process. For some autonomous strategic behaviors, the middle management who proposed them may succeed in convincing top management of their strategic significance, causing a change in top management's view of the company's future direction or resource allocation (strategic context). As a result of this, officially approved ideas are ultimately retained as new strategies (concept of corporate strategy) (Fig. 1). The point is that not only the variation process, as a frontend process, but also the selection and retention processes, which are backend processes, are shown explicitly.

This model comprises two routes. The route for implementing existing strategies is called the "induced strategy process." A "concept of corporate strategy" is an idea that has officially and organizationally been determined as a current strategy. It is intended for organizational implementation and resources are actually allocated for it. A concept of corporate strategy indicates the strategic intent of top management and provides operational- and middle-level managers with a common frame of reference for the direction the organization is heading. Strategies are organizationally "retained" through their establishment as concept of corporate strategy. An "induced strategic

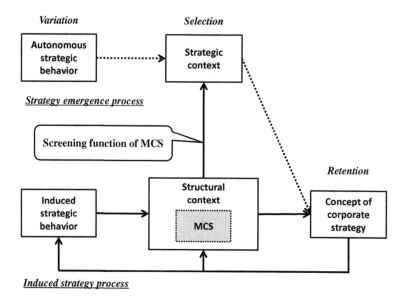

Fig. 1.   Burgelman's model
Source: Adapted from Burgelman (1983), p. 65.

action" is evoked by managers adopting a strategic action that is consistent with current concept of corporate strategy.

A "structural context" refers to the whole structure of a mechanism constructed by top management in order to turn the intended strategy (concept of corporate strategy) into practical action. It encompasses not only organizational structure and management systems but also cultural factors such as ceremonies and codes of conduct. It should be considered to encompass all MCS in a broad sense. A structural context contributes to enforcing and implementing the existing strategies while also functioning as a selection mechanism for new strategic behaviors.

Strategy emergence arises from "autonomous strategic processes." The term "autonomous strategic behavior" refers to various trial and error efforts evoked by managers outside the scope of the current concept of corporate strategy. It is possible for an autonomous strategic behavior to occur at any level of management, but it is most likely to occur at an executive management level that has more opportunities to gain direct contact with the latest technology trends or changes in market conditions and has a certain degree of authority to make budget decisions (Burgelman, 1991, p. 246). Autonomous strategic behavior often occurs accidentally and is difficult to predict, but does not necessarily occur randomly, because it is rooted in and limited by an organization's capabilities (Burgelman, 1991, p. 246).

"Strategic context," which stands alongside "autonomous strategic behavior," refers to top management's "crude strategic intent" (Barnett and Burgelman 1996). Strategic context is a process in which a strategic significance is attached to a successful autonomous strategic behavior. Even if an autonomous strategic behavior has some success, it ends up being eliminated if its significance is not recognized by top management. Thus, in order to justify an autonomous strategic behavior, middle management takes political action and negotiates with or persuades top management. It is assumed that the role top management plays in deciding strategic context is only either approving of or rejecting new project trials (new autonomous strategic behaviors). This is a major difference from Simons (1995). If middle management fails to convince top management about a new project and obtain approval from them, resources necessary for the new project will not be allocated, and the project will ultimately be eliminated and not be included in the concept of corporate strategy.

3.2. *Intel's strategic shift in the 1980s*

In order to construct his model and reinforce its validity, Burgelman conducted a detailed and long-term study of Intel's strategy emergence process. Intel originated as a memory company in 1968, and in the 1980s, a strategic shift from memory to microprocessors was executed against the intent of the top management, who were the founders (Barnett and Burgelman, 1996). The initial strategy intended by the top management was to continue focusing on the memory business. This was because they valued the company's history of being founded as a "memory company" and its role in the development and technologies of the memory business.

The company's subsequent growth proved that the strategic shift from memory to microprocessors was a great success. There were two selection mechanisms at work for the strategic shift to be implemented against top management's intent. The two reasons of criteria for resource allocation (result-oriented evaluation) and organizational culture are given as the structural context that affected the elimination of the memory business.

First, Intel's criteria for resource allocation (factory production capacity allocation) were decided according to the profitability per wafer (product unit). The criteria were chosen to maximize profit obtained from production capacity, which is a scarce resource. Because the criteria worked, more factory production capacity came to be allocated to microprocessors, which had far greater profitability than memory, which top management had focused on.

Second, since its foundation, top management at Intel had been practicing a rule that open discussion should be encouraged (i.e. they shared the idea that "knowledge-based opinions supersede status-based authority"). As a result of this, middle management was able to challenge top management's thinking that memory should be focused on. In addition to middle management being given opportunities to persuade top management of microprocessors' advantage, an atmosphere in which top management would listen to them attentively and consider the validity of their ideas had been present since its foundation.

To allow autonomous strategic behavior to be incorporated into the concept of corporate strategy, a strategic context must be present that makes it possible. In the case of Intel, two structural context factors, namely, result-orientated resource allocation criteria and the organizational culture of data-based thorough discussion, were important in deciding the strategic context.

3.3. Significance of Burgelman's model

According to Burgelman's model, an MCS forms part of the strategic structure, is positioned in induced strategic processes, and plays a role in facilitating efficient implementation of the existing strategy and securing the stability of an organization. Strategy emergence occurs in autonomous strategic processes. The contents of autonomous strategic behaviors by organization members are unpredictable and become the source of strategy emergence. Strategic context is an "agreement" of the precondition of strategy in an organization, and many autonomous strategic behaviors are rejected by the existing strategic context and failed to lead to a change in the strategy contents. When autonomous strategic behaviors continue to attempt to shake up strategic context, part of the action may become successful and strategy contents may ultimately be revised. In such cases, discontinuous change will occur and a new strategy will emerge.

What is important is that structural context can have a significant effect on strategic context. It should be noted that an MCS plays an important role in creating an atmosphere determining whether a new proposal will be adopted. The significance of Burgelman's model lies in the fact that it perceives strategy emergence not only as the stage in which variation, that is, autonomous strategic behavior, occurs but also as a whole, including its survival of the selection process and its retention.

4. Examination of MCS Researches using Burgelman's Model

4.1. *Previous researches citing Burgelman's view*

Previous researches of MCS that referred to Burgelman's strategy emergence model, include Simons (1991, 2010), Marginson (2002), and Davila (2005). In terms of the relation with MCS, all of these researches focused primarily on the variation process, but did not explicitly relate MCS to the selection and retention processes.

Simons (1995) praised Burgelman's researches (1983, 1991) for their usefulness in establishing the concept of ICS. He stated that, with regards to the relationship with strategy emergence, an ICS causes the experimentation and learning necessary for new autonomous strategic behavior. Autonomous strategic behavior corresponds to variation and the process from selection through retention is not considered. It is clear that ICS is a concept focusing on "the upstream process of strategy emergence."

A major difference between Simons' discussion of ICS and Burgelman's model lies in whether the selection process is taken into consideration. We think that the selection process is important when examining strategy emergence. Understanding that an autonomous strategic behavior generated by learning or experimentation does not always immediately lead to strategy emergence is consistent with corporate reality. To be accepted as a strategy, "formalization", "organizational approval", and "resource allocation" should likely be considered essential. Burgelman's model makes it clear that an MCS not only plays a role in promoting autonomous strategic behavior (variation process), but also, as the structural context, functions as a mechanism for evaluating and selecting autonomous strategic behaviors. This role that an

MCS plays in the selection process is extremely important in that it affects the strategic context decision regarding to what extent an autonomous strategic behavior should be accepted.

4.2. Two routes for an MCS to affect strategy emergence

As a result of examining the strategy emergence process of Burgelman's model, the following two routes for an MCS to affect strategy emergence can be found. Route 1, "MCS (structural context) → autonomous strategic behavior," affects autonomous strategic behavior and Route 2, "MCS (structural context) → strategic context," affects strategic context (see Fig. 2). Many theorists, including Simons (1995), have focused on just Route 1.

4.3. Route 1: effect on autonomous strategic behavior

Simons' ICS is one of the leading examples of Route 1, but is not the only controlling method that affects autonomous strategic behavior. Davila (2005)

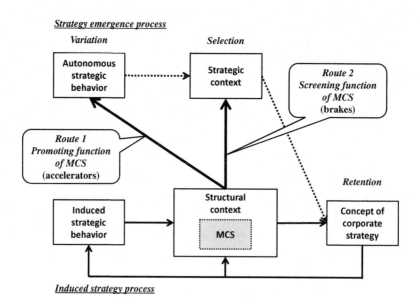

Fig. 2.   Two routes for an MCS to affect strategy emergence
Source: Adapted from Burgelman (1983), p. 65.

proposed an MCS that promotes autonomous strategic behavior and can be divided into the following four components: (1) building a system that promotes autonomous action, (2) increasing exposure to learning opportunities, (3) increasing availability of resources, and (4) building a system that promotes information exchange in an organization. Incidentally, an ICS has two components: promoting autonomous action by superiors' attention and promoting information exchange between superiors and subordinates.

Examples of a "system that promotes autonomous action" include strategic intent (Hamel and Prahalad, 1994), stretch goals (Dess *et al.*, 1998), and belief systems (Simons, 1995). Means to achieve "increasing exposure to learning opportunities" include bringing people with different training and experiences together (Dougherty and Hardy, 1996) and using external collaborations to generate creative abrasion (Leonard-Barton, 1992). Means for "increasing availability of resources" include provision of the slack indispensable for initial experimentation and the funds necessary for the advancement of the project. Measures such as appointment of idea "scouts" and "coaches" (Kanter, 1989) and establishment of innovation departments (innovation hubs) (Leifer *et al.*, 2000) are given as examples of a "system that promotes information exchange in an organization."

In addition to the controlling strategy proposed by Davila (2005) that has the potential to affect autonomous strategic behavior, we think the following measures may also contribute to the activation of autonomous strategic behavior. This is not an exhaustive list, but it gives valuable options.

(i) Promoting autonomous action by organizational culture management or clan control (Ouchi, 1979).

(ii) Restricting scales for evaluation (Simons, 2010)
This can economize managers' workloads and increase discretionary power over the process.

(iii) Controlling employees (Merchant, 1982; Simons, 2010)
Preferentially hiring assertive and enterprising employees and providing them with thorough education and training to promote trial and error and opportunity discovery should increase autonomous actions.

(iv) Results-based control (Merchant, 1982)
This should have an effect similar to that of restricting evaluation scales. It results in the assignment of discretionary power over the process, giving managers more freedom of action.

(v)   Boundary system (Simons, 2010)
By clearly defining business boundaries and levels of risk allowed, discretionary power is assigned within controlled limits.

(vi)   Promoting autonomous action by adopting evaluation scales to measure innovation (e.g. the number of new project proposals).

(vii)   Generating creative tension (Simons, 2010)
Autonomous action is incentivized by putting pressure on managers by announcing rankings (nurturing competition within the organization, utilizing peer pressure), intentional deviation from the controllability principle (developing entrepreneurship), allocating corporate expenses, team matrix structure (deviation from routines), etc.

Among these, (i)–(v) are relevant to an MCS's design principle of aiming to increase the discretionary power of managers without detailed checking of the process, (vi) aims to promote the autonomous behaviors necessary for experimentation and trial and error, and (vii) intends to increase transparency and make the necessity of autonomous action become recognized.

It would appear that there are many possibilities, other than an ICS, that affect autonomous strategic behavior. As pointed out by Marginson (2002), however, what should be focused on here is the importance of the question of not only whether a system or measure is introduced, but also of how managers perceive controlling strategies.

4.4.   *Route 2: effect on the selection process (strategic context decision) for autonomous strategic behaviors*

One advantage of Burgelman's model is that it clearly indicates that an MCS has the potential to have a significant effect on the selection process. Factors extracted from Burgelman's researches fall among the following items.

(i)   Organizational culture
In the case of Intel, the presence of an organizational culture that allows open discussion enabled middle management to challenge top management's intent.

(ii)   Compiling a corporate history
Being given credit at a later date as a manager who started a new project can be an incentive for top managers to support a new project.

(iii) Composition of personnel in top management
Deployment of personnel with prominent experience in developing new projects may help autonomous strategic behavior survive the selection process more easily.

The following are candidates for additional measures that have the potential to affect the above-described selection process for autonomous strategic behaviors (strategic context decision).

(i) Adopting and emphasizing a belief system
The probability that top management accepts middle management's proposals is higher because consensus about priorities in the domains that fit within the corporate mission is formed in advance.

(ii) Implementing an ICS
To begin with, the subjects for an ICS lie only in the domains top management is interested in. When an ICS has already been put into action, the probability that top management accepts middle management's proposals is higher.

(iii) Establishment of an open new project committee (at the top management level)
The purpose of this effort is to institutionalize autonomous strategic processes by devising a formal organization or meeting structure.

(iv) Evaluation using performance scales
In the case of Intel, decisions on resource allocation were made according to the profitability of each product. In such a situation where importance is attached to scales to assess performance that are directly connected to the market, the probability that top management will accept middle management's proposals is higher.

(v) Adopting fewer evaluation scales
This is also related to evaluation using performance scales. When fewer scales are considered in the selection process, the probability that a new project will be highly evaluated is higher; this was the situation in the case of Intel.

We examined how these two routes are operated mainly based on the views of Davila (2005), etc. Going forward, an accumulation of further systematic organization of discussions and empirical research are needed.

5. Conclusions

Mintzberg (1978) conceptualized strategy formed as a pattern from trial and error conducted over time to accommodate factors that differ from the initial assumptions as emergent strategy. In a rapidly changing environment, formulating the optimal strategy in advance is not easy and managing an organizational learning process is important to effectively bring emergent strategies into being.

Conventionally, it was assumed that headquarter staff (strategists) or the top management themselves analytically evaluate the external environment and internal resources of a company and formulate an optimal strategic plan in advance. However, observing business practice has led to support for the view that the actual strategy formation in a company is not necessarily implemented analytically as assumed in the strategic plan, and that strategy, as a pattern of action, is formed a *posteriori* through a process of trial and error in actual business practice conducted at many levels of management.

Previously, in management accounting researches, ICS, advocated by Simons, has come to be known as a concept of an MCS that contributes to the appearance of emergent strategy. Simons' theory formed an excellent and highly important theory that related strategy emergence to the MCS and expanded the range of research on MCS. However, weaknesses can be pointed out: for example, the strategy formation process is not subject to direct consideration because the MCS is the main consideration, and the contribution of the middle management levels responsible for frontline operations is difficult to perceive because emphasis is placed on top management's roles.

In this paper, by focusing on a strategy emergence model and examining whether MCS plays any role in the model, we proposed the possibility that an MCS, other than an ICS, may be related to strategy emergence. As a strategy emergence model, we adopted Burgelman's well-established model, based upon which, we examined from a broader perspective the role an MCS plays in strategy emergence.

The significance of Burgelman's model is that it seems to be consistent with the facts surrounding strategic changes in actual corporate organizations (in particular large corporations in Japan). The model focuses on analyzing resource allocation through vertical interactions between top and middle managements, in particular, the role middle management plays. What is important is that a strategy has no particular meaning when it is simply devised and first gains substantial meaning only when it survives competition within a company and resources are allocated for it.

Also, top management is not always able to collect up-to-date frontline information and only plays the role of evaluator for strategy alternatives that can be proposed by middle management responsible for operation management. The point is that the model appears to be well suited for depicting the real picture for two reasons: attention is also given to competition for survival over resource allocation, which is the backend process of strategy emergence, and the model has middle management as main actor.

The significance of our using Burgelman's model to examine the relationship between strategy emergence and an MCS lies in its usefulness for ascertaining from a broader perspective the effects that an MCS has on strategy emergence. When considering its relation to strategy emergence, an MCS is important in the following two ways.

(i) An MCS affects the direction and total amount of autonomous strategic behavior (variation) generation.

(ii) An MCS affects the selection process (what should be allowed to survive and at which level of probability) for autonomous strategic behaviors.

In this paper, based on previous researches, we proposed MCS strategies to activate each of these. Burgelman's model, which focuses on backend processes, was found to be useful for the examination of (ii).

A role that top management plays in this model, which should not be overlooked, is that they decide when an induced or autonomous strategy process should be used. The probability that autonomous strategic behaviors will be generated, supported, and adopted can be adjusted by the design of the structural context including the MCS.

References

Anthony, R. N. (1965). *Planning and control systems: A framework for analysis*. Division of Research, Graduate School of Business Administration, Harvard University.

Barnett, W. P. and R. A. Burgelman (1996). Evolutionary perspectives on strategy. *Strategic Management Journal* 17: 5–19.

Burgelman, R. A. (1983). A model of the interaction of strategic behavior, corporate context, and the concept of strategy. *Academy of Management Review* 8: 61–70.

Burgelman, R. A. (1991). Intraorganizational ecology of strategy making and organizational adaptation: theory and field research. *Organization Science* 2(3): 239–262.

Burgelman, R. A. (2002). *Strategy is Destiny: How Strategy-Making Shapes a Company's Future*. New York: The Free Press.

Davila, T. (2005). The promise of management control systems for innovation and strategic change. In Chapman, C. S. (Ed.), *Controlling strategy: Management, accounting, and performance measurement* (pp. 37–61), New York, NY: Oxford University Press.

Dess, G. G., J. C. Picken and D. W. Lyon (1998). Transformational leadership: lessons from U.S. experience. *Long Range Planning* 31(5): 722–731.

Dougherty, D. and C. Hardy (1996). Sustained product innovation in large, mature organizations: Overcoming innovation-to-organization problems. *Academy of Management Journal* 39(5): 1120–1153.

Frow, N., D. Marginson and S. Ogden (2010). Continuous budgeting: reconciling budget flexibility with budgetary control. *Accounting, Organizations and Society* 35(4): 444–461.

Hamel, G. and C. K. Prahalad (1994). *Competing for the Future*. MA: Harvard Business School Press.

Kanter, R. M. (1989). *When giants learn to dance: Managing the Challenges of Strategy, Management and Careers in the 1990's*. New York: Simon & Schuster.

Leifer, R., C. M. McDermott, G. C. O'Connor, L. S. Peters, M. P. Rice and R. W. Veryzer (2000). *Radical innovation: How Mature Companies can Outsmart Upstarts*. MA: Harvard Business School Press.

Leonard-Barton, D. (1992). Core capabilities and core rigidities: a paradox in managing new product development. *Strategic Management Journal* 13: 111–125.

Marginson, D. E. W. (2002). Management control systems and their effects on strategy formation at middle-management levels: evidence from a UK organization. *Strategic Management Journal* 23(11): 1019–1031.

Merchant, K. A. (1982). The control function of management. *Sloan Management Review* 23(4): 43–55.

Malmi, T. and D. A. Brown (2008). Management control systems as a package: opportunities, challenges and research directions. *Management Accounting Research* 19(4): 287–300.

Mintzberg, H. (1978). Patterns in strategy formation. *Management Science* 24: 934–948.

Ouchi, W. G. (1979). A conceptual framework for the designs of organizational control mechanisms. *Management Science* 25(9): 833–848.

Simons, R. (1991). Strategic orientation and top management attention to control systems. *Strategic Management Journal* 12(1): 49–62.

Simons, R. (1995). *Levers of control: How Managers Use Innovative Control Systems to Drive Strategic Renewal.* MA: Harvard Business School Press.

Simons, R. (2010). Stress-test your strategy: the 7 questions to ask. *Harvard Business Review* 88(11): 93–100.

Do Management Control Systems Really Contribute to Product Innovation?

Kazunori Fukushima

Associate Professor, Department of Commerce,
Seinan Gakuin University, Japan

1. Introduction

In recent years, researchers have grown increasingly interested in the relationship between management accounting and control systems (MACS) and innovation. In contrast to previous findings in this domain, many contemporary studies have shown MACS to increase innovation (e.g. Bisbe and Malagueño, 2009; Chenhall *et al.*, 2011; Dunk, 2011; Fukushima, 2012; Horii, 2013; Mouritsen *et al.*, 2009; Ylinen and Gullkvist, 2014).

Innovation is not a monolithic phenomenon, but can be classified as one of the several different types. One common distinction between two types of innovation relates to differences between radical and incremental innovations. Radical innovation induces fundamental changes in technologies and products, ultimately disrupting the nature of an existing market (Ettlie *et al.*, 1984; Utterback, 1994). Incremental innovation relates to the use of existing knowledge to gradually improve products and services for customers (Ettlie *et al.*, 1984; Henderson and Clark, 1990). As evidenced by the distinct implications for each, radical and incremental innovations require the implementation of different organizational management strategies (Dewar and Dutton, 1986; Ettlie *et al.*, 1984), and therefore, require different types of

Japanese Management and International Studies Vol. 13:
Management of Innovation Strategy in Japanese Companies
World Scientific Publishing Company, September 2016

MACS (Davila, 2005; Davila *et al.*, 2009; Revellino and Mouritsen, 2009). Few researchers have empirically explored whether MACS exert a similar influence across different types of innovations (Bedford, 2015; Fukushima, 2012; Horii, 2013; Ylinen and Gullkvist, 2014). Moreover, the research that does exist has been unclear and inconsistent with regard to the link between MACS and radical innovation.

To redress this shortcoming of the literature, this paper explores how MACS' capabilities improve radical innovation. MACS capabilities are organizational capacities that allow organizations to realize the desired effects of MACS on performance (Fukushima, 2013). For example, MACS capabilities related to target costing can prevent product design fatigue and decrease costs (Yook, 2003; Yoshida, 2001a, 2001b). Further, MACS capabilities related to performance measurement moderate the effect of performance measurement on achieving organizational objectives positively (Fukushima, 2015). Similar to how previous studies have shown MACS capabilities to exert influence on the consequences of MACS, this study explores how MACS capabilities help foster radical innovation.

To address the issues outlined above, I have organized the remainder of this paper into a series of interrelated sections. In the following section, I provide a brief overview of extant literature and propose a theoretical model. Then, I describe my research method followed by a discussion of the results they produce in Section 3. Finally, I conclude the paper with a consideration of the study's limitations and avenues of future research.

2. Literature Review and Theoretical Framework

The relationship between MACS and innovation has been the topic of focus for a great deal of management accounting research. In the past, researchers thought MACS to exert a negative effect on innovation (e.g. Abernethy and Brownell, 1997; Rockness and Shields, 1988). However, more recent research has come to conclude that MACS actually enhance innovation (e.g. Bisbe and Malagueño, 2009; Chenhall *et al.*, 2011; Dunk, 2011; Fukushima, 2012; Horii, 2013; Mouritsen *et al.*, 2009; Ylinen and Gullkvist, 2014). As a form of management control, management accounting information can improve or hamper innovation (Dunk, 2011). It also facilitates discussion of innovation activities (Mouritsen *et al.*, 2009; Revellino and Mouritsen, 2015).

Several of these studies drew from Simons' (1995, 2000) levers of control framework. Previous research in this domain has primarily explored the effects of interactive control on innovation (Bisbe and Malagueño, 2009; Bisbe and Otley, 2004; Fukushima, 2013; Henri, 2006). Interactive control is designed to assist the organization to identify new methods for strategically positioning itself in a dynamic marketplace. Previous studies consider that interactive control acts as a facilitator of successful innovation. In contrast to the theoretical claims derived from Simons' levers of control framework, Bisbe and Otley (2004) found no evidence to support the notion that interactive use of MACS improves innovation. Henri (2006), however, reported that interactive use of performance measurement systems may positively influence organizational innovativeness.

Though they have contributed to our understanding of innovation, these traditional studies have treated innovation as a monolithic concept. However, innovation can be classified as one of the multiple types. This is an important distinction, as different types of innovations require different strategic organizational management activities (Dewar and Dutton, 1986; Ettlie *et al.*, 1984), including the implementation of different types of MACS (Bedford, 2015; Bisbe and Malgueño, 2009; Davila, 2005; Davila *et al.*, 2009; Revellino and Mouritsen, 2009; Ylinen and Gullkvist, 2014). Bisbe and Malgueño (2009) reported that an organization's choice of individual MACS is associated with its organizational and managerial process by which innovation arises and is managed, regardless of whether the information provided by interactive use of MACS responds to the organization's needs for improving innovation. Similarly, Bedford (2015) reported that individual MACS are associated with improved performance in firms that specialize in exploration or exploitation innovation.[1] Furthermore, Ylinen and Gulkvist (2014) indicated that in exploratory (radical) innovation projects, organic control positively influences innovation.[2] This effect disappears in exploitative (incremental) innovation projects.

---

[1] Exploitation requires "refinement and extension of existing competencies, technologies, and paradigms whereas exploration entails experimentation with new alternatives" (March, 1991, p. 85).

[2] Organic control reflects two characteristics: (i) informal control reflecting norms of cooperation, communication and emphasis on getting "things done", and (ii) open channels of communication and free flow of information between project manager and subordinates (Ylinen and Gullkvist, 2014, p. 94).

In spite of relatively clear research trends in relation to the concepts above, previous scholarship has produced mixed results with regard to the relationship between interactive control and radical innovation (Davila, 2005; Davila *et al.*, 2009; Fukushima, 2012). Whereas some scholars have asserted that interactive control may enhance radical innovation (Davila, 2005; Davila *et al.*, 2009), empirical work to examine this possibility has yet to provide support to this claim (Fukushima, 2012).

In an attempt to resolve these inconsistencies, I focus on the moderating effect of MACS capabilities on the relationship between interactive use of MACS and radical innovation. MACS capabilities are organizational capacities that enable the realization of expected effects of MACS on performance (Fukushima, 2013). Experimental learning affects knowledge acquisition, accumulation, and implementation (Kolb, 1984; Yeung *et al.*, 1999), and may therefore exert a positive influence on the implementation of MACS (Kaplan and Norton, 1996; Tani *et al.*, 1994). For example, Kaplan and Norton (1996) argued that establishing targets and tolerances for balanced scorecard required trial and error. Tani *et al.* (1994) also indicated that when first implemented, target costing was meant to reduce costs. However, over time, it was used for the successful achievement of other objectives, including the timely introduction of new products and the satisfaction of consumer needs. These studies suggested that experimental learning about the use of MACS helps firms to realize expected consequences of MACS.

Figure 1 depicts the theoretical model reflecting the relationships between MACS (interactive control), MACS capabilities (experimental learning capabilities), and innovation (radical innovation). Extant literature suggests that if an organization possesses the capabilities to learn through the

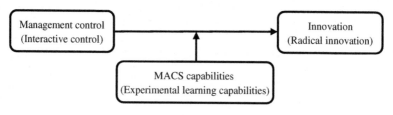

Fig. 1.   Theoretical framework

use of MACS, interactive use of MACS will improve radical innovation. Taken together, these assertions lead to the following hypothesis:

H1: The positive effect of interactive control on radical innovation is more pronounced when the organization possesses experimental learning capabilities.

3. Research Method

3.1. Data collection

In October 2013, a questionnaire with a cover letter and a stamped return, self-addressed envelope was mailed to either the chief of the general accounting department or the business administration department at 847 Japanese manufacturing firms listed in the first section of the Tokyo Stock Exchange.[3] I chose chief controllers as respondents because they are the most knowledgeable about their respective firms' use of MACS. To incentivize potential participants' responses, I promised to provide them with an executive summary of the study at their request. Moreover, I attempted to contact respondents with a follow-up message. Of the 847 questionnaires mailed, 76 (9.0%) were returned. Two questionnaires were discarded as a result of missing data, resulting in a final sample size of 74 (Table 1).

3.2. Variable measurement

3.2.1. Management control: interactive control

To measure interactive control, I used a multiscale instrument developed by Henri (2006) designed to ascertain how managers use performance measurement systems (PMS). This instrument captures whether PMS are used to (1) tie the organization together, (2) provide a common view of the organization's situation, (3) foster discussions in meetings between superiors and peers, and (4) debate action plans. An exploratory factor analysis (see Panel A in Table 2) indicated that the four items loaded on a single factor with an eigenvalue 2.417, explaining 60.42% of the variance in the underlying variable. The reliability estimate for this scale was relatively good ($\alpha = 0.767$).

---

[3] Industry classifications are based on Securities Identification Codes (Shoken Code) in the range of 3050–3800.

Table 1. Response rates for the questionnaire

	Industry classification	Sent	Received	%
3050	Foods	69	5	7.2
3100	Textiles and apparels	41	4	9.8
3150	Pulp and paper	11	1	9.1
3200	Chemicals	128	12	9.4
3250	Pharmaceutical	38	4	10.5
3300	Oil and coal products	11	0	0.0
3350	Rubber products	11	2	18.2
3400	Glass and ceramics products	33	2	6.1
3450	Iron and steel	32	5	15.6
3500	Non-ferrous metals	24	1	4.2
3550	Metal products	37	6	16.2
3600	Machinery	120	5	4.2
3650	Electric appliances	154	13	8.4
3700	Transportation equipment	62	5	8.1
3750	Precision instruments	28	2	7.1
3800	Other products	48	7	14.6
	Total	847	74	8.7

Given that the items loaded onto a single factor, I calculated the mean of the four items as an index measure of interactive control. Higher mean score indicates a higher degree of interactive control.

3.2.2. MACS capabilities: experimental learning capabilities

To measure experimental learning capabilities, I used five questions that asked respondents to assess the extent to which their respective organizations not only reviewed performance measurement activities and business strategies, but also refined them for the following period. These questions were developed on the basis of past research on experimental learning (Huber, 1991; Kolb, 1984). Another exploratory factor analysis (see Panel B of Table 2) resulted in a single factor with an eigenvalue of 2.613, which explained 52.26% of the variance in the underlying data. Like the previous variants, the reliability estimate for this scale was also quite good ($\alpha = 0.766$). Given the scale's internal consistency, I calculated the mean of the five items to generate a composite measure of experimental learning capabilities. Higher mean value indicates possessing better experimental learning capabilities.

3.2.3. Innovation: radical innovation

I operationalized radical innovation as a four-item index variable geared towards measuring the degree to which firms are concerned with the development of next generation technology or new products for emerging customers and markets. This scale was developed on the basis of previous work by Dewar and Dutton (1986) and Ettile *et al.* (1984). Another exploratory factor analysis generated a single-factor solution (see Panel C of Table 2) in which the factor had an eigenvalue of 2.436 and explained 60.89% of all variance in the data. Collectively, these items produced a good reliability estimate ($\alpha = 0.786$). Like the other scales, the high reliability estimate allowed for the calculation of a mean that could serve as the composite score for this scale. Higher mean values signify a greater dedication to radical innovation.

4. Results and Discussion

To explore the interaction effects between interactive control and experimental learning capabilities on radical innovation, I performed a two-way analysis of variance (ANOVA) procedure. Although multiple regression analysis would have been preferable, the relatively small sample size precluded this possibility (Hartmann and Mores, 1999; Hoque and James, 2000). In the two-way ANOVA, I performed a median split for both the interactive control ($M = 4.87$) and experimental learning capabilities ($M = 5.60$) variables to generate "high" and "low" values for each measure.

Table 3 summarizes the results of the ANOVA. These results do not provide support for main effects of interactive control or experimental learning capabilities for radical innovation. However, the interaction of interactive control and experimental learning capabilities (INT * ELC) was shown to exert a significant influence on radical innovation (F-value = 4.013, $p < 0.05$), providing support for H1. Table 3 provides a visual representation of this

Table 2.   Questionnaire items and statistics of measurement analysis

Items in questionnaire	Mean	Std. dev.	
Panel A: Interactive control			
Tie the organization together	4.43	1.008	**0.743**
Provide a common view of the organization	4.99	1.079	**0.732**
Discuss in meetings of superiors and peers	5.36	0.821	**0.700**
Debate action plans continually	4.58	1.314	**0.573**
Eigenvalue			2.417
Value explained			60.424%
Cronbach's α			0.767
Panel B: Experimental learning capabilities			
Review and refine business activities	5.84	0.876	**0.787**
Review and refine business strategy	5.53	1.023	**0.743**
Target setting reflected performance	5.93	0.881	**0.630**
Review and refine performance measurement	4.74	0.777	**0.575**
Explain business performance	5.38	1.107	**0.423**
Eigenvalue			2.613
Variance explained			52.260%
Cronbach's α			0.766
Panel C: Radical innovation			
Emphasis on creating next generation technologies	4.74	1.415	**0.826**
Emphasis on developing new products	4.58	1.385	**0.796**
Emphasis on developing new markets	4.91	1.196	**0.629**
Emphasis on new customers acquisition	5.05	1.109	**0.512**
Eigenvalue			2.436
Value explained			60.891%
Cronbach's α			0.786

Note: In answering each question, use range from 1 to 7, where "1" stands "strong disagree" and "7" stands "strong agree". This table reports the results of factor analyses. Bold indicates the loading of the items wording of survey items.

interaction effect. Consistent with H1, Fig. 2 shows that firms that emphasize interactive control and have substantial experimental learning capabilities tend to foster successful radical innovation.

Table 3. Analysis of variance (ANOVA): two-way interaction effects

Source of variation	Sum of squares	df	Mean square	F	Sig. of F
Panel A: Radical innovation					
INT	2.064	1	2.064	2.183	0.144
ELC	0.655	1	0.655	0.693	0.408
INT × ELC	3.793	1	3.793	4.013	0.049
Residual	66.171	70	0.945		
Total	1792.938	74			

Note: INT, interactive control; ELC, experimental learning capability.

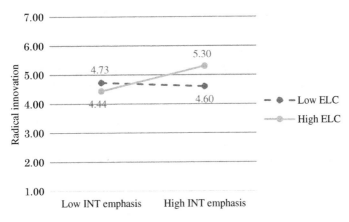

Fig. 2.   INT * ELC interaction effect on radical innovation

Previous research on the relationship between MACS and innovation has suggested that interactive control is positively related to firm performance for exploratory innovation firms (Bedford, 2015), and that organic control positively affects innovation for exploratory innovation projects (Ylinen and Gullkvist, 2014). Because exploratory innovation is closely related to radical innovation, these studies have produced evidence to suggest that MACS can enhance radical innovation as well. Other studies have also shown that interactive control can improve radical innovation (Davila, 2005; Davila *et al.*, 2009), but empirical study has not supported the suggestion (Fukushima, 2013). This study revealed that it is not enough to use interactive control highly for enhancing radical innovation, simultaneously possessing or developing high experimental learning capabilities are key to foster radical innovation.

By measuring performance, organizations with substantial experimental learning capabilities can accumulate procedural knowledge related to where, when, and how managers should utilize PMS as a form of interactive control. Consequently, for organizations with experimental learning capabilities, an emphasis on interactive control can foster successful radical innovation.

5. Conclusion

Previous work has produced inconsistent results regarding the relationship between MACS and radical innovation. This study addresses these inconsistencies by exploring the moderating effect of MACS capabilities on this relationship. By introducing MACS capabilities as a moderator in the analysis, this study shows that MACS do, in fact, foster successful radical innovation. However, the results imply that the interactive use of MACS is simply not sufficient to enhance radical innovation. It is also necessary for a firm to possess experimental learning capabilities to more effectively foster radical innovation.

This study contributes to an extant body literature that has sought to explore the effects of MACS capabilities. A growing stream of research has shown how capabilities play a central role in the effective use of MACS (Fukushima, 2015; Yook, 2003; Yoshida, 2001a, 2001b). Drawing from experimental learning theory, this study contributes to the growing number of studies to reach this conclusion. This study's findings also suggest that reviewing and refining activities related to performance measurement help organizations to achieve expected results.

In spite of the contribution of this study, it does suffer from some limitations. First, this study drew from experimental learning theory (Huber, 1991; Kolb, 1984) to develop an instrument for measuring MACS capabilities. However, these instruments were not originally intended for evaluating MACS; future research should seek to refine a multidimensional measure intended specifically for gauging MACS capabilities. Second, the sample size for this study was relatively low, thereby reducing statistical power and diminishing external validity. Future studies should utilize larger samples to improve the study's statistical power and the generalizability of the findings.

Acknowledgment

This work was supported by JSPS KAKENHI Grant Nos. 2473406, 15K17175.

References

Abernethy, M. A. and P. Brownell (1997). Management control systems in research and development organizations: the role of accounting, behavior and personnel control. *Accounting, Organizations and Society* 22(3/4): 233–248.

Bedford, D. S. (2015). Management control systems across different modes of innovation: implications for firm performance. *Management Accounting Research* 28: 12–30.

Bisbe, J. and D. Otley (2004). The effects of the interactive use of management control systems on product innovation. *Accounting, Organizations and Society* 29(8): 709–737.

Bisbe, J. and R. Malagueño (2009). The choice of interactive control systems under different innovation management modes. *European Accounting Review* 18(2): 371–405.

Chenhall, R. H., J.-P. Kallunki and H. Silvola (2011). Exploring the relationships between strategy, innovation, and management control systems: the roles of social networking, organic innovative culture, and formal controls. *Journal of Management Accounting Research* 23(1): 99–128.

Davila, T. (2005). The promise of management control systems for innovation and strategic change. In Chapman, C. S. (Ed.), *Controlling Strategy: Management Accounting and Performance Measurement* (pp. 37–61), New York, NY: Oxford University Press.

Davila, A., G. Foster and D. Oyon (2009). Accounting and control, entrepreneurship and innovation: venturing into new research opportunities. *European Accounting Review* 18(2): 281–311.

Dewar, R. D. and J. E. Dutton (1986). The adoption of radical and incremental innovations and empirical analysis. *Management Science* 32(11): 1422–1433.

Dunk, A. S. (2011). Product innovation, budgetary control, and the financial performance of firms. *The British Accounting Review* 43(2): 102–111.

Ettlie, J. E., W. P. Bridges and R. D. O'Keefe (1984). Organizational strategy and structural differences for radical versus incremental innovation. *Management Science* 30(6): 682–695.

Fukushima, K. (2012). The effects of management control systems on product innovation: an exploratory study. *The Journal of Management Accounting, Japan* 20(1): 37–51 (in Japanese).

Fukushima, K. (2013). The relationship between management accounting and organizational capabilities: an introduction to management accounting capabilities. *The Commercial Review, Seinan Gakuin University* 60(1/2): 43–58 (in Japanese).

Fukushima, K. (2015). An exploratory study of management accounting capabilities: effects of relationship between performance measurement systems and absorptive capacity on organizational performance. *The Journal of Cost Accounting Research* 39(1): 65–75 (in Japanese).

Hartmann, F. G. H. and F. Moers (1999). Testing contingency hypotheses in budgetary research: an evaluation of the use of moderated regression analysis. *Accounting, Organizations and Society* 24(4): 291–315.

Henderson, R. and K. Clark (1990). Architectural innovation: the reconfiguration of existing product technologies and the failure of established firms. *Administrative Science Quarterly* 35(1): 9–30.

Henri, J.-F. (2006). Management control systems and strategy: a resource-based perspective. *Accounting, Organizations and Society* 31(6): 529–558.

Hoque, Z. and W. James (2000). Linking balanced scorecard measures to size and market factors: impact on organizational performance. *Journal of Management Accounting Research* (12): 1–17.

Horii, S. (2013). The role of budgetary management in product innovation. *The Quarterly Journal of Ritsumeikan University* 51(6): 39–54 (in Japanese).

Huber, G. P. (1991). Organization learning: the contributing processes and the literatures. *Organization Science* 2(1): 88–115.

Kaplan, R. S. and D. P. Norton (1996). *The Balanced Scorecard: Translating Strategy into Action*. Boston, MA: Harvard Business School Press.

Kolb, D. A. (1984). *Experimental Learning: Experience as the Source of Learning and Development*. Upper Saddle River, NJ: Prentice-Hall.

March, J. G. (1991). Exploration and exploitation in organizational learning. *Organization Science* 2(1): 71–87.

Mouritsen, J., A. Hansen and C. Ø. Hansen (2009). Short and long translations: management accounting calculations and innovation management. *Accounting, Organizations and Society* 34(6/7): 738–754.

Revellino, S. and J. Mouritsen (2009). The multiplicity of controls and the making of innovation. *European Accounting Review* 18(2): 341–369.

Revellino, S. and J. Mouritsen (2015). Accounting as an engine: the performativity of calculative practices and the dynamics of innovation. *Management Accounting Research* 28: 31–49.

Rockness, H. O. and M. D. Shields (1988). Organizational control systems in research and development. *Accounting, Organizations and Society* 9(2): 165–177.

Simons, R. (1995). *Levers of Control: How to Managers Use Interactive Control Systems to Drive Strategic Renewal.* Boston, MA: Harvard Business School Press.

Simons, R. (2000). *Performance Measurement and Control Systems for Implementing Strategies.* Upper Saddle River, NJ: Prentice-Hall.

Tani, T., H. Okano, N. Shimizu, Y. Iwabuchi, J. Fukuda and S. Cooray (1994). Target cost management in Japanese companies: current state of the art. *Management Accounting Research* 5(1): 67–81.

Tushman, L. and P. Anderson (1986). Technological discontinuities and organizational environments. *Administrative Science Quarterly* 31(3): 439–465.

Utterback, J. M. (1994). *Mastering the Dynamics of Innovation.* Boston, MA: Harvard Business School Press.

Yeung, A. K., D. O. Ulrich, S. W. Nason and M. A. von Glinow (1999). *Organizational Learning Capability: Generating and generalizing Ideas with Impact.* New York, NY: Oxford University Press.

Ylinen, M. and B. Gullkvist (2014). The effects of organic and mechanistic control in exploratory and exploitative innovation. *Management Accounting Research* 25(1): 93–112.

Yook, K.-H. (2003). The effect of group maturity and organizational capabilities on performance of target cost management. *The Journal of Management Accounting, Japan* 11(1): 3–14 (in Japanese).

Yoshida, E. (2001a). Empirical study about the relationship between organizational capabilities for target cost management and performance: comparison among three division at a Japanese electric company. *The Journal of Cost Accounting Research* 25(2): 1–9 (in Japanese).

Yoshida, E. (2001b). Relationship between performance and organizational capabilities in target cost management: mail survey to design engineers. *The Journal of Management Accounting, Japan* 10(1): 39–52 (in Japanese).

Solving the Wage Differentials Throughout the Supply Chain by Collaborative Innovations for Changing the Parts Prices and Costs

Yasuhiro Monden

Professor Emeritus, The University of Tsukuba, Japan

1. Theme of This Paper

The protesting march called "Occupy Wall Street" in Manhattan, NY began on September 17, 2011. Their slogan was "We are the 99%" and they criticized the wage difference that the amounts of assets and income held by the wealthy people of upper-1% were increasing since 1970s. Likewise, Tom Piketty (2014) has pointed out the existence of the fewer acquirers of the super high amount of income and the fewer owners of the super high amount of assets, and thus he proposed to charge higher progressive taxes on income and owing assets as well as inherited assets.

However, apart from their proposals, the author tries to explore and propose the entirely new method for solving the wage difference among people by changing the transfer prices (or parts prices) between inter-firms of the supply chain, which has been promoted by Japanese companies for their wage differentials.

In this paper, the author will propose and show how the parts prices could be increased during the yen rate (currency exchange rate) depreciation phase, while the parts prices will be decreased during the yen rate appreciation phase,

Japanese Management and International Studies Vol. 13:
Management of Innovation Strategy in Japanese Companies
World Scientific Publishing Company, September 2016

for the purpose of solving wage differences. There are many such practical methods actually adopted by Japanese companies.

Such methods of reducing the wage differences among firms of supply chain have never been proposed and analyzed theoretically in the academic world. However, there exists a variety of useful, practical conventions in Japanese industrial world, for which the government Ministry of Economy, Trade and Industry (METI) and the government Small and Medium Enterprises Agency (SMEA) have also issued many valuable guidances to promote and support the industrial best practices.

2. Japanese Causes of Poverty and How We Should Cope with the Wage Differentials

2.1. History of Japanese inter-firm network after the World War II

The occupation policy of General Headquarters (GHQ) just after the World War II to democratize Japanese society led to agrarian land reform and Zaibatsu reform (i.e. decomposing the big holding company groups) resulting in reallocation of the big-scale lands, stocks, and household assets. As a result, the concentration of wealth was resolved and thus the income based on the wealth (assets) has been much equalized (Moriguchi, 2015).

The driving force of the high growth of the Japanese economy after the occupation period was the *Japanese business system* where the core company of the keiretsu allied business group (i.e. inter-firm network organization) partially owned its member firms and was supported or governed by the "main bank". During the high economic growth period and the stable growth period, Japan almost achieved the economic growth without the income differentials among people and achieved the "middle class family of all of one hundred million people".

2.2. Problem of Japanese domestic employment system under the long period of the yen-currency appreciation: Increase of non-regular employees

After the bubble burst in 1991 originated on account of Plaza Accord which resulted in high yen appreciation in 1986, Japan got into a long period (more than 20 years) of economic depression. During this time, most of the Japanese firms increased the number of *"non-regular employees"* due to which the low-income class people have expanded over the past 25 years or so ranging from 1991 to 2015. This was the appearance of Japanese wage differentials.

The expansion of distribution of the poor people is the unique characteristic of Japanese wage differentials (Abe, 2015). According to Prof. Abe, the "ratio of relative poverty," which is the proportion of the people whose income is below the half amount of the median (central figure) of income data was 12.0% in the year 1985, but it increased up to 16.1% in the year 2012.

When the Lehman shock hit Japanese economy, the non-regular employees had to be totally laid off. After the Lehman shock was over, Japanese companies have again held the non-regular employees of almost 40% among all employees at present (March, 2015), as before Lehman crisis. Further, the red ink SME firms due to yen currency depreciation after 2014 could not enjoy the increased wage unlike the employees of the booming exporting companies. The action due to which Japanese companies have increased the non-regular workers during the age of high yen currency has weakened the social background as a base of stronger Japanese style management of manufacturing (Shimokawa, 2009).

According to the survey of National Tax Agency, Japan, the average annual salary of regular employees in 2013 was 4.73 million yen, while the non-regular employees got only 1.68 million yen, which shows large gap (*The Nikkei*, 2015i). Therefore, almost 40% of working persons got only 35.5% (= 1.68/4.73) of the average amount of annual salary. Thus, it seems somewhat tougher to solve the wage difference for the non-regular employees through the changes of transfer price in the supply chain.

However, in order to approach the essential improvement for the labor conditions of non-regular employees, the Act on *"the same wage for the same job"* is needed to be introduced. Further, some action for changes from the non-regular position to the regular employee position must be taken. The former legislation was introduced in June 2015 (*The Nikkei*, 2015j, 2015k), and the latter actions have begun to be undertaken by companies positively to the employee incentives (First Retailing for Yunikuro brand, as a recent example).

3. Why Can the Inter-firm Network Reduce the Costs? Negative and Positive Aspects

Japanese inter-firm network or supply chain used to reduce the wage costs. Then why can the inter-firm network reduce the costs?

3.1. *The reason 1 is easiness in reducing the wage costs*

(1) Remarkable wage difference actually exists between the big firm and the small or medium firms in the supply chain. Seeing Table 1, the "amount of salary in cash per employee" will be lower when the firm size in terms of the number of employees becomes smaller. The average "amount of salary in cash per employee" for the firm of more than 1,000 employees is 6.36 million yen, while the firm of 4–9 employees is 2.81 million yen

Table 1.   Wage and value-added conditions per employee for each company scale, Ministry of Economy, Trade and Industry (2009). *Manufacturing statistics report*, shown in Noguchi (2012) p. 158

Number of employees	Total annual salary in cash per employee (million yen) A	Sales amount of manufactured products per employee (million yen)	Value added per employee (million yen) B	Salary/value added A/B
Total	**4.24**	**34.29**	**10.38**	**0.41**
4–9	2.81	10.93	5.25	0.54
10–19	3.26	15.49	6.81	0.48
20–29	3.44	19.03	7.71	0.45
30–49	3.61	23.21	7.95	0.45
50–99	3.75	27.46	9.14	0.41
100–199	4.08	33.34	11.14	0.37
200–299	4.38	39.37	11.52	0.38
300–499	4.77	51.02	13.82	0.35
500–999	5.22	49.30	13.75	0.38
1,000	6.36	63.53	14.81	0.43

Notes: Object is manufactures, not-less-than-4 employees.

which is merely 44%. It will exceed 50% when the firm size is bigger than 10–19 employees who receive 3.26 million yen.[1]

(2) Another reason for the wage difference within the supply chain is that the welfare costs (social security costs) will be cheaper as long as the firm size will be smaller. The welfare facilities will be much better in the big company and thus the company house, for example, could be easily available for the employees of big firms that are financially wealthy. The company pension system is also much better and can give a larger amount. Further, since the health insurance system for the big firm is a company union insurance in Japan, their finance is much wealthier.

3.2. The reason 2 is easiness in reducing the outsourced parts costs thanks to close collaborations between the ordering company and the ordered parts suppliers in the supply chain

Let us take a look at the composition rates of various manufacturing costs of automobile industry, especially the material costs as the main target for continuous improvement in the cost reduction.

Table 2 shows the composition rates of each cost element of materials, labor, and overhead costs in Toyota Motor Corporation and Nissan Motor Corporation. The material cost composition rate of more than 80% is corresponding to the purchase of raw materials for the "intra-firm parts manufacturing" and the "purchase of the outsourced parts". Actually, more than 70% of material costs as a whole were paid for the parts purchased from the suppliers (note that of course the amount of payment for the outsourced parts will be used for the labor costs and overheads within the parts supplier in question).[2]

---

[1] One of the factors that has been making the wage of small and medium firms lower may lie in the low level of labor productivity. The figure of the "salary divided by the value-added per employee" (= A/B) becomes larger, if the firm size is smaller than 1,000 employees. Since the value-added (B) includes the depreciation costs of facilities, the figure of B will be lower so long as the firm size becomes smaller; that means the lower equipment rate of facilities so that the labor-intensive production used to appear in the small and medium firms.

[2] The composition ratio of material costs will gradually decrease when we see the automobile industry from final assembler down to the first layer supplier through second and third layer suppliers. This may be due to the decrease in the equipped ratio of facilities in the small and medium companies.

Table 2.   Breakdown of the manufacturing costs of Japanese major automakers

	FY 1989 (%)	FY 1990 (%)	FY 2008 (%)	FY 2009 (%)	FY 2010 (%)	FY 2011 (%)	FY 2012 (%)	FY 2013 (%)
Toyota's Cost Ratios								
Cost elements								
Materials[a]	84.5	84.9	83.3	81.1	82.2	82.3	82.4	83.4
Labor[b]	6.5	6.2	7.0	7.6	7.8	7.7	7.7	7.4
Overhead[c]	9.0	8.9	9.7	11.3	10.0	10.0	9.9	9.2
Total costs	100.0	100.0	100.0	100.0	100.0	100.0	100.0	100.0
Nissan's Cost Ratios								
Cost elements								
Materials[a]	85.4	85.2	80.0	77.8	78.8	79.8	81.4	80.2
Labor[b]	8.9	8.7	7.3	7.8	8.1	7.3	6.2	6.0
Overhead[c]	5.7	6.2	12.7	14.4	13.1	12.9	12.4	13.8
Total costs	100.0	100.0	100.0	100.0	100.0	100.0	100.0	100.0

[a] Material costs include indirect materials.
[b] Labor costs include indirect labor.
[c] Indirect materials and indirect labor are excluded from overhead costs. Depreciation expenses account for 20–30% of overhead costs.

Sources: "Statements of costs of goods manufactured" (FYs 1989, 1990, 2008, 2009, 2010, 2011, 2012, and 2013) of Toyota and Nissan.

On the other hand, the big three auto companies in North America have been manufacturing 60–70% of autoparts in their intra-firm plants until the end of 1980s; that means only 30–40% of parts were procured from outsides PAC (1986), Desrosiers (1986), and Monden (1987). However, the US auto companies have increased the outsourcing ratio during the late 80s and 90s, their outsourcing ratio at present must have approached Japanese ratio.

The fact that the ratio of material costs is very high in the cost structure of the Japanese automobile industry is the background that the automakers used to request the parts suppliers to reduce the parts transaction prices by reducing their costs through their continuous cost improvement (or "Kaizen cost management") in every half a year. This is because it would be easier for the automaker to reduce the variable material costs as a main cost reduction target than aiming at reducing the labor costs and overhead costs as the target, though the latter costs must be one of the major cost reduction targets in the product development phases of both automakers and suppliers.

Therefore, Toyota motors, for example, has promoted 30% reduction of their manufacturing costs in the year 2000, by selecting the major 173 product items through the project of "Construction of Cost Competitiveness 21st Century," thereby tried to achieve the world's cheapest cars. In December 2009, again, Toyota requested their allied ("keiretsu") parts makers to reduce the parts prices down to more than 30% (Toyota Motor Corporation, 2012).

4. Demand for Higher Wages by the Japanese Government to the Industrial World: The First Phase Movement

Since December 2014, the "Abe" government (headed by Premier Sintaro Abe) has demanded the wage increase for the top management people of the industrial world in their labor-management negotiations in the ending stage of budget year 2014 (i.e. during March and April, 2015). This was to boost the people's consumption, which was under depression due to the increase in sales tax rates in April 2014, in order to get out of deflation (i.e. to achieve effective 2% inflation that was targeted by the so-called "*Abenomics*"). This request for higher wage was called the "wage increase by government leadership" (*The Nikkei*, 2015e).

Accepting this demand, the biggest company in Japan, Toyota Motors, had first decided their "policy" of not requesting the parts-price reduction in January 2015 (*The Nikkei*, 2015a, 2015b). Then Toyota formally declared *not to demand the parts-price reduction* for the parts to be procured after the first half of 2015 (April through September, succeeding to the second half period of 2014) (*The Nikkei*, 2015c).

Further, following the action of Toyota, most of the larger affiliated auto parts manufacturers of Toyota group also have expressed their declination to request the sub-parts price reduction. Aishin Seiki, Toyota Manufacturing Industry and JTEKT, etc. have immediately followed Toyota's policy (*The Nikkei*, 2015a, 2015d).

However, as I see it, it is not enough that Toyota and the bigger parts makers just express declination to request for price reduction. Rather, they were expected to declare the parts-price *increase*, which was also the next proposal of the government to be explained in the next section.

5. Increase in the Parts Prices Facing the Yen Currency Depreciation: The Second Phase Movement of Demand for Higher Wage by Premier Abe in the Government/Labor/Management Conference

Prime Minister Abe has expressed that he wished to "request for the wage increase in the SMEs for the *"good circulation of economy"* to the very best efforts of yours," in the government/labor/management conference held at the premier's office ("Kantei"; Prime Minister of Japan and His Cabinet) (*The Nikkei*, 2015f, 2015g, 2015h). The "good circulation" implies the good cycle of "higher business earnings (as well as higher investment and employment) → higher wages → higher consumption → higher business earnings."

In this conference, the minister and bureaucrats of the *Ministry of Economy, Trade and Industry* (METI), the SMEA, and the *Fair Trade Commission* showed up as government side. The labor stands for the *Japanese Trade Union Confederation* (JTUC; abbreviated RENGO). The management stands for *Japan Business Federation* (or abbreviated Keidanren) and the *National Federation of Small Business Associations* (NFSBA).

Prime Minister aimed at increasing the consumption as a macro economy through increasing the higher wages in the small and medium firms as well as larger firms. In order to cause the *"trickle down"* of pay raise from big firms to SME firms, it is indispensable to be able to shift the increased prices of the imported raw materials due to the yen currency depreciation on to the rise of parts prices of suppliers.

In the above conference, the government and Japan Business Federation prepared the policies to facilitate shifting the increase of imported raw materials cost onto the transaction price, in order for the SME firms to easily raise their wage. This is *the second phase movement* of the government demand for higher wage.

The concrete policy of the government is to demand **16** industries such as automobile and aircraft industries to abide by the guidelines that suggest "that there should be price negotiations regularly when the raw material prices fluctuate largely" and other rules, based on the "*Act against Delay in*

Payment of Subcontract Proceeds, etc. to Subcontractors" (abbreviated as *Subcontractors Law*, originally enacted on July 1, 1956), and the *"Act on Prohibition of Private Monopolization and Maintenance of Fair Trade*" (abbreviated as the *Antimonopoly (or Antitrust) Act*) conducted by Japan Fair Trade Commission.

The detailed guidelines have already been shown as publications by the *Ministry of Economy, Trade and Industry* (2010, 2014). There is also another guideline of the *Small and Medium Enterprise Agency* (2013). To enforce the 14 industries to abide by these guidelines, the *Fair Trade Commission* (2004, 2010) will make inspections in the 500 big companies by the end of September 2015. Those companies who violate the above laws will be guided and further punished (i.e. fined).

The actual result of pay raise in FY 2014 and FY 2015 (*The Nikkei*, 2015f)

RENGO reported that the performance of labor/management negotiations in the spring season of 2015 was as follows: The average wage increase as a sum of the regular (routine) pay raise and the "base-up" of wage table itself for all employees is 6,944 yen, which is larger than the last year pay raise by 449 yen, and wage increase rate is 2.33% which is higher than last year by 0.13 points.

Also, according to the survey by the METI, more than 90% of big companies raised their wages in 2014, while only 65% of SME have raised their pay. Further, 65% of big companies have achieved the "base-up" of wage tables for all employees, but only 23% of SME have achieved it when we see the firms below 300 employees.

6. Problem to be Considered in the Pay Raise by the Government Leadership

The pay raise policy should be based on the following rule by the company management and the economic policymaker[3]:

---

[3] Regarding the wage raise problem, the theories of "*Lewisian Turning Point*" advocated by William Arthur Lewis (1954) in his "dual-sector model" and the "*Reserve Army of Labor*" concept by Karl Heinrich Marx (see Dobb (1958) for this concept) are useful. In the labor market of dual-sector economy, when the supply of the labor is bigger than its demand, the unlimited number of labor could be procured with the cheaper wages. However, when the demand for

From the relation between demand (D) and supply (S) in the labor market,

(1) In the period of D < S, the wage level is suppressed.
(2) In the period of D ≧ S, the wage level can be raised.

Thus, under the booming phase of the exports-related big enterprises thanks to the currency depreciation, pay raise could be recommended as a reallocation of wages within the supply chain to achieve the equilibrium in the labor market of D ≧ S, while economy is under depression of D < S, there must be mutual efforts for survival through the collaboration as will be suggested in the following sections.

7. Collaborations During the Yen Currency Depreciation Periods

7.1. *How to treat the request for shifting the increase in the acquisition cost of raw materials onto the parts-price increase, which will be made by the parts seller to the parts buyer*

The material price increase will happen in the following situations:

(1) During the period of yen currency depreciation, the price of the imported materials in terms of yen denominated price will increase.
(2) Even though the yen currency is not depreciated, the market prices of the crude oil and iron ore, etc. in their auction markets may increase.
(3) During the Lehman economic crisis, for example, all of the companies' facility-usage-rates have been reduced due to demand shortage and thus the costs of all companies have increased.

In such situations, the guidelines for the subcontractors (i.e. parts sellers) rendered by the METI (2014) and the SMEA (2013) pose the following "desirable transaction conventions" and "the best practices":

Step 1: The seller (parts supplier) should show the clear reason why the costs have increased, to the buyer.

---

labor begins to exceed its supply, such time-point is denoted as "*Lewisian Turning Point*," and the wage level of the country will begin to increase. The "*Reserve Army of Labor*" of Marx is also equivalent to the affluent labor to be supplied for the growing industry in the period of [D < S].

Step 2: Sufficient discussions must be carried out between the buyer and the seller.

It is desirable to have an agreement on the methods of calculating the parts prices beforehand, so that both parties can determine the *rational* price of the parts in question. The procedures of these two steps will be as per the following practices.

How can the increased market price of raw materials be shifted on to the parts price?

As stated above, the following agreement on the methods of calculating the parts price that reflects the increase of raw material price is the introduction of the *sliding* system or the *surcharge* system. Especially for the fuel costs, the so-called fuel surcharge system is applied and thus the parts prices will be regularly changed by this system. The transportation costs by trucks that use the diesel oil will be computed by the following formula, and this system is agreed as a transportation contract between the transportation company and the consigner (shipper), who will be charged the transportation cost by this system; that is,

Transportation cost
= fuel cost as a fixed base + [amount of fuel-surcharge],

where, the fuel surcharge = [miles/(mileage per liter)] × [monetary amount per liter].

7.2. How will the wage raise in the parts supplier be treated in computing the parts prices?

Although such shift of imported raw material costs on to the parts prices could be admitted by the purchasers (parts users such as the automobile makers and the like), the purchasers usually will not admit the increase in parts prices based on the wage increase of suppliers. Their wage increase must be absorbed by the collaborative efforts between supplier and buyer, which include innovations and continuous process improvements at the supplier end. The innovation includes the changes in the manufacturing technologies such as facility investment that replaces human operations with the machine operations. On the other hand, continuous improvements include the effective labor usage through *reduction of man-hours* per unit of production throughout the whole plant. The surplus gained by such activities could absorb the wage rise in parts suppliers. Detailed know-how will be described in the following sections.

8. Collaborations During the Yen Currency Appreciation Periods

8.1. How should the automaker's request for the parts price reduction be treated during automaker's depression period?

During the long-term depression period caused by highly evaluated yen currency, even the big Japanese companies were ailing and they used to demand their parts suppliers in the lower layers of the supply chain to reduce the parts prices twice each year. To prevent "beating the parts price down" by the core companies of the supply chain, METI and SMEA of Japanese government have guided the bigger customer companies not to exploit the parts companies.

The concept of "**beating the parts price down**" is defined in the *Subcontractors Law*, as follows: It is to determine *in one sided view the incredibly lower price* than the **amount to be paid in** *a normal business transaction* and pay such lower amount to the subcontractor. Here, the "amount to be paid in *a normal business transaction*"[4] means the amount of payment that will be *usually* paid for the *same or similar goods or services* as the ordered objects. In addition, the determination of the price "in one sided view" is also strongly prohibited, and the mutual discussion between the buyer and the seller must be done for the price determination (Notice No.18 by the head official of *Fair Trade Commission* (2004)).

8.2. Collaboration steps between the ordering company and the ordered company: Three steps as the best practice

The following collaboration steps will be taken in the product development phase as well as the manufacturing phase after development.

---

[4]This price of a normal business transaction is similar to the **arms' length transfer price of comparable transaction object** in the international transfer pricing. Also, this is similar to the "**gain to be acquired by the independent action**" of the team member of the cooperative game theory.

Step 1: Proposals from the ordering company (e.g. automobile maker)

On the side of an ordering company (i.e. final assembler or core-company in the supply chain), they will establish the *cross-functional team* for a new model in the development phase (or for the existing representative model in the manufacturing phase), which is composed of the procurement department, production engineering department (for facilities preparation), product-design department, and manufacturing and assembly departments. And then the staff of each department of this team will examine their various cost reduction ideas as well as the ideas for supplier's cost reduction, and make their proposal to the ordered company (i.e. parts manufacturer).

The staff of the procurement department will re-examine the purchase methods and look for the new suppliers. The staff of production engineering department will develop the new manufacturing methods and approaches for the die-cost reduction, which were proposed to the supplier. The staff of the design department will propose the new blueprints that could enable low-cost production.

Step 2: Proposals from the ordered company (i.e. parts manufacturer)

The ordered company (i.e. subcontracted firm for the parts) will also make a report to the ordered company about the examined results of their cost reduction activities by their own efforts, and try to achieve the appropriate parts prices.

When they are requested by the ordering company to reduce the costs, the ordered company will investigate various ideas and methods that could be adopted by their own efforts to meet the demanded amount of cost reduction such as:

(1) Changes in energy resources,
(2) Improvements of production processes,
(3) Plans to increase the capacity-usage rate by adding the ordered quantity from various customers (users), and
(4) Utilization of the existing capacity without introducing the new facility, etc.

Step 3: Bringing both the cost reduction proposals together to reduce the parts prices for the new model, or for the regular request for the parts-price reduction for the existing model

Bringing both the proposals together and through the collaboration between the ordering firm and the ordered firm, the target amount of cost reduction could be achieved, and finally meet the target price of new product and parts and the regular request for the reduced parts-price.

For the details of the above three steps in the product development phase, please see Monden (1993) and Monden (1995, Chapter 18).

9. Negotiation Between Automaker and Parts Supplier for Determining the Parts Prices in the Product-Development Phase: Application of VE or Target Costing

Value Engineering (VE) is a technique to achieve the target cost and quality in the *development phase* by changing the designs through selecting better materials and manufacturing methods, etc. while Value Analysis (VA) is a technique to achieve the revised target cost and quality in the *manufacturing phase* by changing the designs for selecting the materials and manufacturing methods, etc. Both VE and VA are almost similar techniques, but their terms are used separately as explained here in the Japanese automotive industry.

The VE technique is a main tool in the so-called "*Target Costing*" that achieves the product target cost to realize the target profit under the target sales price of the product. On the other hand, the VA technique is used in the "*Kaizen Costing*," which is roughly defined as the continuous improvement activities for cost reduction by using lean manufacturing techniques and VA in the manufacturing phase.

(For details of Target Costing (or VE) and Kaizen Costing (or VA), see Monden (1983, 1986a, 1995) and also Monden and Hamada (1991)).

9.1. "Full cost principle" as a computation method of the "estimated parts prices" by the parts supplier

In the early stage of the product development process of a new automobile model, the automaker will divide the "*target-cost per vehicle unit*" into the "*target-cost per unit of part*" for various parts. Such "*target-cost per unit of part*" will be transmitted to each parts maker. This parts target-cost will be regarded as a tentative "*sales price of the parts*" for the parts maker and a tentative "purchase price of the part" for the automaker. However, the actual parts sales-price (or parts purchase-price in the automaker side) will be determined through the negotiation between the automaker (i.e. its purchase department) and the parts maker in the final stage of product-development (Noboru and Monden, 1983; Monden, 1986a,b).

However, the parts makers have to determine their own target-cost per unit of their parts, which is below the tentative sales price of the parts in question, by applying the principle of the *full cost plus markup* (Monden, 1994, pp. 83–84, 1995, pp. 107–109; Asanuma, 1984, 1997).

The procedure of the *full cost principle*[5] will be formalized as follows:

$$\text{Full cost} = \text{Direct material costs} + \text{Direct processing costs} + \text{Processing costs}, \tag{1}$$

where the direct material costs = raw material costs + procured parts costs, the direct processing costs = commissions for outsourced processing job, and the processing costs = direct labor costs + manufacturing overhead costs.

$$\text{Markup rate} = \frac{\text{Estimated gross sales margin}}{\text{Manufacturing full cost}}. \tag{2}$$

Since the markup is for covering the operating profit and the sales and general administrative expenses, it corresponds to the gross sales margin.

The readers should note that the markup rate is neither the return on sales (i.e. ROS) nor the return on investment (i.e. ROI) or return on asset (i.e. ROA), but it is the **return on full cost**. In other words, the markup stands for the gross profit that should be normally gained when a certain amount of production resources is consumed.

---

[5]The "full cost principle" was first found as a practically used method for establishing the sales-price of products in the monopoly market. It was first found as the "full cost plus markup" method by Hall and Hitch (1939) in examining their pricing methods actually used in England monopoly market. Also, the full cost principle is often used for *international transfer pricing* for the goods and services transferred between the parent firm and their subsidiary firms in different global locations. In addition, this method is also often used for measuring the *intra-company transfer price* in the division-based company where there is no market price of the transferred goods.

From Equations (1) and (2), the estimated sales-price P* of the parts

$$= \text{Full cost } C^* + \text{markup rate} \times \text{full cost}$$
$$= \text{Full cost } C^* (1 + \text{markup rate}). \tag{3}$$

9.2. *"Cooperative game" based on the long-term reliability relationship between automaker and parts maker regarding the markup rate*

The *markup* rate as a normal margin or opportunity cost

Now let us consider how the markup rate will be determined in the Japanese automobile industry. The markup rate for automobile parts in the Japanese automobile industry will be setup, for example, as [8% of the manufacturing full costs] for covering the sales and general administrative expenses and as [5% of the manufacturing full costs] for covering the operating income, thus totalizing the 13% as "*margin rate to the total manufacturing full costs*" per unit of the parts in question.

Such amount of markup figure will be approved by the automaker, because such *markup rate for each part is predetermined in the long-term historical experiences of the transactions between automaker and several suppliers of the parts in question in the market, and it is regarded as a given condition (or given data) at each point in time of the negotiation* (Asanuma, 1984, p. 42, 1997, p. 177).

Thus, the amount of markup is determined in the competitive parts market and through the long run transactions between automaker and parts makers. The markup is a kind of *normal margin* to be acquired when the supplier worked in the competitive market of the parts in question and could be regarded as a kind of normal profit to be gained through the transaction between the automaker and the parts maker, both of whom are located in the *arm's length distance*.

Therefore, it corresponds to the profit to be gained through the *arm's length transaction* in the international transfer pricing logic. Also, the margin in the markup rate corresponds to the "cooperative game theory," in which the gain acquired through the *independent* single member activity outside the cooperative network will be regarded as an **opportunity cost for participating in the cooperative network**.

9.3. *The additional extra-margin that exceeds the normal markup margin will be acquired through the cost reduction activities conducted by both automaker and the parts maker in question*

Difference between the target parts cost determined by automaker and the target parts cost determined by parts maker

As stated before, the ***target parts cost*** will be designated and assigned to the parts supplier by the buyer (i.e. customer or automobile maker, for example), which will be the most important factor as a *tentative target parts price* for both buyer and seller. This *target parts cost* of each parts is determined by decomposing the target-product cost of the final product (for example, automobile in case of automobile industry).

Thus, since the target parts cost determined by the automaker is regarded as a tentative target parts price or an estimated sales price of the part by the automaker and the parts maker, Equation (3) will be derived from the following formula:

From Equations (1) and (2), the estimated sales-price P* of the part
= Full cost C* + markup rate × full cost
= Full cost C* (1 + markup rate). $\qquad$ (3)

∴ *Full cost* **C** *of the part* = the **estimated sales-price P***of the part/
(1 + markup rate). $\qquad$ (4)

Target parts cost **C** for the parts supplier

$$= \frac{\text{the estimated parts price P * assigned by the automobile manufacturer}}{(1 + \text{markup rate})}. \qquad (4')$$

However, the target cost for part A, for instance, in the left-hand side of Equation (4′) must be achieved or realized by the parts maker A within their plant.

The reader should note that there are two kinds of target parts costs in the above explanation. One is determined by the automotive maker and will be given to the parts maker as an estimated (tentative) parts price. The other is determined by the parts maker and should be regarded as the real target to be attained by the parts maker. Figure 1 shows the relations between these two kinds of target costs.

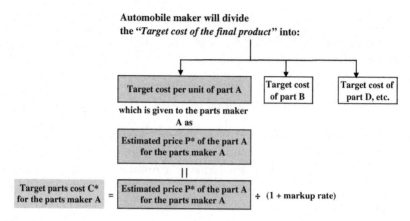

Fig. 1. The relationship between the target parts cost given by the automaker and the target parts cost determined by the parts maker in question

Therefore,

if

Actual full cost C^* of part A

$\leq$ Target cost C of part A within the plant of parts supplier A,   (5)

where the right-hand side is equal to the left-hand side of (4').
Then, it follows that;

Actual profit gained by the part supplier A

$\geq$ Profit planned by the markup rate,   (6)

where the right-hand side is equal to [the full cost × markup rate] in the right-hand side of (3).

The above [if ---, then ---] clause covering Equations (5) and (6) implies that in order for the parts supplier to get larger profits, which is bigger than the normal margin of markup, the *final actual cost C^* of part A* actually achieved by the parts maker A must be smaller than the **target cost C of part A determined by Equation (4)** or (4') (Monden, 1994, pp. 83–84, 1995, pp. 107–109).[6]

---

[6] Equation (4') based on the "full cost plus target markup rate" is the one that the author has reformed the "sales price method" so-called in Japanese auto-industry, in order for the

10. How to Adapt to the Parts-Price Reduction Requested by the Automaker Twice a Year: VA or "Kaizen Costing" Applied to Achieve the Newly Reduced Target Cost for the Part in the Manufacturing Phase

Japanese automaker used to request to reduce the parts price twice a year. For example, suppose an automaker has requested the parts-price reduction by 2% to a certain parts maker to be attained in the next six months.

---

readers to easily understand it as a kind of "full cost principle" method. In general, there are two main different methods that calculate the *target parts cost* inside the parts supplier. But these two methods will calculate the identical *target parts cost* inside the parts supplier. This logic can be proved through a simple mathematical derivation as follows, though such proof of equivalence has not yet been made so far:

The first method is the one I have shown in the above as (4′), which applied the target (or normal) markup rate:

Target parts cost C for the parts supplier
= the estimated parts price P* assigned by the automobile manufacturer/
(1 + markup rate). (a)

On the other hand, there exists another method, which uses the "target (or normal) rate of the manufacturing costs on sales amount". The method of utilizing Equations (b) and (c) was suggested to me by Dr. Koji Umeda (City University of Nagoya) as another method also widely utilized in Japanese auto-industry. Some companies call this method as the "sales price less method".

Target rate of the manufacturing costs on sales amount
= target rate of (**manufacturing costs/sales amount**), (b)

Target parts cost for the parts supplier
= (estimated parts price P* assigned by the automaker)
× (target manufacturing costs rate), (c)

where the target manufacturing costs rate in the right side is (b).

Method (c) is to assure the predetermined target manufacturing costs rate that assures target margin of sales and administrative costs plus operating profit irrespective of any amount of P*.

Let us take the reciprocal number of target manufacturing costs rate, which is the target rate of (sales amount/manufacturing costs).

Thus, the reciprocal number of target manufacturing costs rate

= target rate of (sales amount/manufacturing costs)
= target rate of

In such situation, the following formula will be introduced by applying Equation (4'):

[The parts price in the beginning of mass-production
  × (1–0.02)]/(1 + markup rate)
= Newly reduced target-cost for the parts.   (7)

When the parts maker achieved this new target-cost of the parts, then it follows that the parts price could be reduced by 2% as requested by the automaker. Further if the parts maker could have achieved much lower cost than the new target-cost of (7), then the following "*extra margin*" will be gained:

Extra margin = new target-cost of the parts of (7)
        – actually achieved cost of the parts.   (8)

This extra margin will be the additional profit to the parts maker, which will be utilized for paying the raised wages and new facility investment, etc. However, if 40% of the reduced cost were made by the ideas of the automaker, then the extra margin × 0.40 will be attributed to the automaker in a form of additional parts-price reduction, and the extra margin × 0.60 will be kept in the parts maker. In this way, the *joint extra margin will be allocated between automaker and parts maker based on each of their contribution ratio to the cost reduction.*

{[manufacturing costs + (sales and administrative costs
+ operating income)}/(manufacturing costs)}

= target rate of [1 + {(sales and administrative costs
+ operating income)/(manufacturing costs)]}

= [1 + target markup rate].
Then, Equation (c) of target parts cost for the parts supplier

= (estimated parts price P* assigned by the automaker)
    × (target manufacturing costs rate)
= (estimated parts price P* assigned by the automaker)
    × (reciprocal of [1 + target markup rate])
= (estimated parts price P* assigned by the automaker)
    × (1/[1 + target markup rate])
= (estimated parts price P* assigned by the automaker)/
    [1 + target markup rate]
= the right-hand side of Equation (a).   (QFD)

Three steps of collaborations between the ordering company and the ordered company

In Section 8.2, we have discussed how the collaborations will be made between the buyer (i.e. automaker) and the seller (i.e. parts supplier) through the three steps. Such collaborations will be done for reducing the supplier's costs. When the supplier's cost is reduced in the product development stage as well as the mass production stage, the benefits will be allocated as a reduced parts-price to the automaker and as an increased profit to the parts maker. It should be emphasized that the origin of such benefit allocation lies in the reduction of the parts costs achieved through contribution grade of both parties.

11. For the Assurance of Sustainable Supply Chain: Incentives to Induce the Members' Contributions

Sustainability of the firm will be assured by considering the sociality, environment, and economy, which could be rephrased by people, planet, and profit; the three P goals. Since traditional economics and corporate finance considered merely the *economic* profit to explain the behavior of the firm, it has some limitation for the sustainability. Thus, let us consider the *behavioral* (human) aspect of the firm.

The first person in the business management who introduced the basis of the behavioral theory of the firm is Chester I. Barnard (1938), who was followed by Simon (1957) and Cyert and March (1963), etc. Barnard has advocated the proposition that the organization could survive so long as the contributions rendered by the organization members were balanced by the incentives (or called side-payments or rewards) paid by the firm itself. He called this theory as the **organizational equilibrium theory**.

When such theory is applied to the supply chain, the chain (or network) can not only get the contribution or cooperation of each member firm, but also get especially contributions of the employees of each member firm of the chain network. Matsuo (2014) also emphasized the viewpoint of sociality and sustainability of the supply chain.

Similar theory also exists in the cooperative game theory that requires the following two conditions for the existence of the cooperative game network.

(1) Condition of the "*total rationality*": If the coalition of plural members yields the *synergetic effect*, then the total gain acquired by the grand coalition of all members will exceed the sum of each gain acquired by each member who works independently outside of the network organization.

(2) Condition of the "*individual rationality*": The gain allocated to each member of the network from the joint gain of the cooperative network consisting of all members working together, can exceed the amount of gain which is supposed to be acquired by each member acting independently of the cooperative network.

The above two conditions will assure payment of the *incentive reward* to all participating members in the network of the ordering company (i.e. carmaker) and the ordered member companies (i.e. parts makers). Such incentive reward is what the author coins as the "incentive price," which is the price for allocation of the joint profit according to the contribution grade of each participating member of network organization.

12. Concluding Summary for Continuous Evolution

The theme of this paper is to investigate how the profit differences among the companies could be resolved through changing the transaction price and costs of the parts in the supply chain, thereby reducing the wage differentials among companies. Here, the transaction price of the parts has the function to allocate the profit to be jointly attained by the ordering company (i.e. the buyer) of the parts and the ordered company (i.e. seller who will manufacture and supply the parts). For allocating the joint profit, both companies must have a negotiation or the collaborative activities in determining the transaction price or reducing the parts costs. Such collaboration is actually required by the laws or government.

The negotiation or collaboration between the buyer and the seller of the parts implies that both companies will mutually provide the ideas for reducing the manufacturing cost of the parts. Depending on how each company has contributed to reduce the parts costs by applying the ideas of each party, the total reduced amount of costs will be allocated as benefits to each partner, namely, according to the contributing grade of each company, and thus the transaction price of the parts will be finally determined.

The collaborative activities for reducing the parts cost in the product and parts development phase between the multilayer companies in the inter-firm network (i.e. supply chain) are called *"concurrent engineering"* or *"design-in"* approach. Since the terms of *"concurrent engineering"* or *"design-in"* are often used in European and American companies, the collaborative innovations and improvements could be adopted in those western countries, though such collaborative activities especially emphasized in the Japanese manufacturing industry. They can create not only the *"Win–Win"* relationship through the fair allocation of joint margin, but also provide the incentives to enhance the morale of employees of both buyer and seller for development and production of the attractive product to the final customers in the consumer market.

Therefore, such transaction convention will comply with the gain allocation rule of the *cooperative game theory*, rather than following the competitive market principle. It will also comply with the proposition of the *"organizational equilibrium theory"* of Chester Barnard.

Finally, the author adds another implication contained in the resolution of differences in the profits and wages via changes in the parts transaction price. This method will not merely reshuffle the joint profit, which is regarded as a "zero-sum" within a supply chain, but also dig out the *"hidden or overlooked good-opportunity,"* which is called an *organizational slack* by Cyert and March (1963). In other words, it will reduce the costs by eliminating the so-far overlooked wastes in the company and dig out the additional profit hidden as a "plus-sum" game inside the supply chain.

In the Japanese automobile industry, the carmaker used to request the parts maker to decrease the costs and improve the quality, thereby the decrease in the parts prices has been continuously demanded by the automobile maker. However, such convention should not necessarily be criticized as "beating the price down".

As explained in the beginning of Section 9 (about VE or "Target Costing" for *"innovation"*) and in Section 10 (about VA or "Kaizen" costing for *"continuous improvement"*), both the carmaker and the parts maker have tried to reduce costs and improve quality in the long-term transaction relations. They have actually encouraged each other to make efforts for their many times of *evolutions*. The evolutions include technological innovations of parts suppliers from the "drawings-supplied" parts maker to the "drawings-approved" parts maker, who would further evolve from the early-stage supplier having a few customers (automakers) to the advanced "mega-supplier" having many customers. Such process has contributed to enhance the *competitive power of technology, productivity, and quality* of both parties. Thus, there are many cases of the parts makers of even SMEs who could have extended their business to the overseas to make and sell their products to new customers (new automakers) in the overseas and in the domestic market as an excellent parts supplier thanks to their cultivated competitive technology.

References

Abe, A. (2015). Income differentials reconsidered (2): Social solidarity is required by wider burdening for resolving the poverty. *The Nikkei*, "Economic Seminar" February 12 (in Japanese).

Asanuma, B. (1984, 1985). The contractual practice for parts supply in the Japanese automotive industry: *Japanese Economic Studies*, summer: 54–78 (Japanese original version of this paper appeared in *Seasonal Issue: Contemporary Economics*, 1984 Summer: 38–48).

Asanuma, B. (1997). *Japanese Business Organization: Its Evolutional Adaptation Mechanism: Structure and Function of the Long-term Transaction Relations.* Tokyo: Toyo Keizai, Inc. (in Japanese).

Barnard, C. I. (1938). *The Functions of the Executive.* Boston: Harvard University Press.

Cyert, R. M. and J. G. March (1963). *A Behavioral Theory of the Firm.* Englewood Cliffs, NJ: Prentice-Hall.

Desrosiers, D. (1986). Canadian Suppliers at the Critical Crossroads: Strategies for Success. Paper presented at APMA (Automobile Parts Manufacturing Associate), April.

Dobb, M. (1958). *Capitalism Yesterday and Today.* London: Lawrence & Wishart.

Fair Trade Commission (2004). *Application standard of Subcontractors Law.* Notice No.18 by the head official of Fair Trade Commission (in Japanese).

Government /labor /management conference for the good circulation of economy (2015). *Policies to facilitate the shift of the cost-increase to the transaction price and to enhance the productivity of service industry.* Prime Minister of Japan and His Cabinet, April 2, pp. 1–5.

Hall, R. L. and C. J. Hitch (1939). Price theory and business behavior. Oxford Economic papers, May, pp. 12–45 contained in *A Survey of Contemporary Eeconomics*, (ed.) H. S. Ellis.

Iwamoto, Y. (2015). Discussion points on the second round wage raise (1): "The spring labor offensive lead by government" may cause trouble to economy. *The Nikkei*, Economic Seminar, March 4 (in Japanese)

Lee, J. Y. and Y. Monden (1996). Kaizen costing: its structure and cost management functions. *Advances in Management Accounting* 5: 27–40.

Lewis, W. A. (1954). Economic development with unlimited supplies of labor. *Manchester School of Economics and Social Studies* 22: 139–91.

Matsuo, H. (2014). Repercussion effect of yen currency depreciation from the exporting firms to the importing firms could not be expected: Supply chain must be reconsidered from the viewpoint of sociality and sustainability. *The Nikkei*, Economic Seminar, October 31 (in Japanese).

Ministry of Economy, Trade and Industry, the Small and Medium Enterprise Agency (2010). *On the Fair Transaction of Subcontracting in the Period of High Yen Appreciation*, November (in Japanese).

Ministry of Economy, Trade and Industry (2014). *Guideline for the Right Transaction of Automobile Industry* January, 3rd edition (in Japanese).

Monden, Y. (1983). *Toyota Production System: Practical Approach to Production Management*. Norcross, GA: Industrial Engineering and Management Press. IIE.

Monden, Y. (1986a). Production strategy of Japanese automakers and partsmakers in Canada. *Fair Trade* (Fair Trade Commission) 434: 29–35 (in Japanese).

Monden, Y. (1986b). Total cost management system in Japanese automobile corporation. In Monden, Y. (Ed.), *Applying Just In Time*, Norcroess, GA: Industrial Engineering and Mangement Press. IIE (pp. 171–184).

Monden, Y. (1987). *Just-In-Time: Toyota Production System Crosses the Ocean*, Tokyo: Japan Productivity Center (in Japanese).

Monden, Y. and K. Hamada (1991). Target costing and Kaizen costing in Japanese automobile companies. *Journal of Management Accounting Research* 3 (Fall): 16–34.

Monden, Y. (1993). Japanese new-product development techniques: the target-costing system in the automotive industry. *Journal of Industry Studies* 1(1): 43–49.

Monden, Y. (1994). Target Cosing and Kaizen Costing, Tokyo, Toyokeizai-shinnposha. (in Japanese).

Monden, Y. (1995). *Cost Reduction Systems: Target Costing and Kaizen Costing*. Portland, OR: Productivity Press.

Moriguchi, C. (2015). Income differentials reconsidered (1): Concentration of wealth in post-war Japan is low, but the equalized society also has problem for growth. *The Nikkei* "Economic Seminar," February 11 (in Japanese).

National Tax Agency Japan (1986). *Special Action Law on Tax*, Article 66 (Taxation on the transaction with the related overseas company) (in Japanese).

National Tax Agency Japan (2007a). On Partial Revision of "*Guideline of International Transfer Pricing*", June 25 (in Japanese).

National Tax Agency Japan (2007b). *Reference Cases for Applications of International Transfer Pricing*, June 25 (in Japanese).

Noboru, Y. and Monden, Y. (1983). Total cost management system in Japanese automobile corporation. *Accounting* 35(2): 104–112 (in Japanese).

Noguch, Y. (2012). *Defeated Japanese Manufacturing*, Tokyo: Toyo Keizai, Inc. (in Japanese) Pacific Automotive Corporation (PAC) (1986). *Material for 2nd exhibition meeting of the Canadian Auto-market*, July.

Piketty, T. (2014). *Capital in the Twenty-First Century*. Translated by Arthur Goldhammer, Cambridge Massachusetts, Belknap Press of Harvard University Press (Original French version was published in 2013).

Shimokawa, K. (2009). On non-regular employees of the automotive plants, in Shimokawa, K. (2009). *Is there any prosperous future in the automobile business?* Tokyo: Takarajima. Chapter 3 (in Japanese).

Simon, H. A. (1957). *Administrative Behavior — A study of Decision-Making Process in Administrative Organization*. 3rd Edition, New York. Macmillan Company.

Small and Medium Enterprise Agency (2013). *Guideline for the Right Transaction of Subcontracts: Collections of the Best Practices*, 4th September, Edition (in Japanese).

Takahashi, S. (2015). Discussion points on the second round wage raise (2): positive business attitude may boost the good circulation of economy. *The Nikkei*, "Economic Seminar," March 5 (in Japanese).

The Nikkei (2015a). Toyota is worried for its strong position for not requesting the part price reduction. Which is followed by the 1st layer suppliers, February 4 (in Japanese).

The Nikkei (2015b). Improved business performance should be returned to the suppliers of Toyota, February 5 (in Japanese).

The Nikkei (2015c). No demand to the suppliers for reducing their parts price: Toyota's special policy, February, 28 (in Japanese).

The Nikkei (2015d). Toyota backs up the wage raise of keiretsu firms, March 16 (in Japanese).

The Nikkei (2015e). For the purpose of continuous pay-raise, March 2 (in Japanese).

The Nikkei (2015f). Wage raise was requested to the SMEs by premier Abe, who backed up to shift the rise of raw materials costs to the parts prices, April 3 (in Japanese).

The Nikkei (2015g). Unprecedented intervene to extend the wage raise: Government/labor/management conference made policy to facilitate the "*good circulation of economy,*" April 3 (In Japanese).

The Nikkei (2015h). Subcontractor's law: Restriction on forced demand for the rice reduction, April 3 (in Japanese).

The Nikkei (2015i). Industrial policy forced by administrative guidance will be worried, April 21 (in Japanese).

The Nikkei (2015j). "*The same wage*" must be determined by each company's policy, June 19 (in Japanese).

The Nikkei (2015k). The act on *"the same wage for the same job"* was enacted for the non-regular and regular employees to resolve the wage difference, June 20 (in Japanese).

Toyota Motor Corporation (2012). *75 Years of Toyota; Ever-better Cars*, Toyoda city, Toyota Motor Corporation (in Japanese).

Supplementary Reference Resources

Act against Delay in Payment of Subcontract Proceeds, Etc. to Subcontractors (abbreviated as *Subcontractors Law*, originally enacted on July 1, 1956).

Act on Prohibition of Private Monopolization and Maintenance of Fair Trade (the Antimonopoly [Antitrust] Act).

Statements of costs of goods manufactured (FYs 1989, 1990, 2008, 2009, 2010, 2011, 2012, and 2013) of Toyota and Nissan.

The Inherent Roles
of Management Accounting
for Promoting Innovation: The Case
of Material Flow Cost Accounting

Tatsumasa Tennojiya

Associate Professor, Faculty of Economics,
Hiroshima University of Economics, Japan

1. Introduction

Since Robert Simons presented the concept of "interactive control systems" (Simons, 1995), researchers have come to understand the relationship between innovation and management accounting to be positive in kind. Simons (1995) provided "a comprehensive theory illustrating how managers control strategy using four basic levers: beliefs systems, boundary systems, diagnostic control systems, and interactive control systems" (p. 4). Recognizing the differences between diagnostic control systems and interactive control systems is critical for understanding the nature of the relationship between innovation and management accounting.

Whereas diagnostic control systems are defined as "the formal information systems that managers use to monitor organizational outcomes and correct deviations from present standards of performance" (Simons, 1995, p. 59), interactive control systems are "formal information systems managers use to involve themselves regularly and personally in the decision activities of

Japanese Management and International Studies Vol. 13:
Management of Innovation Strategy in Japanese Companies
World Scientific Publishing Company, September 2016

subordinates" (Simons, 1995, p. 95). The use of diagnostic control systems represents a conventional type of management accounting. The use of management accounting as diagnostic control systems assists in the implementation of specific intended strategies through the improving performance on critical variables.

However, when organizations operate under conditions of uncertainty (including the strategies they mean to execute), the use of management accounting as diagnostic control systems can be difficult. In these situations, managers cannot know what kind of critical variables will lead to positive outcomes. To address issues related to uncertainty, Simons (1995) introduced the concept of "interactive control systems".

Simons' (1995) work was derivative of Galbraith's (1977) conceptualization of uncertainty. Galbraith (1977) described uncertainty as derived "from a difference in the information required to perform a task and the amount of information possessed by the organization" (Galbraith, 1977, p. 36). Interactive control systems collect new information and present methods for using information. Owing to their capacity to stimulate learning among organizational participants and effectively respond to perceived opportunities and threats, interactive control systems may be useful when organizations face strategic uncertainties (Simons, 1995, p. 91). Managers who identify strategic uncertainties can use interactive control systems to activate search for new information, as they provide frameworks or agendas for debate, and motivate information gathering outside of routine channels (Simons, 1995, p. 96).

The promotion of innovation requires attending to uncertainty. Using control systems interactively is one method for doing so. By searching for new information, interactive control systems can increase an organization's information capacity. Therefore, interactive control systems are capable of reducing the uncertainty, as defined by Galbraith (1977). Furthermore, through the use of interactive control systems, learning effects (which are critical for promoting innovation) emerge. Taken together, these benefits clearly indicate that interactive control systems assist in the promotion of innovation.

Simons' (1995) work spearheaded a changing understanding of the relationship between management accounting and innovation. To illustrate, a number of studies that adopted this new understanding emerged as a result of his seminal work (e.g. Abernethy and Brownell, 1999; Davila, 2000; Bisbe and Otley, 2004; Henri, 2006; Bisbe and Malagueño, 2009). These studies have empirically demonstrated a positive effect of interactive control systems on innovation, and are located at the mainstream research by Davila *et al.* (2009), who performed a comprehensive review of the studies related to innovation and management accounting.

In this way, the emergence of interactive control systems has changed the general thinking regarding the relationship between innovation and management accounting; whereas this relationship may have been considered to be negative in kind, Simons' (1995) work (and other research derived from it) has demonstrated the association to be positive. Despite this shift, there remains limited understanding of *how* management accounting promotes innovation, as interactive control systems relate solely to how information is used and focus on reducing the uncertainty or improving the learning effects for innovation.

Any discussion of innovation requires a consideration of Schumpeter's (1926) "new combination". A more common understanding of interactive control systems seems possible only through an exploration of the relationship between information gathering and innovation. Although management accounting creates various types of information, interactive control systems do not focus on this subject. The nature of the relationship between the information created by management accounting calculation and the "new combination" as innovation remains an open question.

To further our understanding of how management accounting promotes innovation, this paper focuses on the information that is created by management accounting tools. This paper considers the relationship between information created by material flow cost accounting (MFCA) and the "new combination." Following this, the paper will turn to a consideration of the inherent roles of management accounting for promoting innovation inductively.

To accomplish these goals, the remainder of this paper is divided into four sections. The next section introduces the MFCA method. The third section describes a case of innovation promoted through MFCA. The fourth section describes the inherent roles of management accounting in promoting innovation. Finally, the last section offers some concluding remarks and future avenues of research.

2. What is Material Flow Cost Accounting?

2.1. *MFCA as an environmental management accounting tool*

MFCA is an environmental management accounting (EMA) tool developed by Institut für Management und Umwelt (IMU; Research Institute of Environmental Management) in Augsburg, Germany (Ministry of Economy, Trade and Industry [METI], 2002; Nakajima and Kokubu, 2008). In Japan, academic researchers introduced MFCA to METI as an EMA tool. Following its introduction to METI, a number of companies have implemented MFCA. Owing to the number of organizations that employ it, Japan is one of the most advanced countries in terms of MFCA research and practice. To illustrate, Christ and Burritt (2016) describe Japan and Germany as "the prime instigators responsible for early development of the MFCA tool" (p. 2).

In 2011, MFCA was integrated into the ISO 14000 family as ISO 14051 (International Organization for Standardization [ISO], 2011). ISO (2011) describes MFCA as "a management tool that can assist organizations to better understand the potential, environmental, and financial consequences of their material and energy use practices, and seek opportunities to achieve both environmental and financial improvements via changes in those practice" (p. v). Through its integration into environmental management standards, many researchers expect MFCA to diffuse around the world rapidly (Christ and Burritt, 2016).

A number of case studies have illustrated the usefulness of MFCA (e.g. Kokubu, 2008). Moreover, other researchers (Kokubu *et al.*, 2006; Kokubu *et al.*, 2012; Kokubu *et al.*, 2013) have begun attempting to combine MFCA with other environmental management tools (e.g. Life-cycle Impact Assessment Method based on Endpoint Modelling [LIME] and Carbon Footprint of Products [CFP]). Given its pervasiveness and adoption by academics, practitioners, and governments, it is clear that MFCA has been recognized as an effective tool for EMA.

2.2. *Information created by MFCA*

Material balance — a comparison of physical quantities of inputs and outputs — is one of the fundamental elements of MFCA (METI, 2002; ISO, 2011). Because inputs and outputs are equal in quantity, the term "material

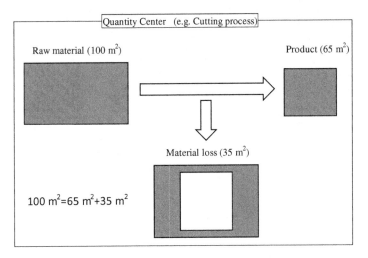

Fig. 1. Image of material balance and quantity center

balance" is appropriate. Material balance can be used to compare the physical quantities of inputs to products or material losses as outputs.

MFCA requires the achievement of material balance in quantity centers. Material balance within a quantity center is illustrated in Fig. 1. The ratio of materials intrinsic to products to material inputs is "resource efficiency." In Fig. 1 for example, the resource efficiency equals 65%.

Because MFCA treats resource efficiency as the key basis of cost allocation, it can be useful for improving this ratio (Schmidt and Nakajima, 2013). During MFCA calculations, process costs (except waste management costs) are allocated to product and material loss by using resource efficiency as an allocation criterion.[1] Waste management costs are assigned to material loss. Through these accounting methods, it is possible to calculate the costs associated with producing waste products.

Figure 2 presents a simple example of the MFCA calculation method. In this example, material costs are assigned to product and material loss. Although process costs are allocated to product and material loss in accordance with the resource efficiency criterion, waste management costs are all attributed as material loss.

---

[1] This doesn't mean "resource efficiency" is an exclusive criterion of allocation.

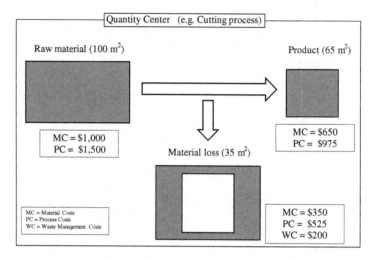

Fig. 2. MFCA calculation example

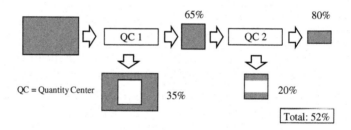

Fig. 3. Material flow model example

It is also important to recognize and understand material flow. Figure 3 presents an example of a model depicting material flow. Raw materials are generally involved in multiple processes. The product (i.e. output) of one process becomes an input for the next process. MFCA allows for the calculation of each process's resource efficiency, as well as the resource efficiency across all process. These figures allow for the calculation of costs related to material losses. In this example, the resource efficiencies for quantity centers A and B are 65% and 80%, respectively. Further, the resource efficiency across all processes is 52% (i.e. 0.65×0.80). Process costs for each quantity center are allocated into product and material loss by 65% and 80%, respectively. Finally, waste management costs are assigned or allocated to each process's material loss and total costs associated with product and material loss are calculated.

Through an adherence to resource efficiency, MFCA creates information related to material losses. If a company succeeds in improving its resource efficiency, it would purchase less material and create less waste. As a result, the costs associated with both materials and waste management would be reduced, thereby minimizing the organization's impact on the environment. As such, MFCA encourages companies to improve the resource efficiency of their raw materials through the calculation and visualization of material loss costs.

3. Innovation Through MFCA: Canon

3.1. Implementing MFCA into the camera lens line

One of the most famous cases related to the implementation of MFCA concerns the circumstances surrounding Canon's success with respect to the manufacturing line for single reflex camera's lens in 2000. This case was described not only by its promoter (Anjo, 2007), but also in instructional materials (METI, 2002; Nakajima and Kokubu, 2008; ISO, 2011).

Given the success of MFCA in this case, it is often identified as the specific incident that showed MFCA to promote innovation (Nakajima, 2006; ISO, 2011). So, the final goal of this paper will be to illustrate how management accounting promotes innovation. The Canon case will be used to achieve this goal. To effectively describe the Canon case, I consider prior studies (Nakajima, 2006; Anjo, 2007; Schmidt and Nakajima, 2013), established guidelines (METI, 2002; Nakajima and Kokubu, 2008; ISO, 2011), and interview data[2] collected from Mr. Yasuo Anjo, who was the promoter that implemented MFCA at Canon in 2000.

Figure 4 presents a basic illustration of a manufacturing process in which MFCA is implemented. First, the glass is placed in the line as a raw material. Secondly, the glass is ground, smoothed, and polished to create the required shape and thickness. Following the polishing of the glass lenses, they are then centered and coated. The coated glass lenses are the final products of this

---

[2]The three-hour interview was conducted on December 27, 2012. This interview was recorded and transcribed by the author.

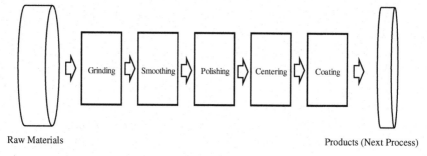

Raw Materials   Products (Next Process)

Fig. 4.   Manufacturing process in which MFCA was implemented

process and are then used as input in the next processes. Testing and cleaning are typically included in this process (METI, 2002; Nakajima, 2006; Nakajima and Kokubu, 2008; ISO, 2011; Schmidt and Nakajima, 2013). For the sake of simplicity, however, these steps have been omitted from Fig. 4.

3.2. The effects of implementing MFCA: Mobilization of technology

Because the raw materials in this process are fragile by nature, Canon long-sought to reduce defects using the ratio of defects to inputs. Around 1970, this ratio was roughly 30%, indicating the process to be somewhat problematic. As a result of Canon's efforts, however, this ratio had dropped to 1% by 2000, showing the process to be vastly improved in terms of the problems causing product defects.

After MFCA was implemented, however, the process once again was shown to be problematic. MFCA showed the ratio of costs from material losses to input costs to be approximately 32% in total. Furthermore, MFCA showed that 67% of costs due to material loss accrued in the grinding process. Handling material losses due to the grinding processes also increased the costs of waste management, which accounted for 43% of all material loss costs from the grinding process.

Before MFCA was used at Canon, material losses were recognized (sludge from the raw materials was visible), but not monetarily calculated. That MFCA allows for the expression of material losses as a monetary term is one of the key reasons it was adopted at Canon. Quantification of waste management costs was also a contributing factor for its adoption. Because the factory performed closed effluent treatment for sludge, waste management costs were huge. These costs were included in process costs and allocated to each product. However, these costs accrued only because of the sludge, not because of the products. Therefore, the promoter thought these costs should be treated exclusively as material loss.

The information derived from MFCA methods induced Canon to reduce material loss costs in the grinding process. To reduce material costs, it is first imperative to improve resource efficiency. Therefore, Canon sought to improve resource efficiency during the grinding process, and developed the "near-shaping" lens in collaboration with suppliers. The near-shaping lens is shaved to a lesser degree than a conventional lens. By using the near-shaping lenses in place of a conventional lens, Canon was able to improve its resource efficiency, as there was less room for grinding.

In actuality, the technologies used to develop near-shaping lenses were adapted to the production of other products (e.g. aspheric lens), but they were not adapted for the single-lens reflex camera. The degree of curvature needed for a lens on the single-lens camera made it seem difficult to adopt near-shaping technologies for it.

However, the information derived from the MFCA methods helped induce Canon to adopt these technologies to improve resource efficiency and reduce costs associated with material losses. As a result, the technologies needed to produce the near-shaping lens were placed in the object line, after information produced by MFCA showed that line to be problematic.

The accuracy of near-shaping technologies improved following this change, and costs from material losses were reduced substantially. By mobilizing the technologies for near-shaping lens in the production line, the "new combination" (innovation) was realized. In this way, researchers and practitioners can point to Canon's case as one in which management accounting helped promote innovation.

4. The Inherent Role of Management Accounting in the Promotion of Innovation

This section considers the Canon case to illustrate the relationship between the information created by MFCA and the "new combination" as innovation.

Moreover, this section demonstrates the inherent role of management accounting in the promotion of innovation through the Canon case and another study.

4.1. Creating "tension"

In the case of Canon, although material losses were visible before the implementation of MFCA, technologies for developing the near-shaping lens were not adopted. Because the process was recognized as nearly perfect in terms of the old performance indicator (ratio of defects to input), there seemed to be no need to implement new technologies.

However, information created by MFCA changed perceptions of the extant production process. Specifically, the MFCA showed the process to be problematic, thereby causing Canon to adopt technologies adapted to the near-shaping lens. In a sense, the information produced by the MFCA method created "tension" in the production line.

As in the case of Canon, this "tension" can be produced by the introduction of new calculation logics. Mouritsen *et al.* (2009) provided a good example. Through a case analysis of three firms, they argued that "management accounting calculation problematizes the firm, its innovation and technologies and its boundaries" (Mouritsen *et al.*, 2009, p. 753).

The authors described all the cases with a focus on two management accounting calculations — one old and one new. Similarly, for all cases, the specific calculations for the old and new tabulation methods differed, and management accounting information created by new calculation logic procedures revealed existing activities to be problematic. The Canon case presented here, as well as the cases presented by Mouritsen *et al.* (2009), show that management accounting can create "tension" through the introduction of calculation logics that differ from those that have been used in the past.

4.2. Legitimatizing resource mobilization

In the case of Canon, the technologies for the near-shaping lens were mobilized after MFCA created monetary "tension" resulting from the grinding process. These technologies were mobilized because they were effective in improving the resource efficiency of raw materials, thereby reducing costs associated with both materials and waste management. In this way, resource efficiency can be said to the ultimate outcome of MFCA. Given the attractiveness of resource efficiency, it can further be said that the information created by MFCA legitimatized the mobilization of technologies for producing Canon's near-shaping lens.

Mouritsen *et al.* (2009) also addressed the relationship between the information created by management accounting and resource mobilization. For example, they showed that SuitTech, which "produced and sold measurement systems to R&D departments and university laboratories whose measurement problems varied considerably" (Mouritsen *et al.*, 2009, p. 741), used sales as a performance indicator for sales engineers, thereby incentivizing sales engineers to generate greater numbers of sales. Therefore, "sales engineers could, in cooperation with the customer, choose from special and customized components delivered by a broad range of suppliers or developed and produced by SuitTech itself" (Mouritsen *et al.*, 2009, p. 741).

However, these activities were problematized after the company introduced "contribution margin" as a new performance measure. Contribution margin incorporates not only sales figures, but also direct costs incurred. While "sales performance motivated a strategy of tight customization through liberal use of externally sourced special and customized components" (Mouritsen *et al.*, 2009, p. 742), the use of contribution margin as a performance indicator problematized these activities because of high direct costs. So, by using contribution margin as its key performance indicator, SuitTech legitimized the use of programmable standard components and the upgrading of internal software competences. Both the Canon case, and those presented by Mouritsen *et al.* (2009), show that management accounting information can be used to legitimize the mobilization of resources associated with its calculation logics.

5. Conclusions and Future Research

This paper considered the inherent roles of management accounting in the promotion of innovation through multiple case illustrations. Figure 5 illustrates one of the key conclusions of this paper. Specifically, management accounting can create "tension" by introducing a new method for calculating

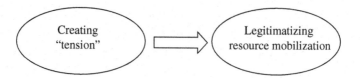

Fig. 5.   The inherent role of management accounting

costs. The new information gleaned from the new calculation method can illustrate production shortcomings in monetary terms, thereby leading the organization to view existing conditions as problematic.

After producing tension, management accounting can be used to legitimize resource mobilization. New information created by new calculation logics 'opens the organization's eyes' to new resources and promote innovation as the "new combination". The expression of production shortcomings in monetary terms helps to legitimize resource mobilization.

Whereas the approach employing the concept of interactive control systems helped to clarify the relationship between information gathering and the innovation, the approach illustrated in this paper helps to evaluate the relationship between information created through management accounting calculation logic and mobilized resources. As a result, another role of management accounting in the promotion of innovation emerged: creating "tension" and legitimatizing resource mobilization. The approach described in this paper can complement the approach that employs the concept of interactive control systems to provide a more comprehensive understanding of the role of management accounting in innovation.

The framework described above is adaptable to other cases. It requires future researchers to address issues like process tension, and the conditions under which resource mobilization is legitimized. For instance, future research should explore organizational resistance to implementing new management accounting tools (Malmi, 1997; Tennojiya, 2014). Further, there exist other control tools (e.g. technology roadmap) that express common expectations (Miller and O'Leary, 2005). In addition, future research in this domain should examine the relationship between various mobilized objects and the reasons for their mobilization (Revellino and Mouritsen, 2009; Takeishi *et al.*, 2012). Finally, more case studies that employ the framework described here would allow for the accumulation of useful and actionable knowledge.

Acknowledgment

This work was supported by JSPS KAKENHI Grant No. 26780266.

References

Abernethy, M. A. and P. Brownell (1999). The role of budgets in organizations facing strategic change: an exploratory study. *Accounting, Organizations and Society* 24(3): 233–249.

Anjo, Y. (2007). Implementing material flow cost accounting in canon. *Kigyo-Kaikei* 59(11): 40–47 (In Japanese).

Bisbe, J. and R. Malagueňo (2009). The choice of interactive control systems under different innovation management models. *European Accounting Review* 18(2): 371–405.

Bisbe, J. and D. Otley (2004). The effects of the interactive use of management control systems on product innovation. *Accounting, Organizations and Society* 29(8): 709–737.

Christ, K. L. and R. L. Burritt (2016). ISO 14051: A new era for MFCA implementation and research. *Spanish Accounting Review* 19(1): 1–9.

Davila, T. (2000). An empirical study on the drivers of management control system's design in new product development. *Accounting, Organizations and Society* 25(4/5): 383–409.

Davila, A., G. Foster and D. Oyon (2009). Accounting and control, entrepreneurship and innovation: venturing into new research opportunities. *European Accounting Review* 18(2): 288–311.

Galbraith, J. (1977). *Organization Design*. Boston, MA: Addison-Wesley.

Henri, J-F. (2006). Management control system and strategy: a resource-based perspective. *Accounting, Organizations and Society* 31(6): 529–558.

International Organization for Standardization (ISO) (2011). *ISO14051: Environmental Management: Material Flow Cost Accounting: General Framework*, International Organization for Standardization.

Kokubu, K. (eds.) (2008). *Practice of Material Flow Cost Accounting*. Japan Environmental Management Association for Industry.

Kokubu, K., H. Kitada, T. Fuchigami, and D. Tanaka (2013). Applicability of integrated model of MFCA-CFP to practice. *Environmental Management* 49(1): 73–77 (In Japanese).

Kokubu, K., T. Fuchigami and A. Yamada (2012). The development of integrated model of MFCA and CFP. *Environmental Management* 48(2): 66–76 (In Japanese).

Kokubu, K., N. Itsubo and M. Nakajima (2006). Integration of material flow cost accounting and LIME. *Journal of Economics & Business Administration* 194(3): 1–11 (In Japanese).

Malmi, T. (1997). Towards explaining activity-based costing failure: accounting and control in a decentralized organization. *Management Accounting Research* 8(4): 459–480.

Miller, P. and L. O'Leary (2005). Capital budgeting, coordination, and strategy: a field study of interfirm and intrafirm mechanisms. in Chapman, C. S. (ed.), *Controlling Strategy: Management, Accounting, and Performance Measurement.* Oxford University Press.

Ministry of Economy, Trade and Industry (METI). (2002). *Workbook on Environmental Management Accounting Methods.* Ministry of Economy, Trade and Industry (In Japanese).

Mouritsen, J., A. Hansen and Ø. C. Hansen (2009). Short and long translations: management accounting calculations and innovation management. *Accounting, Organizations and Society* 34(6/7): 738–754.

Nakajima, M. (2006). "Possibilities of promoting innovation through the environmental management accounting. in Amano, A., Kokubu, K., Matsumura, K. and Genba, K. (eds.), *Innovation of Environmental Management*, Seisansei-Syuppan (In Japanese).

Nakajima, M. and K. Kokubu (2008). *Material Flow Cost Accounting (Second Edition).* Nikkei Publishing (In Japanese).

Revellino, S. and J. Mouritsen (2009). The multiplicity of controls and the making of innovation. *European Accounting Review* 18(2): 341–369.

Simons, R. (1995). *Levers of Control.* Boston, MA: Harvard Business School Press.

Schmidt, M. and M. Nakajima (2013). Material flow cost accounting as an approach to improve resource efficiency in manufacturing companies. *Resource* 2(3): 358–369.

Schumpeter, J. A. (1926). *Theorie Der Wirtschaftlichen Entwicklung, 2.* Duncker and Humblot (In German).

Takeishi, A., Y. Aoshima and M. Karube (2012). *Reasons for Innovation: Creating Legitimacy for Resource Mobilization,* Yuhikaku. (In Japanese).

Tennojiya, T. (2014). Consideration of the resistance when the management accounting innovation are introduced: exploratory research toward the deepening of understanding. *HUE Journal of Economics and Business* 37(3): 155–165 (In Japanese).

Part 2

Considerations of Innovation Management From the Perspective of Individual Industries and Companies

Innovation Strategies and Segment Reporting: A Case Study of Corporate Electronics Groups in Japan

Shufuku Hiraoka

Professor, Faculty of Business Administration,
Soka University, Japan

1. Introduction

Japan's corporate electronics groups have faced numerous challenges over the last decade. In reaction, these corporate groups have executed innovation strategies and re-structured their business portfolios to improve their financial performance. Resolving environmental and social problems within businesses is crucial to success. In this paper, I analyze the innovation strategies and re-structuring approaches of six major corporate groups involved in the business of electrical goods.

First, I classify these company groups into three types based on their performance under given circumstances. The groups of the first type have had unfavorable histories of performance with regard to stakeholders. The groups of the second type have recovered in terms of their performance. The groups of the third type have had stable favorable histories of firm performance.

Next, I analyze the impacts of innovation strategies and re-structuring on the financial performance of business segments of the corporate groups in question.

Japanese Management and International Studies Vol. 13:
Management of Innovation Strategy in Japanese Companies
World Scientific Publishing Company, September 2016

2. Corporate Groups with Unfavorable Performance

2.1. *SHARP*

The business segments of SHARP are as follows:

(1) Product business segment, consisting of consumer electronics, energy solutions, and business solutions divisions.
(2) Device business segment, consisting of electronic device and display device divisions.

The consumer electronics division includes businesses related to digital appliances, communications, healthcare, and the environment. The energy solutions division mainly includes solar cell businesses. The business solutions division mainly consists of multifunctional products and digital signage. The electronic devices division is almost completely focused on semiconductors. The display device division is focused on liquid crystal displays. SHARP's performance primarily depended on its device, energy solution, and digital businesses. SHARP has been concentrating its resources on small and mid-sized solar cells named IGZO for smart phones and tablets in recent years. Its financial performance temporarily improved in the fiscal year 2013. However, the prices of liquid crystal displays sagged significantly in the fiscal year 2014. The performance of its energy solutions division also fell, because the prices of mega solar cells decreased. SHARP also decided to drop out of the mega solar business at the same time. Multifunctional products and camera modules are highly competitive product areas. The former belongs to SHARP's business solutions division, while the latter belongs to its electronic device division. Its communication business is also highly profitable. SHARP needs to innovate by creating products and services related to new businesses. Its healthcare and environment businesses should also be a focus. Its digital appliance division needs to create products that are not only for advanced nations but also for rising nations.

The performance of its business segments in the fiscal years 2013 and 2014 is shown in Table 1.

The impact of business performance on consolidated financial performance is shown in Table 2.

Table 1.   Performance of SHARP's business segments

Fiscal year	Return on sales (%)		Sales distribution ratio (%)		Operating profits: Yen (millions)	
	2013	2014	2013	2014	2013	2014
Product business	5.3	−0.8	62.1	57.3	96,802	−12,295
Digital appliance	1.8	−3.1	16.6	15.7	8.926	−13,477
Communication	1.6	7.1	8.4	8.4	3,914	16,501
Healthcare and environment	6.4	5.1	11.2	11.3	21.018	15,927
Energy solution	7.4	−23.1	15.0	9.7	32,400	−62,679
Business solution	9.6	9.6	10.9	12.2	30,544	31,403
Device business	3.4	0.09	45.0	48.4	44,853	1,270
Electronic device	1.0	0.15	11.1	15.8	3,265	676
Display device	4.2	0.07	33.9	32.6	41,588	594

Table 2.   Performance based on SHARP's consolidated financial statements (%)

Fiscal year	2013	2014	Deterioration points
Return on equity	7.2	−197.4	204.6
Return on sales	3.7	−1.7	5.4
Capital to assets ratio	8.9	1.5	7.4
Current ratio	88	77	11
Quick assets ratio	63	51	12
Fixed long-term conformity ratio	128	241	113

SHARP has to improve its financial performance. The policies planned and executed by SHARP are as follows:

(1) Improving the capital to asset ratio through debts equity swaps.
(2) Introducing a company system for the delegation of authority.
(3) Re-structuring non-profitable businesses and assets.
(4) Looking for employees that will voluntarily retire in Japan.

However, it is most important for SHARP to innovate in its main businesses so as to improve sales growth rates and profitability at the corporate group level.

2.2. TOSHIBA

The business segments of TOSHIBA are as follows:

(1) Electric power and social infrastructure
(2) Community solutions
(3) Healthcare
(4) Electronic devices
(5) Lifestyle
(6) Others

The electric power and social infrastructure segment consists of transportation systems, machinery, and equipment for producing energy. The community solutions segment consists of elevator machines, air conditioning units, LEDs, POS systems, and multifunction products. The healthcare segment consists of medical devices and healthcare solutions. The electronic device segment includes semiconductors and hard disk drives. The lifestyle segment consists of appliances, personal computers, and video equipment. The "others" segment includes cloud solutions and physical distribution services.

TOSHIBA has been particularly good at innovating in the areas of electronic devices, healthcare, and electric power. Its NAND flash memory is highly competitive in the electronic device market, while its computerized tomography offerings have been competitive in the healthcare field. Its hydrogen energy systems will be a new business in the clean energy sector in the future.

TOSHIBA has introduced a company system in which each company manager is heavily responsible for the profits of the company. TOSHIBA has been also cross-functionally carrying out the Kaizen activity project named "GAIN" to reduce costs since April 2014. However, dysfunction has arisen in the company, putting great pressure on many managers to achieve target profits. A third party has pointed out that modifications have been

Table 3. Business segment profits and revisions in TOSHIBA: Yen (billions)

Fiscal year	Operating profits 2012	Operating profits 2013	Overstated past operating profits	Estimated impairment loss
Electric power and social infrastructure	85.1	32.3	47.7	—
Community solutions	42.7	51.9	—	—
Healthcare	23.8	28.6	—	—
Electronic devices	95.5	238.4	36.0	50
Lifestyle	−42.3	−51.0	68.0	20
Others	−6.5	−8.7	—	—

made in the many cases of inappropriate accounting of TOSHIBA. It estimates that the group still has to revise past operating profits by ¥56.2 billion, inclusive of independent checks by TOSHIBA. It will also have to add up impairment losses of ¥70 billion. The operating profits of its business segments for the past two years and the overstated amounts are shown in Table 3.

President Hisao Tanaka recently stepped down and took responsibility for TOSHIBA's accounting irregularities. Former President and Vice Chairman Norio Sasaki also resigned as a board member due to scandal. Investigations revealed that the company's main missing profits involved the following:

(1) Overestimating profits related to the smart meter business and ETC with the percent of completion method.
(2) Adding the fee reimbursements for materials as realized profits in the personal computer business.
(3) Overestimating profits and inventory value in the semiconductor business.
(4) Underestimating or delaying some expenses in the TV business.

Inappropriate accounting hinders innovation. If TOSHIBA sincerely hopes to increase its innovation, not only its financial accounting but also its management accounting must be carried out correctly.

3. Corporate Groups with Recovering the Performance

3.1. SONY

The business segments of SONY are as follows:

(1) Mobile communication, within which smartphone products make up the main business.
(2) Game and network services, consisting of PlayStation®4, software, and network businesses.
(3) Imaging products and solutions, which include camera and broadcast equipment businesses.
(4) Home entertainment and sound, which consists of TV, audio, and video products.
(5) Devices, which consists of COMS image sensors and components.
(6) Movie, which consists of filmmaking, TV production, and media networks.
(7) Music, which consists of music production, and publishing.
(8) Finance, which involves the insurance business and banking.
(9) Others.

The ROS (return on sales) of SONY business segments in the fiscal years 2013–2014 is shown in Table 4. The changes in the mobile communication and

Table 4.   ROS for business segments of SONY

Fiscal year	Return on sales (%)		Improvement or deterioration
	2013	2014	
Mobile communication	1.1	−16.7	Deterioration
Game and network service	−1.8	3.5	Improvement
Imaging products and solution	3.6	7.6	Improvement
Home entertainment and sound	−2.2	1.7	Improvement
Devices	−1.7	9.7	Improvement
Movie	6.2	6.7	Improvement
Music	6.1	10.8	Improvement
Finance	17.1	17.8	Improvement
Consolidated	0.34	0.83	Improvement

devices divisions are remarkable. The former has been affected by a depression affecting sales of smartphone products, while the latter has been affected by the satisfactory performance of COMS sensors. The "others" segment has faced operating losses related to the PC business and disk production.

SONY has disposed of its PC business. It has also spun off its smartphone and TV businesses because of the business slump. Its TV business has been restructured and its resources have been centralized in 4K. Therefore, it has moved into the black. However, its smartphone business continues to be in the red.

Although SONY has reduced the number of departments and personnel in its smartphone division, it has continued to sell the "Xperia® Z4" as its flagship model, which has a stronger camera and high-tech audio. Within its TV business, the company has also been developing a high-resolution TV model for emerging markets. Both the COMS sensor and the PlayStation®4 are top global products. The market share of the COMS sensor is about 40%, because of smartphone and tablet terminals. An example of SONY's application domains is shown in Fig. 1.

SONY has carried out organizational reforms. The percentage of its managerial-class employees has been reduced from a little over 40% to 20%. The personnel affairs pay system has also been reformed completely, after an interval of 10 years. Some of the other key approaches that it has followed are:

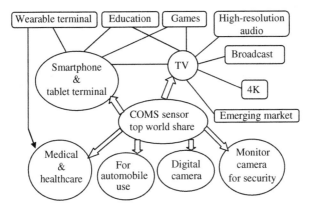

Fig. 1.   Example of SONY's application domains

(1) Evaluating based on current roles rather than past results.
(2) Abolishing the long service element and seniority.
(3) Skipping grades based on motivation and abilities.
(4) Setting new career paths for professionals.
(5) Establishing a new offer system, making it easy for employees to move to desired posts within the company.
(6) Benchmarking competitive domestic companies to get talented employees and reviewing group pay levels.

The financial performance of SONY over the past five years is shown in Table 5.

SONY's profitability improved in the fiscal year 2012, but deteriorated again in the fiscal years 2013–2014. However, it improved in the fiscal year 2015. Its net income in the fiscal year 2015 improved about ¥148 billion. Its ROE increased, while its ROS became 3.6. Its financial soundness is also improving. Sony has announced a new management plan that will be applied until March, 2018. Its target ROE was set at more than 10% for the fiscal year 2017. Sony has also proposed some new innovation strategies to achieve its goals.

SONY's new business model, named "recurring type," aims to continuously gain profits from customers. For example, SONY has begun a cloud TV delivery service with a game machine controller, in order to create new value through innovation in the U.S. Users will be able to reproduce and view TV programs stored on servers. SONY will thus completely reform cable TV service in the U.S. and aim for a transfer of audience.

Table 5.   Financial performance of SONY (%)

Fiscal year	2010	2011	2012	2013	2014
Return on equity	−9.4	−20	2.0	−5.8	−5.5
Return on sales	2.8	−1.0	3.4	0.3	0.8
Capital to assets ratio	19.7	15.3	15.5	14.7	14.6
Current ratio	93	83	85	88	88
Quick assets ratio	62	57	58	62	65
Fixed long-term conformity ratio	106	106	107	105	105

SONY also uses corporate venture capital. It is essential for big companies to accelerate innovation. SONY has been financing a venture company named ZMP that is developing automatic operation systems. The companies are putting the SONY CMOS sensor and the artificial intelligence technology of ZMP together to develop the camera parts needed for driving automatically.

In addition, SONY has created the "First Flight" website, which features products involving new technology or unique ideas. SONY asks potential customers whether they want those products and if so, it commercializes them.

Finally, SONY has adopted the "open innovation" approach proposed by Chesbrough (2003). It has cooperated with a venture company in the U.S. in order to compete in the smart home market. It is possible for that business to utilize SONY's COMS sensor and image processing technology.

SONY's device business has been targeting a large amount of investment because of application domains. SONY has decided to invest a total ¥150 billion in such businesses, which will continue until June 2016, and is offering new stocks and bonds for public investment.

3.2. *Panasonic*

The business segments of Panasonic are as follows:

(1) Appliances, consisting of white home appliances, audio systems, TVs, large air conditioners, cold chains, motors, and compressors.
(2) Eco solutions, consisting of lighting equipment, lamps, wiring appliances, solar power systems, water supply facilities, interior decoration building materials, ventilation, air conditioning and cleaning units, and care facilities.
(3) AVC networks, consisting of AV systems in planes, PCs, projectors, digital cameras, cellphones, monitoring and security cameras, landline phones, fax machines, and social infrastructure systems.
(4) Automotive and industrial systems, consisting of multimedia-related apparatuses for automobiles, electrical components, lithium ion batteries, other batteries, dry cells, electronic parts, electronic materials, control equipment, semiconductors, liquid crystal panels, optical devices,

electronic parts, automated implementation systems, and welding apparatuses.

(5) Others, including Pana-Home Corp. Co. Ltd.

Panasonic faced final deficits of more than ¥750 billion in the fiscal years of 2011–2012. However, it has more recently restructured some of its problematic businesses. Therefore, its bottom lines have been recovered and entered the black in the fiscal year 2013. Panasonic has withdrawn from its plasma television business and sold the real estate associated with it. With the favorable performance of its 4K television sets, the deficits in its TV business have decreased, and its TV business is aiming to become profitable in the fiscal year 2015. It has withdrawn from its smartphone business for individuals and fused its remaining smartphone business with its digital camera business. The engineers in its smartphone business were moved to its digital camera business and some strategic products were developed. Panasonic decided to sell its circuit board production subsidiary to Shinasahi Electronics Ind. Co. Ltd.

Panasonic also decided to sell some of the domestic and foreign factories involved in its semiconductor business. Its control technology for appliances and automotive information terminal technology have been fused and its semiconductor business for automobile and appliance networking has been strengthened. Panasonic's sales have improved in Asia and its operating profit has been increasing.

Panasonic has also established "AP Asia" as a unified company dealing with appliances in Asia, and has accordingly moved many authorities in the fields of product planning, development, production, marketing, and sales. The Panasonic household appliance brand has been cosigning the production and development of items with local specifications in Europe. Its eco solutions segment creates equipment for houses and competitively supplies electric-power-related businesses. Panasonic's solar power generation system for houses is highly profitable and holds a significant market share, because of its high generation efficiency. Its main businesses involving automotive and industrial systems include lithium ion batteries for electric and hybrid cars, car navigation systems, and in-vehicle illumination products. Panasonic has also invested a total of ¥100 billion in a factory for electric vehicles with Tesla Motors in the U.S.

Table 6.   Performance of Panasonic business segments

Fiscal year	2013	2014			
Index	ROS	ROS	ROA	ATR	SGR
Appliance	1.7	2.3	4.5	1.98	−0.43
Eco solutions	5.5	5.7	7.9	1.38	−0.50
Avc networks	3.1	4.5	7.0	1.56	0.15
Automotive and industrial systems	2.5	3.8	5.9	1.56	2.23
Others	3.1	1.9	2.4	1.25	−14.2
Consolidated	3.9	5.0	6.8	1.38	−0.28

ROS(%) = (operating profit/sales) × 100.
ROA(%) = (operating profit/assets) × 100.
ATR(rounds) = sales/assets.
SGR(%) = (sales for 2014/sales for 2013 − 1)×100.

Table 7.   Distribution ratios of Panasonic business segments

Distribution ratio	Sales (%)		Operating profits (%)	
Fiscal year	2013	2014	2013	2014
Appliance	21.6	21.7	11.8	13.2
Eco solutions	20.4	20.5	36.7	31.0
Avc networks	14.0	14.2	14.2	16.8
Automotive and industrial systems	33.1	34.2	27.6	34.3
Others	10.9	9.4	9.7	4.7

The performance of Panasonic's specific business segments is shown in Tables 6 and 7. The ROSs of all segments have improved except for the others segment in the fiscal year 2014. The sales-growth rates increased in for the AVC networks and the automotive and industrial systems segments. Panasonic prioritized improving profitability rather than sales growth by reducing costs and restructuring in the fiscal years of 2013–2014. It then achieved its target operating profit and target free cash flow one year ahead of schedule.

As shown in Table 7, the distribution ratios for appliance, AVC networks, automotive and industrial systems increased. In particular, the operating profit distribution ratios for the automotive and industrial segments changed remarkably. Panasonic has recently been focused on a growth pathway. For the fiscal year 2015, its expected net income was reported as roughly ¥180 billion, its sales were predicted to reach ¥8 trillion and its operating profit was forecast at roughly ¥430 billion. Panasonic has decided to integrate the organic electroluminescence panel business in its industrial segment with that of SONY and to find an R&D base in the spring of 2016, so as to compete with that of Samsung. The distribution ratios of the AVC networks segment increased as well. The automotive and eco solutions segments will be likely to gain a lot of income as growth businesses. The AVC networks segment will also need to gain profits through innovation in the future. With this in mind, Panasonic has established an "innovation center" for its AVC networks segment. The target sales for AVC networks are expected to reach ¥1,500 billion in the fiscal year 2018.

As mentioned above, Panasonic has also been adopting strategies for markets in Asia and Europe, so as to improve the profitability and the sales growth rate of its appliance segment. The consolidated sales amount of the Panasonic group is expected to be ¥10 trillion in the period until the fiscal year 2018.

As shown in Table 8, Panasonic improved not only its profitability but its safety during the fiscal years 2013–2014. It is essential to improve profitability. Panasonic named the method "Capital Cost Management (CCM)". It is also an EVA-type valuation system. Panasonic's CCM has been already explained by Hiraoka (2006, 2007, 2010). Panasonic also brought back its division system in 2013, after an interval of 12 years, and introduced an

Table 8.   Main financial performance of Panasonic (%)

Fiscal year	2010	2011	2012	2013	2014
Return on equity	2.8	−34.4	−47.2	8.6	10.6
Return on sales	3.5	0.56	2.20	3.9	5.0
Capital to assets ratio	32.7	29.2	23.4	29.7	30.6
Current ratio	123	100	96	109	125
Quick assets ratio	74	56	55	66	84
Fixed long-term conformity ratio	94	101	97	94	79

internal capital system in all divisions. Panasonic has decided to apply CCM to each division and raise the weighted average cost of capital before taxes from 8.4% across the board in the group to 9%. However, there is a different rate corresponding to the risk involved in each business (4–16%).

4. Groups Maintaining High Performance

4.1. *Hitachi*

The business segments of Hitachi are as follows (Hitachi, 2015):

(1) Information and telecommunication systems, consisting of financial information systems, government and public information systems, enterprise information systems, infrastructure information systems, consulting, ATMs, cloud services, IT platforms (servers, storage, etc.), and telecommunication systems.

(2) Power systems, consisting of nuclear power generation systems, wind power generation system monitoring/advanced plant maintenance, and solar power generation systems.

(3) Social infrastructure and industrial systems, consisting of escalators, elevators, industrial machinery and plants, and railway vehicles and systems.

(4) Electric systems and equipment, consisting of medical electronic equipment, electronic parts manufacturing system, semiconductor and LCD manufacturing equipment, testing and measurement equipment, and power tools.

(5) Construction machinery, consisting of hydraulic excavators, mining dump trucks, and wheel loaders.

(6) High-functional material and components, consisting of wire, cable, semiconductors, display-related materials, specialty steels, high-grade casting components and materials, copper products, circuit boards and materials, and magnetic materials and components.

(7) Automotive systems, consisting of engine management systems, drive control systems, batteries, electric powertrain systems, and car information systems.

(8) Smart life and eco-friendly systems, consisting of air-conditioning equipment, room air conditioners, refrigerators, and washing machines.

(9)   Others, consisting of logistics and property management.

(10) Financial services, consisting of leasing and loan guarantees.

Hitachi faced a record-high final deficit of ¥ 787,300 million in the fiscal year 2008. A company-wide reform activity called the "Hitachi Smart Transformation Project" was subsequently carried out, in which unprofitable businesses withdrew or were downsized. Some businesses were sold or unified with similar businesses in other company groups. At the same time, M&A were carried out. The company's information and telecommunication systems segment has failed to hit its targets over the past three years. Therefore, Hitachi has set out growth strategies for fusing its social infrastructure and information technology with social innovation. Innovation in conjunction with the internet of things (IoT) will be one of the keys to the company's future success. With regard to its IT-related business, Hitachi has set the goal of increasing sales to ¥3 trillion and its ROS to 10% as part of its mid-range planning for the period until 2018.

The power system segment integrated its thermal power generation business with that of Mitsubishi Heavy Industries and established a joint venture named "Mitsubishi Hitachi Power Systems" in 2014. It then became an equity method application company of Hitachi. Hitachi's Power Systems have been carrying out joint management and collaborative research initiatives together with global companies (GE, LE, and ABB) as a means of realizing its innovation strategies. For its social infrastructure and industrial systems segment, Hitachi has decided to deliver the world's fastest elevator to China. Its railway business has also been developing in Europe and Asia. The main company of the electric systems and equipment segment is Hitachi High-Technologies Corp. Its net income for 2014 was its highest ever. The medical electronics and semiconductor manufacturing equipment segment is also competitive. In addition, Hitachi's construction machinery segment has grown in the U.S., Europe, and Africa. The major consolidated subsidiaries of the high functional material and components segment are Hitachi Chemical Co. Ltd and Hitachi Metals Ltd. Both subsidiaries have achieved high levels of performance. Hitachi Chemical also recently decided to build a factory for the component parts of Panasonic's lithium ion batteries by the fiscal year 2018. As described above, Panasonic has long been supplying lithium ion batteries for Tesla Motors in the U.S. Hitachi Metals has also decided to establish a joint venture to produce and sell rare earth element magnets in China. The automotive systems segment aims to use its know-how in the areas of appliances and cloud computing for business, in order to achieve sales of ¥2 trillion yearly. Big data analysis and cloud computing will also lead to innovation and new demand. In addition, Hitachi has decided to invest in a new automotive engine parts factory in India. Its smart life and eco-friendly system segment has implemented innovation strategies to cope with the weak yen. The break-even points for all parts and materials have been set. Procurement has been reviewed, and the domestic production ratio has been raised. As an example, Hitachi has decided to produce and sell all of its domestic home air-conditioners in Japan, because this allows it to sell higher-priced products of a high quality. The logistics segment has reduced the company's distribution costs by 10–20%, while improving the distribution efficiency of group companies in China. A smart logistics service division has also been established in China. Hitachi aims to raise the total sales of its business to ¥70 billion by the fiscal year 2018.

As for its financial service segment, Hitachi has been boosting its finance business in the U.K., its loan business for trucks in the U.S.

The performance of its business segments is shown in Table 9. The ROS of the financial services segment was the highest. In contrast, the contributions of sales and profits were not very high. The profit contribution degree of the power systems segment was the greatest in the fiscal year 2013. It was lowest in the fiscal year 2014.

Instead of the power systems segment, the contributions of three business segments (information and telecommunications systems, social infrastructure and industrial systems, and high functional material and components) were greater. Those appear to be the pillars of Hitachi's innovation strategies.

The main financial performance of Hitachi is shown in Table 10. Its profitability has been improving smoothly since the fiscal year 2012. Its operating profit was slightly over ¥580 billion in the fiscal year 2014, and rose 10% as compared with the fiscal year 2013. Hitachi has set its target ROS as more than 7%. Its R&D costs are predicted to be ¥500 billion per annum from the fiscal year of 2016 and to increase by 30% over the fiscal year of 2015. Hitachi's Key Performance Indicator (KPI) target is based on the following formula:

Return on R&D Investment = Operating profit/R&D Investment.

Table 9. Performance of Hitachi business segments

Index	ROS (%)		Distribution ratio (%)			
The fiscal year	2013	2014	2013		2014	
Consolidated	5.5	6.6	Sales	OP	Sales	OP
Information and telecommunication systems	5.9	5.2	18.1	16.9	18.6	17.1
Power systems	2.5	0.8	6.7	26.3	4.1	0.6
Social infrastructure and industrial systems	5.2	6.7	13.3	11.5	14.2	17.2
Electric systems and equipment	4.7	5.6	10.2	7.7	10.4	10.3
Construction machinery	7.9	7.4	8.2	9.3	8.3	9.8
High functional material and components	7.5	8.1	13.6	15.4	14.9	20.0
Automotive systems	0.4	3.7	9.2	0.5	9.6	5.6
Smart life and eco-friendly systems	3.8	4.6	7.3	4.1	7.3	5.6
Others	1.6	4.0	10.1	3.5	9.2	8.1
Financial services	9.6	9.9	3.3	4.8	3.4	5.7

Note: OP: Operating profit.

Table 10. Main financial performances of Hitachi (%)

Fiscal year	2010	2011	2012	2013	2014
Return on equity	17.5	21.6	9.1	11.2	12.2
Return on sales	4.8	4.3	4.7	5.5	6.6
Capital to assets ratio	15.7	18.8	21.2	24.1	23.7
Current ratio	120	126	131	133	123
Quick assets ratio	75	80	82	86	82
Fixed long-term conformity ratio	84	80	79	79	86

4.2 *Mitsubishi Electric*

The business segments of Mitsubishi Electric are as follows:

(1) Energy and electric systems
(2) Industrial automation systems

(3) Information and communication systems
(4) Electronic devices
(5) Home appliances
(6) Others

Mitsubishi has been adopting strategies to develop its early selection and concentration on businesses. Within its energy and electrical systems segment, its elevator and transportation system businesses are competitive. Both have decided to build factories in India. Its transformer business is also competitive. Mitsubishi has also been moving forward in its overseas development. Its industrial automation systems are competitive in the FA business in emerging market economies, because of the remarkable rise in personnel expenses there. The company also has some opportunities to get into automotive-related business. Its information and communication systems segment is competitive in business related to satellites, while its electronic devices segment includes a power module business that is the most competitive in the world. Its home appliances segment does not include any TV panel factories. Mitsubishi has withdrawn from the washing machine business and concentrated its resources on the air conditioning business.

The performance of Mitsubishi's business segments is shown in Table 11. Not only for 2007, before the Lehman shock, but also for 2014, the degree

Table 11. Performances of Mitsubishi business segments

| | Distribution ratio (%) | | | | ROS | g(s) |
| | Sales | | OP | | (%) | (%) |
Fiscal year	2007	2014	2007	2014	2014	2014
Energy and electric systems	23.1	24.6	23.5	21.0	5.9	4.4
Industrial automation systems	22.3	25.7	44.4	42.2	11.4	16.7
Information and communication systems	14.1	11.2	0.8	5.5	3.4	2.1
Electronic devices	4.2	4.8	2.9	8.7	12.7	22.5
Home appliances	21.9	18.9	22.6	15.7	5.7	1.8
Others	14.5	14.8	5.8	6.9	3.2	9.5

Note: OP: Operating profit g(s): sales growth.

Table 12.　Main financial performances of Mitsubishi (%)

Fiscal year	2010	2011	2012	2013	2014
Return on equity	12.4	10.3	5.7	10.9	13.9
Return on sales	6.4	6.2	4.3	5.8	7.3
Capital to assets ratio	31.5	33.4	38.1	42.2	45.4
Current ratio	141	153	154	153	163
Quick assets ratio	87	94	92	94	100
Fixed long-term conformity ratio	68	61	63	62	58

of contribution of the industrial automation systems segment is the highest. Mitsubishi's operating profit trends have been particularly remarkable. The ROS and sales growth of its electronic devices segment are the highest. Although the degree of contribution of Mitsubishi's home appliances segment has declined in comparison with the situation in 2007, it continues to be steady.

The main financial performance of Mitsubishi is shown in Table 12. Its ROE increased to approximately 14%, while its ROS exceeded 7%. Mitsubishi is aiming to achieve an ROS of 8% in the fiscal year 2020. Its capital-to-assets ratios have consistently been the highest among the six companies described in this paper. As for the fiscal year 2014, its capital-to-assets ratio was higher than 45%. This made it clear that not only its short-term solvency, but also its long-term fund conformity situation improved.

5. Summary

This paper has done the following:

(1) Reviewed the strengths of existing businesses hand innovating to create synergy with new businesses.
(2) Recognized the period of predominant competition before main products are commoditized.
(3) Explored the opportunities for social infrastructure businesses to strengthen "B to B" efforts.

Most corporate groups need to have main businesses that act as multiple pillars. Even if their market sizes are initially not big enough, corporate groups should pour large amounts of money from cash cows into selected new businesses, until they grow and shine. Business portfolio theory is important. Needless to say, corporate groups should avoid overconcentrating investments in businesses without growth possibilities. It is also important for them to adopt real options. Not only managing solidly, but innovating at the same time is the real challenge.

References

Chesbrough, H. W. (2003). *Open Innovation: The New Imperative for Creating and Profiting from Technology.*

Hiraoka, S. (2006). Valuation of Business Based on EVA-Type Metrics in Japanese Companies, in *Value-Based Management of the Rising Sun*, (eds.) Monden. Y., Miyamoto. K., Hamada. K., Lee. G., and Asada. T. Singapore: World Scientific, pp. 75–87.

Hiraoka, S. (2007). Changes in the Concept of Capital and Their Effects on Economic Profit in Japan, in *Japanese Management Accounting Today*, (eds.) Monden, Y., Kosuga, M., Nagasaka, Y., Hiraoka, S. and Hoshi, N., Singapore, World Scientific, pp. 23–34.

Hiraoka, S. (2010). Business Valuation of a Company Group in Japan: A Case Study of Segment Reporting by Panasonic Electric Works, in *Business Group Management in Japan*, (eds.) Hamada, K. Singapore: World Scientific, pp. 105–118.

Hiraoka, S. (2010). *The Study of Financial Metrics for Corporate and Business Valuation.* Tokyo, So-sei- sya (in Japanese).

Hitachi (2015). *Annual Report.* Tokyo, Hitachi, Ltd.

Front Loading: Key Concept of Strategy for Business Innovation in Japanese Automobile Industry

Noriyuki Imai

Part-time Professor, Graduate School of Business,
Meijo University, Japan

1. Introduction

The expression "lost 20 years" is associated with the Japanese economy. A bubble economy was developed in Japan in the late 1980s and collapsed in the early 1990s. Since then, the Japanese economy has plunged into a long-term deflationary recession. The expression "lost 20 years" refers to the long-term recession during this period.

To break away from this long-term recession, the Japanese government promotes growth strategies as key policies along with monetary and fiscal policies, encouraging Japanese companies to revive and revitalize industries. One of the means to achieve this is for Japanese companies to strengthen innovation strategies.

Innovation is an economic concept advocated by Schumpeter (1912), who refers to economic development as the variations in the economic life cycle that the economy generates from within. Furthermore, economic development is realized only when innovations emerge intermittently. Schumpeter (1912) also states that innovation is accomplished under the following five scenarios: (1) a product, that is still unknown among consumers or has innovative quality, is created, (2) a new production method is introduced, (3) new sales channels

Japanese Management and International Studies Vol. 13:
Management of Innovation Strategy in Japanese Companies
World Scientific Publishing Company, September 2016

and markets are developed, (4) new supply sources for raw materials or semi-finished goods are acquired, and (5) a monopoly position is formed or eliminated (realization of a new organization). In addition, Schumpeter (1912) states that companies and production plants that achieve innovation do so in conjunction with conventional methods, rather than by replacing them.

Based on the aforementioned innovation concept of Schumpeter (1912), this paper aims to focus on and explore the essential elements of the modern innovation strategy of the automobile industry in Japan.

This paper concludes with the following observations: For more than half a century, the automobile industry in Japan has strategically pursued innovation to strengthen and maintain competitiveness mainly from three perspectives, including (1) strengthening cost competitiveness, (2) improving productivity, and (3) achieving economies of scale. One of the major common trends among these innovations is front loading. Its leading cause is the change in innovation strategies in the Japanese automobile industry. By shifting innovation itself from the externally observable stages of mass production and mass marketing to the externally unobservable stage of product development, imitability has been reduced while profitability has been enhanced through innovations in the upstream stage of the product life cycle. In this paper, I will attempt to conceptualize this as "Invisible Competitive Strategy."

The contents of this paper are based on the author's practical experience and knowledge in the automobile industry. This paper discusses the innovations and strategies commonly observed in the automobile industry in Japan; this paper is not intended to include cases of individual companies.

2. Innovation Perspectives in the Automobile Industry in Japan

With 12 core automakers, the automobile industry in Japan is one of the key industries supporting the national economy. The industry has strategically facilitated innovations to strengthen and maintain their competitiveness. Their innovation perspectives stem from the following inherent attributes of the automobile business.

(1) As a product, automobiles are unusually expensive compared with a wide variety of mass-produced consumer products generally available in the

market. Therefore, the price competitiveness of an automobile as a product would improve considerably, if the cost of the product could be reduced and the sales price could be lowered. Consequently, the possibilities for greater customer acceptance, higher market share, and improved profitability will increase.

(2) Automobiles are a typical mass production kind of product. Therefore, improved productivity in the production process leads to improved profitability.

(3) The automobile industry is a typical process industry requiring a large amount of research and development (R&D) expenses and capital investments. For example, in order to develop a new model, a standard model change generally requires about 40–50 billion yen of investment. It is also believed that constructing a new automobile assembly factory usually requires 50–100 billion yen of investment. Therefore, economies of scale play a role in the automobile industry.

Given the above attributes of the automobile industry, the automobile industry in Japan has strategically facilitated innovations for more than half a century to strengthen and maintain its competitiveness primarily from the following three perspectives.

(1) Strengthening cost competitiveness (mainly reducing material costs).
(2) Improving productivity (mainly improving labor and capital productivities).
(3) Achieving economies of scale (reducing the ratio of fixed costs to sales).

3. Traditional Innovation in the Automotive Industry in Japan

Next, traditional innovation in the automobile industry in Japan is described based on the above three perspectives.

First, in terms of the first perspective of strengthening cost competitiveness, innovations from this point of view originated from total quality control (TQC) by Deming (1982). Deming was a leading theorist who widely popularized the quality management movement throughout industries in Japan and rendered a tremendous contribution to enhancing the international competitiveness of Japan's manufacturing industry. To improve the quality of products and services, Deming (1982) presented the principles of TQC management, including (1) institute leadership, (2) breakdown barriers among departments, and (3) constantly improve the system of production and service. These principles were aggressively incorporated by the automobile industry in Japan as well.

For example, Toyota introduced statistical quality control (SQC) in 1949 and then TQC in 1961. It also launched quality control (QC) group activities (kaizen activities in small groups) by having all employees participate in 1962. As a result, Toyota was recognized for its unified, company wide promotion of TQC involving everyone from the top management down to factory workers and won the Deming Prize (Application Prize) in 1965 (Toyota Motor Corporation, 2012).

During the process that led to winning the Deming Prize (Application Prize), Toyota established a functional management system in 1964 in order to enable high-quality, low-cost product manufacturing as well as to facilitate a groundbreaking business management reform. Specifically, it created a business management system that facilitates overall cross-sectional and horizontal cooperation for each of the four functions — namely, quality assurance, cost management, human resource management, and administrative management — in a way to enhance TQC that it has already been practicing (Toyota Motor Corporation, 2012).

This function-based management system at Toyota was revolutionary in the sense that the core production division gained cooperation from other divisions to create a system to facilitate company-wide cost reduction. Subsequently, production divisions in the Japanese automobile industry began actively pursuing cost improvement in the mass production stage.

An example of traditional innovation from the perspective of strengthening cost competitiveness that originated from such a background is cost improvement with indirect materials, consumables, consumable tools, appliances, and fixtures. In other words, it is an activity in which the production division reduces the purchase price of these items in collaboration with the procurement division, substitutes a variety of these items with ones having a cheaper purchase price based on the information provided by the procurement division, or cuts the quantity of these items used in the production process by improving the way they are used.

Next, in terms of the second perspective of improving productivity, a major example of traditional innovation based on this point of view is the Toyota Production System (TPS).

According to Ohno (1978), the originator of TPS, production system enables productivity enhancement by completely eliminating muda. Here, muda in the production process refers to various production elements that only increase the cost, such as too many workers, excessive capacity, and surplus inventory. As for "completely eliminating muda", it means thoroughly identifying and eliminating seven types of muda including (1) muda of overproduction, (2) muda of waiting, (3) muda of conveyance, (4) muda in processing, (5) muda in inventory, (6) muda of motion, and (7) muda of producing defects.

According to Monden (2006), the ultimate purpose of the above TPS created by Ohno (1978) is to thoroughly eliminate excess labor, excess capacity, and excess inventory to improve productivity and increase profits. Monden (2006) states that a chain of muda — the first-order muda (excess production personnel and excess production capacity) → the second-order muda (overproduction) → the third-order muda (excess inventory) → the fourth-order muda (extra warehousing, extra transport personnel, extra transportation facilities, extra inventory management personnel, extra quality control personnel, and extra computer usage) — generally results in extra costs in labor, depreciation, and interest expenses at the point of production. In contrast, the TPS suppresses extra costs from incurring by setting "production at the speed of sales" as its central task. As a mean to do so, the TPS is said to install techniques such as just-in-time (JIT) production, the Kanban method, leveled production, shortening of production lead time, small lot production or one-piece-at-a-time production, shortening of setup change time, multi-skill development, jidoka, and kaizen activities. Based on that, Monden (2006) notes that the TPS is a revolutionary production method that emerged after Taylorism (scientific management method) and the Ford system (mass production assembly line method), since it can improve productivity through unique methods and generate profits even in an era of low growth.

Next, in terms of the third perspective of achieving economies of scale, a major example of traditional innovation based on this point of view is the creation of a mass marketing system in response to motorization.

In general, the creation of a mass marketing system is based on the marketing management theories advocated by Howard (1957), McCarthy (1960), and Kotler (1967). Howard (1957) emphasized the importance of handling marketing comprehensively from the standpoint of management and positioned marketing as a business management area that deals with a wide range of sales and marketing issues. In addition, McCarthy (1960) deemed that formulating an optimal marketing mix of the four P's — product, price, place, and promotion — and aiming to acquire customers while adapting to the company's internal and external environmental changes are the basics of marketing management.

Such marketing management theories created and developed in the United States in the late 1950s–1960s also spread in Japan and were proactively incorporated by the Japanese automobile industry.

In particular, Toyota promoted the creation of a sales network in cooperation with local capitalists not only in Japan but also in major countries worldwide in response to the advancement of motorization. It was Toyota's unique marketing strategy to identify local capitalists who are interested in automobile sales, execute a franchise contract that allows them exclusive rights to sell Toyota vehicles within a certain territory, and build a network of Toyota dealers by having the capitalists to make own investments. The effectiveness of this strategy lies in three attributes: (1) having the capitalists make their own investments increases the motivation to sell Toyota vehicles in their dealership network, (2) Toyota is not required to invest in building the network of dealers, and (3) Toyota can ultimately achieve economies of scale by reducing the ratio of fixed costs to sales.

In other words, Toyota achieved economies of scale by facilitating innovations around the distribution factors, particularly the four aforementioned factors of product, price, place, and promotion when building a mass marketing system in response to motorization.

4. New Innovations in the Automobile Industry in Japan

Now, I will describe the new innovations that emerged from the late 1980s to the 1990s in the automobile industry in Japan based on the three previously described perspectives.

First, in terms of the first perspective of strengthening of cost competitiveness, a major example of new innovations based on this point of view is cost planning by the technology development division during the product development stage.

According to Tanaka (1995), the term "cost planning" was coined to refer to cost management of a new product in the product development stage. In addition, the term is said to originate from the time when it was positioned as one of the three pillars of cost management at Toyota (cost maintenance, cost improvement, and cost planning) in 1963.

Tanaka (1995) defines cost planning as a series of tasks to manage the cost determination process of a new product undertaken by the core technology development division in collaboration with the related divisions such as procurement, parts suppliers, and accounting. It considers under its purview all activities that take place starting from the product planning throughout the product development stage.

In addition, according to the Japan Accounting Association (1996), although cost planning includes a variety of objectives, contents, and application stages, it evolves to a certain ideal state as corporate activity as those objectives, contents, and application stages develop. The ideal state involves comprehensive profit management activities to monitor all activities in the product development stage when planning and developing a new product and try to simultaneously achieve targets for quality, price, reliability, delivery time, etc., that are set to suit the customer needs.

Examples of such cost planning in the automobile industry in Japan include activities at the time of automobile model change (new product planning, development, and design), such as reviewing the quality of the main materials for the vehicle, switching to less expensive materials, developing multiple parts together, reducing the quantity of a main material, and making the parts smaller or lighter at the same time.

Next, in terms of the second perspective of improving productivity, a major example of new innovations based on this point of view is the pursuit of manufacturability by the technology development division during the product development stage.

According to Fujimoto (2004), a man-made product is constituted of a combination of design information and the medium that embodies the design information. In other words, product development proposes to create the design information, and the purpose of procurement is to acquire the raw materials, or the medium, from outside the company. Production involves workers and equipment in the production process to repeatedly transfer the design information to the medium — raw materials and work in progress (WIP) — while sales and marketing send out the design information to customers placed on the medium.

Furthermore, according to the proposition by Fujimoto (1997), labor productivity and equipment productivity reflect the efficiency in transferring the design information from the workers and equipment to the raw materials and WIP. For example, labor productivity during the final automobile assembly process is measured by the number of actual working hours per finished vehicle. Actual working hours are composed of the net operating time for actually transferring the design information and the contingency time of conveyance and the accompanying time when the design information transfer does not take place. Therefore, the shorter the net operating time and the higher the percentage of the net operating time to account for the actual working hours, the higher the labor productivity will be.

The pursuit of manufacturability primarily aims to increase the percentage of net operating time during the mass production stage. It is a productivity enhancing activity in which the core technology development division collaborates with associated divisions, such as production technology, procurement, and parts suppliers, to simultaneously develop the product structure (design information) and production process layout from the early stages of product development.

Examples of pursuit of manufacturability in the Japanese automobile industry include activities such as reducing the wait time by rearranging worker's task elements, shortening the walk time for workers to fetch parts and tools, and cutting unnecessary operations of equipment. These can be performed at the time of model change (development and design of a new product) when task elements for workers in the mass production stage are simplified, and the product structure is designed to increase the flexibility of equipment.

Next, in terms of the third perspective of achieving economies of scale, a major example of new innovations based on this point of view is the promotion of parts commonization in the technology development division during the product development stage.

Commonization of parts in the automobile industry began when European automobile manufacturers commonized platforms (chassis) in the mid-1990s. In particular, Volkswagen AG (VW) facilitated modularization of the automobile after the year 2000 in addition to commonizing platforms as a response to the lean production model of Japanese automakers. It was a strategy to share modules, such as the engine, brake system, and fuel system, among multiple car models to reduce the number of parts and to improve the efficiency of the R&D expenses and capital investment. Furthermore, in recent years, VW has been promoting a system called Modularer Querbaukasten (MQB), which enables the utilization of platforms, modules, and main parts in different models just like using Lego blocks.

In response to such trends among European automakers, initiatives in recent years to commonize parts are increasing among Japanese automakers as well, for example, Nissan's Common Module Family (CMF) and Toyota's Toyota New Global Architecture (TNGA).

This type of parts commonization aims to lower the cost of automobiles through economies of scale by sharing automobile platforms, modules, and main parts among different models to reduce R&D expenses and capital investment and lower the ratio of fixed costs to sales.

5. Front Loading

So far, this paper has provided an overview of both the traditional innovations and new innovations, which have emerged mainly after the late 1980s, by considering the innovation viewpoints in the Japanese automobile industry.

One of the major trends that is common among these innovations is front loading. In other words, whereas traditional innovation (the cost improvement and the TPS in the production division as well as the creation of a mass marketing system, as described above) takes place during the mass production and mass marketing stages in the product life cycle, new innovations (cost planning, the pursuit of manufacturability, and the promotion of parts communization, as described above) are upstream innovations that occur during the product development stage.

This can be regarded as a reflection of the Japanese automobile industry's strategic change at the time to focus more on product innovation in addition to the conventional process innovation. This is symbolized by the introduction of Prius, the world's first mass-produced hybrid car, in 1997.

The automobile industry in Japan strategically initiated the front-loading innovation during the period between the late 1980s and 1990s.

6. The Concept of Invisible Competitive Strategy

So why did they front-load innovation?

There are two environmental changes that describe this: the maturation of the automobile markets in developed countries and the homogenized strategies in the Japanese automobile industry.

The period between the late 1980s and 1990s coincides with the maturation period in which the post-war high economic growth ended and motorization settled down in the automobile markets in many developed countries. It was also the period that saw considerable increase in the variety of automobiles and their product life cycles became considerably shorter. As a result, the Japanese automobile industry was forced to shift from sales-oriented management to profit-oriented management coupled with product development.

In addition, strategies in the Japanese automobile industry became increasingly comparable with those of the automobile markets in developed countries that were undergoing the above-described maturation. In other words, as Imai (2006) showed, while there are three major processes — namely, (1) supply chain process, (2) sales process, and (3) product development process — in automobile industry, as far as (1) and (2) go, the creation of mass production and mass marketing systems to deal with motorization in the developed countries has been almost completed and the difference in strategies among automobile manufacturers in Japan has become insignificant.

Under these circumstances, the Japanese automobile industry wound up changing its innovation strategy in a way to shift innovation itself from the externally observable mass production and mass marketing stages to the externally unobservable product development stage. That enabled it to reduce imitability and increase the profit improvement effect through innovations in an upstream stage in the product life cycle.

In this paper, I will try to conceptualize this as Invisible Competitive Strategy. This concept has two main premises: (1) reduced imitability of

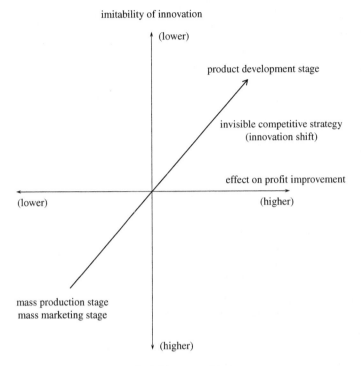

Fig. 1.   Invisible competitive strategy

innovation and (2) enhanced effect on profit improvement. The requirements for each of these two premises are as described below. In other words, an innovation strategy that meets these two requirements will be Invisible Competitive Strategy (Fig. 1).

(1) The visibility of innovation from outside the company decreases (invisibility increases) when innovation is shifted from the mass production and mass marketing stages to the product development stage. There are two reasons for this: it is generally difficult for outsiders to physically enter the company's technology development division, and it is extremely difficult for outsiders to understand internal information related to the planning, development, and design of new products. Consequently, innovation that emerges during the product development stage becomes a core competency with a low imitability, resulting in strategy differentiation (Hamel and Prahalad, 1994).

(2) The areas to be considered for profit improvement expand from the conventional supply chain and marketing processes to the product development process when innovation is shifted from the mass production and mass marketing stages to the product development stage. In addition, the cost planning performed during the product development stage — where more than 80% of the product cost at the mass production stage is determined — by going back to the source of a cost and thoroughly analyzing its mechanism enables drastic cost reduction (Kato, 1993). As a result, the effect on profit improvement increases through innovation in the upstream stage of the product life cycle.

7. Conclusion

In this paper, I explored both traditional innovation and new innovation from recent years in the Japanese automobile industry, explored the essential elements in innovation strategies in this industry, and identified a major trend of front loading. Based on that, I examined the management thinking behind front loading and derived a new concept called Invisible Competitive Strategy.

Based on the above discussion, we can say that front loading is a key concept for innovation strategies in the automobile industry in Japan.

In terms of the concept of Invisible Competitive Strategy that this paper has derived, it is necessary to further refine the requirements and examine cases in a wide range of industries, business types, and companies, in order to generalize the concept.

As global competition in the 21st century intensifies even more by transcending the boundaries of regions and industries, corporate managements will be required to further differentiate their strategies and improve profitability. In such circumstances, front loading as an innovation strategy and the concept of Invisible Competitive Strategy presented in this paper should become even more important in the future.

References

Deming, W. E. (1982). *Out of the Crisis*. Cambridge, MA: Massachusetts Institute of Technology Press.

Fujimoto, T. (1997). *Evolution of Production Systems: Organizational Capabilities and Emergent Process as Seen in Toyota Motor Corporation.* Tokyo: Yuhikaku Publishing Co (in Japanese).

Fujimoto, T. (2004). *Manufacturing Philosophy in Japan.* Tokyo: Nikkei, Inc (in Japanese).

Hamel, G. and C. K. Prahalad (1994). *Competing for the Future.* Boston, MA: Harvard Business School Press.

Howard, J. A. (1957). *Marketing Management: Analysis and Decision.* Homewood, IL: Richard D. Irwin.

Imai, N. (2006). An examination on the relationship between management quality and accounting function: Given the background of establishing toyota's production system. *The Meijo Review* 7(2): 83–100 (in Japanese).

Japan Accounting Association. (1996). *Challenges with Cost Planning Research.* Tokyo: Moriyama Shoten (in Japanese).

Kato, Y. (1993). *Cost Planning: Strategic Cost Management.* Tokyo: Nikkei, Inc (in Japanese).

Kotler, P. (1967). *Marketing Management: Analysis, Planning, Implementation, and Control.* Upper Saddle River, NJ: Prentice-Hall.

McCarthy, E. J. (1960). *Basic Marketing: A Managerial Approach.* Homewood, IL: Richard D. Irwin.

Monden, Y. (2006). *Toyota Production System: Its Theory and System.* Tokyo: Diamond, Inc (in Japanese).

Ohno, T. (1978). *Toyota Production System: Aiming to De-scale the management.* Tokyo: Diamond, Inc (in Japanese).

Schumpeter, J. A. (1912). *Theorie der wirtschaftlichen Entwicklung.* Berlin: Duncker & Humblot GmbH.

Tanaka, M. (1995). *Target Cost Management and Profit Engineering.* Tokyo: Chuokeizai-Sha, Inc (in Japanese).

Toyota Motor Corporation. Official corporate site. (2012). *75 Years of Toyota Motor Corporation's History* (in Japanese). Retrieved from http://www.toyota.co.jp/jpn/company/history/75years/. (accessed 03-01-2015).

Changes in Product Development Approaches and Target Costing

Naoya Yamaguchi

Associate Professor, Graduate School of Professional Accountancy,
Aoyama Gakuin University, Japan

1. Introduction

Target Costing is a cost management technique in the product development and design phase. As Target Costing practices in Japan developed, its importance increased and its purpose was extended.

In the beginning, the main purpose of Target Costing was to reduce costs during the new product development stage. However, through a survey, the Japan Accounting Association (1996) determined that the importance of not only cost reduction, but also of other purposes, such as product development suitable for customer needs, quality improvements, and timely introduction of new products, increased as time passed.

Given such a change in purpose and the development of Target Costing activities, the Japan Accounting Association (1996) presumed the ideal state of Target Costing as the cost management, which was performed as part of the synthetic profit control activities that aim to set targets, such as quality, price, reliability, delivery time, and so on. Ideally, Target Costing was also involved in simultaneously achieving these targets for all of an organization's activities, from the upper stream to the lower stream. Furthermore, the Japan Accounting Association pointed out that near optimal situations were observed in many successful cases.

Japanese Management and International Studies Vol. 13:
Management of Innovation Strategy in Japanese Companies
World Scientific Publishing Company, September 2016

Thus, because Target Costing is regarded as the management technique for the simultaneous achievement of various targets in the product development stage and its function is extendable, its approach depends significantly on a product development approach. Regarding this point, the movements toward changes in the product development approach are observed in automakers that have, to date, made advanced efforts in Target Costing. In recent years, Volkswagen, Nissan Motor, Mazda Motor, and Toyota Motor have successfully reformed their product development approaches to strengthen their ability to stop complicated product development, diversify the product portfolio, shorten development lead time, improve product attractiveness, and reduce development and manufacturing costs.

This paper clarifies the changes in the product development approaches of automakers and suggests a fundamental framework for determining how the Target Costing approach is modified as a result of such changes.

2. Outline of New Product Development Approaches in Automakers

Fujimoto (1997) indicated that the problem of *superfluous design* was observed at Japanese automakers around 1990, and that *design simplification* (*lean products design*) is performed as an adjustment. *Superfluous design* represents a series of problematic groups, such as a superfluous variety of products, superfluous frequency of model changes, too few common parts among models, superfluous equipment, superfluous quality, and superfluous specifications. Moreover, Fujimoto (1997) presented parts communalization, reduction in variations, and cost reductions through value engineering (VE) as *design simplification* efforts.

In contrast, Table 1 provides outlines of the new product development approaches being adopted by Volkswagen, Nissan Motor, Mazda, and Toyota Motor. Mokudai and Iwaki (2013) called these approaches the *new module/ platform strategy*. They further categorized the *new module/platform strategy* into the *new module strategy* and the *new platform strategy* according to the size of the communalization unit. The former is the approach adopted by Volkswagen and Nissan, and the latter is the approach adopted by Mazda and Toyota.

Table 1.   New product development approaches in some global automakers

Volkswagen MQB (modular transverse matrix)	— The engineering dimension is unified. (unifying the distance from an accelerator pedal to a front axle) — All engines share a mounting position. — A modular structure is adopted in new gasoline engines. — The number of parts is reduced by simplifying the variations. — Thorough modularization is attained. (modularization of all parts from the chassis system components, power trains, harnesses, and electrical components, down to the self-manufactured components) — Parts communalization is performed in the cross-brand.
Nissan motor CMF (common module family)	— The structure of the body is divided into the 4 + 1 *big module*, which are the modules of the engine compartment (two types), cockpit (three types), front under-body (three types), central and rear under-body (three types), and E/E (electric/electronics) architecture. Cars are produced using these modular combinations beyond vehicle types and ranks. — Although moderate variations are made to the parts that constitute each module according to differences in vehicle type, cars are generally produced from the same parts. — The interfaces among the modules are not disclosed to the public.
Mazda motor common architecture vision	— The *Package Planning*, *Common Architecture Vision*, and *Flexible Manufacturing Vision* approaches are expected to realize *manufacturing innovation* by achieving both diversity, which increases the competitive power of products, and communality, which improves mass-production efficiency at higher dimensions. — The *Package Planning* (collectively developing new vehicle types on the basis of common development concepts that exceed the classification of sizes and ranks (segments)) defines the *fixed domains* (the forms and structures common to vehicle types and models) and the *variable domains* (what should be changed or modified according to types and models). — The *fixed domains* are developed from the *Common Architecture Vision*, which aims to efficiently develop individual vehicle types by sharing common design concepts that exceed those for every main domain constituting vehicles, and by transcribing these concepts into individual vehicle types. — The *Common Architecture Vision* is a view that has the same design concepts for smaller and larger cars, and the only difference among the types and ranks is the scale of the components. If the scale of a component is different, the component mounting structure and mounting method are the same (design of *similar figures*). — The *Flexible Manufacturing Vision* is expected to realize product variations through technical innovation of the design structure and the productive process for the *variable domains*.

(*Continued*)

Table 1. (*continued*)

Toyota motor	1. Improvement in Product Attraction
TNGA (toyota new global architecture)	2. *Production of Much Better Cars* through *Grouping Development* and improvement in development efficiency — Toyota first decides on its medium- to long-term product lineup and defines the units carried in them, the arrangements, driving position, and so on, as its *architecture* (the design concepts of the production of vehicles). — Toyota promotes the *Production of Much Better Cars* and improves development efficiency by increasing the sharing of parts and units through *Grouping Development*, which performs the simultaneous development of several vehicle types on the basis of the defined *architecture*. — Although this goal will change with parts and units, TNGA aims for 20–30% improvement in development efficiency. Toyota will further supply the resources obtained by the TNGA to the *Production of Much Better Cars*. 3. Manufacturing Reform 4. Approach to Global Standardization — Although formerly parts developments were based only on the Toyota's exclusive standard, it corresponds from now on to global standards, enabling the standard parts to be adopted which many automakers have adopted globally. 5. Procurement Strategy connected with TNGA — The procurement section corresponds to sharing parts and units through *Grouping Development* and carries out the *combined orders* that exceed vehicles' types, areas, and time.

Source: This table is produced by the author using each company's homepage, annual report, Motor fan illustrated No. 68 (2012), Shiomi (2012), and Mokudai and Iwaki (2013).

Mokudai and Iwaki (2013) pointed out the *repetitious utilization of design information* and *parts communalization* as features common to both strategies. They also noted the following additional common features:

— Sharing a modular matrix or platform (PF) that exceeds a segment;
— Collectively planning and developing several vehicle types;
— Cost reductions from sharing parts and/or units or from the capital investment savings; and

— Sharing approaches that differ among Volkswagen, Nissan, Toyota, and Mazda.

In contrast, Mokudai and Iwaki (2013) indicated that the difference between both strategies is that the *new module strategy* aims at communalizing the design itself and the *new platform strategy* aims at communalizing the design concept. According to Mokudai and Iwaki (2013), the features of each strategy are as follows.

1. *New module strategy* (Volkswagen, Nissan)
   — The product development approach aims to subdivide the conventional platform into smaller parts and to create various vehicle types through these combinations.
   — In the precedence development stage, automakers subdivide the entire vehicles system into subsystems, such as engine, chassis, and body, and define in advance the interface states among those subsystems.
   — They also develop in advance variations in the subsystems and consider them design elements (building blocks) that can be used to design various vehicles.
   — The strategy aims to produce various vehicle types through fewer development processes by pulling out and combining these design elements in the phase in which individual vehicle types are developed.
2. *New platform strategy* (Mazda, Toyota)
   — Although the product development approach preserves the view of a conventional platform, it formulates the object, system, and so on of communalization in a manner that differs from the conventional platform approach.
   — The groups of vehicle types that have a common platform share parts and units.
   — Several vehicle types use information on the common platform design.

3. Feature of New Product Development Approaches Seen from Product Architecture

Ulrich (1995) defined *product architecture* as a scheme by which the function of a product is allocated to physical components. He also defined *product architecture* as the following three features: *arrangement of functional elements, mapping from functional elements to physical components,* and *specification of the interfaces among interacting physical components.*

Furthermore, Ulrich (1995) categorized product architecture into *modular architecture* and *integral architecture* according to differences in the aforementioned features.

1. *Modular architecture*
   Modular Architecture includes a one-to-one mapping from functional elements in the functional structure to physical components of the product and specifies de-coupled interfaces between components.
2. *Integral architecture*
   Integral Architecture includes a complex (not one-to-one) mapping from functional elements to physical components and/or coupled interfaces between components.

Fujimoto (2001a) classified modular architecture into *open architecture* and *closed architecture* according to cooperative relationships among several companies.

A. *Open architecture*
   The interfaces among the modules are standardized on an industry level across companies.
B. *Closed architecture*
   The interface design rule among modules is fundamentally closed in one company.

Furthermore, Fujimoto (2001a) noted that because a product's functions, structure, and process structure are generally expressed in a hierarchical form, the product architecture is originally specified between a product functional hierarchy and a product structure hierarchy (further between process hierarchy). He indicated that, according to the features, whether the product type is modular or integral depends on the hierarchical levels of the parts. Moreover, modular products are viewed as those in which a modular nature appears at a higher level (level of a certain integration degree) in the product function and product structure hierarchy.

Baldwin and Clark (2000) defined a *module* as *a unit whose structural elements are powerfully connected among themselves and relatively weakly connected to elements in other units.* Furthermore, they defined *modularity* as *a particular design structure in which parameters and tasks are interdependent within units (modules) and independent across them.*

Baldwin and Clark (2000) classified *modularity* into *the one in design, the one in production,* and *the one in use.* In contrast, Takeishi *et al.* (2001) and Fujimoto (2002) classified *modularity* into *the one in product architecture* (modularity in product development), *the one in production,* and *the one in systems among companies* (aggregation of supply parts).

Based on these arguments, the features of the new product development approaches as viewed from a product's architecture can be defined as the extension of a *closed modular architecture* domain through *modularity in design (modularity in product architecture).*

4. Components of New Product Development Approaches

The three components of the new product development approaches are as follows: *preceding development of common elements across vehicle types, deployment of the outcome of the development of common elements to individual product development,* and an *increase in module/parts communalization that accompanies an increase in common elements.*

In the *preceding development of common elements across vehicle types,* automakers define a design concept (architecture) as common elements across vehicle types, decide on the domain to modularize, and develop the interfaces among the modules.

In the *deployment of the outcome of the development of common elements to individual product development,* common design concepts, common modules, and interfaces among the modules are utilized in the individual product development. The deployment aims to obtain the following outcomes: improvement in design quality, reduction in development costs, and shortening of the development lead time. However, the level at which these outcomes are realized depends on the range of the target vehicle types in the preceding development (segment), the range of the common elements, and the interface between the preceding development and individual product development (the ease of utilization of the outcome of the preceding development).

The *increase in the module/parts communalization that accompanies an increase in the common elements* indicates not the mere communalization of generic parts but the communalization of modules/parts accompanying the increase in the common elements by the preceding development.

5. Effects Expected by New Product Development Approaches

If the new product development approaches function effectively, they would contribute to *improvements in quality, cost, and lead time in the development phase*, a *reduction in manufacturing costs in the production phase*, and *improvements in quality and a reduction in quality cost in the use phase*. These effects are presented in Table 2.

Table 2. Effects expected by new product development approach

	Quality	Cost	Lead time (delivery)
Development	Improvement in design quality based on peculiar design reduction	Reduction in development cost based on a reduction in development labor hours (Preceding development and individual development)	Shortening of development lead time based on a reduction in development labor hours
Production		Reduction in manufacturing costs based on modules/parts communalization	
Use	Improvement in product quality based on peculiar design reduction	Quality cost reduction based on peculiar design reduction (Reduction in the cost of internal and external failures)	

Regarding the effects of the new product development approaches, Uyama (2014) discussed the general effects, and Shiomi (2012) and Mokudai and Iwaki (2013) discussed the reduction in development costs based on reductions in development labor hours.

Uyama (2014) analyzed the contemporary roles of parts communalization in Toyota. He indicated that although the company has adopted the individual design approach by vehicle type and area to accelerate bringing new vehicles into growing global markets, since approximately 2002, the overseas markets have expanded rapidly. The individual design approach is suitable for rapidly growing markets, but has caused some problems, including an unnecessary increase in design costs, a shortage of resources for quality control, and complications in parts management. Uyama (2014) discussed the Toyota New Global Architecture (TNGA), a new product development approach that enables Toyota to realize advanced parts communalization (substantial reduction in the type of parts) by changing its product development approach from individual development to packaged development. TNGA is expected to have the following effects: a reduction in design costs, a reduction in quality control resources, and a reduction in the burden related to parts management.

Shiomi (2012) analyzed the feature of the Common Architecture Vision concept, which is Mazda's new product development approach. He indicated that the approach's *transfer nature of the parts structure* reduces prototyping costs by reducing the prototyping processes from the securitization of the transfer nature of the parts functions in the development phase of new parts. The *transfer nature of the parts structure* indicates a reduction and expansion of not only the functional effect of some or all of the entire parts and assembly structure used for a certain product but also of the function of the state of gasoline sprayed in an engine piston cylinder.

Mokudai and Iwaki (2013) analyzed the relationships between the number of development vehicle types and the development labor hours for the three approaches — individual development, platform strategy, and new module strategy — by assuming the preceding development labor hours as the fixed cost and the individual development labor hours as the variable costs. They concluded that because the new module strategy has the largest amount of preceding development processes and the smallest number of individual vehicle type development processes among the three approaches, an increase in the number of development vehicle types makes the new module strategy most advantageous with respect to accumulative development labor hours (preceding labor hours and individual labor hours) and average development labor hours (accumulative labor hours divided by the number of development types).

In contrast, Fujimoto (2001b) indicated that communalizing parts designs between models and generations might not necessarily reduce development labor hours. He indicated that because the existence of common parts for newly designed parts indicates an optimal design of conditions with severe constraints, the design labor hours of newly designed parts and the labor hours of design adjustments among the parts increase. This increase might counteract the labor hours saved through parts communalization. Alternatively, Fujimoto (2001b) indicated that, clearly, communalized parts save on design labor hours and that parts communalization leads to a substantial reduction in experimental labor hours. He concluded that, considered comprehensively, a more substantial reduction in total labor hours is achieved through parts communalization when the parts being communalized (a) have a modular design with minimal interdependence with other parts or (b) are important functional components with a large reduction effect on design and experiment labor hours.

6. Reduction in Manufacturing Costs through Modules/Parts Communalization

To understand how the Target Costing approach may change as product development approaches change, how manufacturing costs — on which the Target Costing primarily focuses — are reduced needs to be shown. In other words, the source of the reduction in manufacturing costs through Target Costing must be shown. To reduce manufacturing costs through modules/parts communalization as exhibited in Table 2, the following four sources of cost reductions are considered, of which sources 1 and 2 are the most important:

1. Reduction in parts costs by applying VE to common modules/parts;
2. Reduction in parts costs through economies of scale in the production and procurement of common modules/parts;

3. Reduction in transaction costs through a reduction in the types and kinds of modules/parts (procurement, distribution, storage, and risk management); and,
4. Reduction in equipment costs through production facility communalization.

The *reduction in parts costs by applying VE to common modules/parts* indicates that cost reductions are obtained through VE, which is particularly important in Target Costing under conventional product development approaches (individual design oriented), for common modules/parts. Cost reductions are also achieved by removing excessive and uneconomical specifications in common modules/parts. Under the new product development approaches, although the cost reduction created by VE in an individual product development stage declines as common modules/parts are extended, the importance of VE in the development/design phase of common modules/parts increases significantly.

According to Cooper and Slagmulder (1999), *excessive specification* means the specification that users do not accept or recognize the value. *Uneconomical specification* means the state in which the cost increase that a maker pays exceeds the value that the users accept.

Table 3 provides viewpoints of excessive specification and uneconomical specification. Whether a certain product has excessive and/or uneconomical specification is eventually judged on the basis of customers' required specifications. Because customers' required specifications are not obvious in the development phase of new products, discovering and removing potential excessive and/or uneconomical specifications through a comparison with other companies' products and a close investigation of the specifications of products and modules is important.

The advanced parts communalization of conventional product development approaches center on generic parts. In contrast, new product development approaches seek to communalize not only generic parts, but also — more or less — modules and parts inside module units through modularity in design. However, parts and module communalization might create risks of excessive and/or uneconomical specifications at the product level (when some modules/parts are communalized across product classes, low-end products may have excessive and/or uneconomical specifications). These risks may also occur in the modules/submodules level (submodules/parts with a specification

Table 3.   Viewpoint of excessive specification and uneconomical specification

External viewpoint	Customer	Definition of excessive specification and uneconomical specification (Cooper and Slagmulder, 1999) Excessive specification: — Specification for which users do not accept its value — Specification for which users do not recognize its value Uneconomical specification (a premise about the reservation of an indispensable specification): — Cost increase that a maker pays exceeds the value that users accept
	Competitor	More excessive than the specification of other companies' products
Internal viewpoint	Product	Required performance changes with product classes: — If the modules/parts carried in high-end products are carried in low-end products, low-end products represent excessive and/or uneconomical specification
	Modules/ Submodules	Submodules/parts with a specification that exceed submodules/parts with a bottleneck specification (specification with the lowest quality and performance that determines the quality and performance of a module/submodule) has an excessive and/or uneconomical specification

exceeding that of submodules/parts with a bottleneck specification, which have an excessive and/or uneconomical specification).

The *reduction in parts costs through economies of scale in the production and procurement of common modules/parts* indicates that economics of scale are realized and that the product cost per unit is reduced by using the same modules/parts for many more products. Economies of scale represent a most important cost reduction resource in new product development approaches. Table 4 shows the approaches and risks to realizing economies of scale in the production and procurement of common modules/parts.

Segment expansion, practical use of the market, and a reduction in the number of suppliers are listed as approaches to realizing economies of scale. However, certain specific risks exist for every approach, including the risk of excessive or inadequate specifications for segment expansion, the risk of declines in competitive advantages and supply chain breakdowns regarding

Table 4. Approaches and risks to realizing economies of scale in production and procurement of common modules/parts

Expansion of segments	Increase in the number of vehicle types that communalize modules/parts — If vehicle types of different classes are communalized, some types might have excessive or inadequate specifications
Practical use of the market	1. In-Out type (in-house initiative) — The company also sells to other companies modules/parts that it develops and produces — The company's competitive advantage might decline 2. Out-In type (dependence on other companies) — The company purchases modules/parts that other companies develop and produce — The company's competitive advantage might decline — When production problems occur from internal and/or external factors, the possibility exists that the required modules/parts and/or the required quantity cannot be supplied
Reduction in the number of suppliers	The company reduces the number of suppliers and increases the order quantity per supplier — Competitive pressures among suppliers and their cost reduction efforts might decline — When a quality problem occurs, the influence might be far-reaching — When production problems occur from internal and/or external factors, the possibility exists that the required modules/parts and/or the required quantity cannot be supplied

the practical use of the market, the risk of declines in suppliers' efforts and the quality of modules/parts, and breakdowns in the supply chain regarding the reduction in the number of suppliers. Therefore, sufficiently taking into account these risks makes it necessary to select the best approaches for every module/parts unit.

This discussion shows that, to realize the cost reduction effects on the basis of the previously mentioned sources 1 and 2, determining the segment (the range of vehicle types that communalizes some modules/parts), the modules/parts communalized, and the scope of VE for common modules/parts are necessary. Weighing cost reductions resulting from economies of scale against cost increases that accompany excessive and/or uneconomical specifications, and the risks associated with pursuing economies of scale, must also be considered.

7. Conclusion: Target Costing under New Product Development Approaches

Using these arguments, the following three features can be listed as part of the Target Costing approaches called for under new product development approaches:

1. Importance of Target Costing in the preceding development phase of common elements;
2. Importance of the development interface between the common elements and individual product development; and,
3. Importance of cost reductions through economies of scale.

Target Costing in the preceding development phase of common elements is important. This importance increases through the development of common elements performed in advance of the individual product development phase because the cost reduction resulting from Target Costing in this phase is reduced through the expansion of common element (design concepts, modules/parts, and interfaces) under new product development approaches.

However, even if the cost reduction of common modules/parts is realized through Target Costing in the common element development phase, the cost reduction effects of new products cannot be realized if the common modules/parts cannot be utilized in individual products.

The *development interface between common elements and individual product development* is also important. To realize cost reduction effects, making it easier to make practical use of the common elements in advance through an interface between the preceding development and individual product development is important.

The *importance of cost reductions through economies of scale* indicates that the range of economies of scale expands and production costs per unit decline from utilizing more common elements in individual product development. Utilizing the cost reduction effects by extending the common elements is important in Target Costing under new product development approaches. However, such utilization depends on the *range of common elements* and the *degree of practical use of the common elements in individual product development*. The *range of common elements* constrains individual product development and the *degree of practical use of the common elements in the individual product development* depends on their ease of practical use (the interface between common elements and individual product development). Furthermore, as previously noted, pursuing economies of scale for every approach has risks. Therefore, to account for these risks in advance, determining the range of common elements and their degree of practical use in individual product development is necessary.

As a matter of course, new product development approaches aim at not only cost reductions but also the simultaneous achievement of various targets. Such targets include strengthening the ability to adapt to the complications in product development and diversifying the product portfolio, shortening the development lead time, improving product attraction, and reducing development and manufacturing costs. Therefore, establishing a Target Costing process with the previously noted features and reconciling with these other targets is necessary.

This paper merely suggests a fundamental framework for how Target Costing approaches change with respect to the change in product development approaches. Analyzing the type of changes that have actually occurred in these companies through interviews is necessary.

References

Baldwin, C. Y. and K. B. Clark (2000). *Design Rules: Volume 1. The Power of Modularity*. Cambridge, MA: Massachusetts Institute of Technology.

Cooper, R. and R. Slagmulder (1999). *Supply Chain Development for the Lean Enterprises — Interorganizational Cost Management*. Productivity Press, NY.

Fujimoto, T. (1997). *An Evolutionary Theory of Production Systems*. Yuhikaku Publishing, Tokyo (in Japanese).

Fujimoto, T. (2001a). Chapter 1: Architecture-Based Industrial Theory, in Fujimoto, T., Takeishi, A. and Y. Aoshima (eds.), *Business Architecture: Strategic Design of Product, Organization, and Process*. Yuhikaku Publishing (in Japanese).

Fujimoto, T. (2001b). *Introduction to Production Management Vol. II: Management of Production Resource and Technology*. Nikkei Publishing, Tokyo (in Japanese).

Fujimoto, T. (2002). Chapter 6: Japanese Supplier System and Modularity — A Case of Automobile Industry, in Aoki, M. and H. Ando (eds.), *Modularity: Essence of New Industrial Architecture*. Toyo Keizai, Tokyo (in Japanese).

Japan Accounting Association (1996). *Research Issues of Target Costing*. Moriyama Shoten, Tokyo (in Japanese).

Mokudai, T. and F. Iwaki (2013). Challenging new vehicle development approaches: VW MQB, Nissan CMF, Mazda CA, and Toyota TNGA. *Akámon Management Review (Global Business Research Center)* 12(9): 613–652 (in Japanese).

Motor Fan illustrated No. 68 (2012). San-eishobo Publishing, Tokyo (in Japanese).

Shiomi, K. (2012). The report of MAZDA's common architecture vision: The one of the common architecture vision features. *Hiroshima University Management Review* 13: 47–56 (in Japanese).

Takeishi, A., T. Fujimoto and S. H. Ku (2001). Chapter 4: Modularity in Automobile Industry: Compound Hierarchy of Product, Production, and Procurement Systems, in Fujimoto, T., Takeishi, A. and Y. Aoshima (eds.), *Business Architecture: Strategic Design of Product, Organization, and Process*. Yuhikaku Publishing (in Japanese).

Ulrich, K. (1995). The role of product architecture in the manufacturing firm. *Research Policy* 24: 419–440.

Uyama, T. (2014). New development of part communalization in Toyota: The problems accumulated in the huge expansion phase of the oversea markets and the change of product development method. *Kyushu Sangyo University Business Review* 25(2): 47–73 (in Japanese).

Organizational Learning via Strategy Formulation and the Role of MCS in That Process: The Case of Kikkoman Corporation

Junji Fukuda

Professor, Faculty of Business Administration,
Hosei University, Japan

1. Introduction

Who formulates strategy? The answer to this question has considerable bearing upon managerial roles throughout various hierarchies and the role of the Management Control System (MCS) in the process of strategy formulation and implementation.

At the early discussion stage, strategy is typically formulated by top managers. In this situation, the roles of middle and lower managers are restricted to strategy implementation. The function of the MCS is to support strategy implementation by middle and lower managers (Davila, 2005).

Based on observations of the strategy formulation processes of some organizations, Mintzberg (1978) demonstrated that strategy is not necessarily formulated by top managers but initiated by the bottom levels of organizations. In the process of emerging strategy, middle and lower managers play important roles, and the role of the MCS is recognized as not being restricted to strategy implementation. Therefore, the influence of MCS on strategy formulation continues to be discussed (Simons, 1995).

Japanese Management and International Studies Vol. 13:
Management of Innovation Strategy in Japanese Companies
World Scientific Publishing Company, September 2016

Burgelman (1983, 2002) proposed the conceptual model describing the roles of managers at various hierarchies and the function of the MCS in the strategy formulation process. He applied this model to the strategic decision-making process at Intel Co., Ltd.

The purpose of this research is to demonstrate whether the model developed by Burgelman, which is based on observations of some western firms, can be applied to Japanese firms, which have a different cultural background. To accomplish this, I refer to the case of strategic decision-making at Kikkoman Co., Ltd. (hereafter, Kikkoman), a traditional Japanese firm, which decided to make a direct investment in the U.S. I found evidence of differences between the Burgelman model and the case of Kikkoman. The roles of their middle managers differ significantly. In addition, Kikkoman promoted the person in charge of the lower manager role to a middle manager role during the long time span spent in decision-making.

Another purpose of this research is to interpret the strategic decision-making process from the perspective of organizational learning. Kikkoman postponed the final decision for constructing a local factory in the U.S. Instead, the company decided to transfer only a part of the production process to the U.S. This decision gave them enough time to develop production-specific technological knowledge, gain more information on new trends in the local market, and arrive at a final decision.

The structure of this article is as follows. In the next section, I review the past literature concerning the role of the MCS in the strategy formulation process. In Section 3, I illustrate the process of strategic decision-making at Kikkoman, beginning with the initiation of its direct investment in the U.S. market and ending with its final decision. Section 4 discusses the similarities and differences between the Burgelman model and the Kikkoman case. Finally, I conclude by noting the contributions and limitations of this research and provide directions for future research.

2. Role of the MCS in the Strategy Formulation Process

There are various perspectives on the relationship between strategy formulation and implementation. In early discussions, strategy tends to be characterized as "(a) explicit, (b) developed consciously and purposefully, and (c) made in advance of the specific decisions to which it applies" (Mintzberg,

1978, p. 935). The roles of middle and lower managers are constrained to the implementation of the strategy. The task of the MCS is to "measure progress, which is monitored by senior managers who may need to take corrective action" (Simons, 1995, p. 19).

However, Anthony *et al.* (1972) pointed out that in large multi-division firms, strategy at the division level was derived from the activities of each division instead of being formulated by the top manager.

After observing the strategy formulation process in practice, Mintzberg (1978) defined strategy as "a *Pattern in a Stream of Decisions*" (p. 935; italics are original). In this perspective, strategies "have to form as well as be formulated" (Mintzberg *et al.*, 1998, p. 11). This recognition dramatically changed the focus of researchers concerning the roles of various managers and that of the MCS in organizations. Simons (1995) proposed the concept of the interactive control system (ICS) and suggested that the MCS impacts the emergence of a strategy. The ICS communicates the strategic uncertainties[1] perceived by the top managers to their subordinates and fosters organizational learning through continued debates and discussions on the topic. Based on Simons' understanding, Kober *et al.* (2007) reported that strategic change is fostered by debate and discussion between participants who used the ICS. Abernathy and Brownell (1999) conducted a mail survey of large-sized hospitals in Australia and found that the interactive use of budgeting functions as "an integrative liaison device that breaks down the functional and hierarchical barriers that inhibit information flows" (p. 192) and fosters strategic change. A survey study among Spanish hospitals led Naranjo-Gil and Hartmann (2007) to conclude that the ICS mediates the effects of the heterogeneity of the top management team on strategic change.

Burgelman (1983, 1991, 2002) considered the MCS to be an element of the organization. He examined how strategic initiatives emerged at the bottom level of an organization, to be eventually realized as a corporate strategy by way of an internal selection process. Using structural context to realize the current corporate strategy, top managers "influence the type of proposals that will be defined and given impetus" (Burgelman, 1983, p. 64). The ICS, as part of the organization's structural context, impacts its emergent strategy by

---

[1] Simons (1995) defined strategic uncertainties as "uncertainties and contingencies that could threaten or invalidate the current strategy of business" (p. 94).

"stimulat[ing] the discussion and exchange of knowledge around critical assumptions of an organization's current business model" (Davila *et al.*, 2009, p. 288).

As opposed to this, strategic initiatives "that fall outside the scope of the current concept of corporate strategy" (Burgelman, 1983, p. 61) are evaluated and selected "through interactions between various types of 'champions' and top management" (Burgelman, 1991, p. 247), because no one in an organization understands the strategic meaning of those initiatives. Therefore, strategic context needs to be created. The role of top managers in the autonomous strategic process is "to facilitate the activation of strategic context determination processes to find out which of the autonomous initiatives have adaptive value for the organization and deserve to become part of the organization's strategy" (p. 256). Middle managers "must make sense out of these autonomous strategic initiatives and formulate workable, attractive strategies for the corresponding areas of new business development," and "they must engage in political activities to convince top management to rationalize, retroactively, these successful initiatives by amending the concept of strategy to accommodate the strategic initiatives" (Burgelman, 1983, p. 66). However, as Davila (2005) suggested, the role of the MCS during this phase are not yet understood. In the following section, I refer to the example of the Japanese firm Kikkoman to understand the process through which autonomous activity by lower managers produces corporate strategy.

3. The Case of Kikkoman Corporation and its Direct Investment in the U.S.

3.1. *The current situation at Kikkoman*

Kikkoman (previously known as Noda Shoyu Co., Ltd.) was established by merging the businesses of the six Mogi families, the Takanashi family, and the Horikiri family about 100 years ago. While Kikkoman is not an affiliated company under Japan's tax law, it is positioned as one because the founding families bear substantial responsibility for its management. However, the eight founder families have an unwritten law that "one person of each generation will be admitted to work for Kikkoman, but to be a board member is not guaranteed" (Mogi, 2007, p. 50).

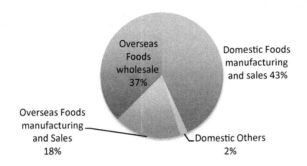

Fig. 1.   Segment sales (FY 2014)
Source: Created by the author using data from the Annual Securities Report of Kikkoman.

The ratios of sales for each segment in fiscal year 2014 are shown in Fig. 1. In 2014, 55% of Kikkoman's sales and about 86% of its operating profit were earned from foreign countries. Although Kikkoman's products constitute traditional Japanese seasonings and food, it is "obviously one of the 'global enterprises'" (Mogi, 2007, p. 2). Next, I describe Kikkoman's initiative to establish local production in the U.S., a major turning point for the company in its quest to become a global corporation.

3.2. Kikkoman's strategy (1955–the early 1960s)

After a rapid increase in shipped amounts of soy sauce, as part of the recovery process of the production capacity lost during World War II, the demand for the product stagnated. Mogi reasoned that while "soy sauce is necessary for life," "the amount of daily consumption at home is constant, and it only increases at the same rate as the population growth rate" (Mogi, 2007, p. 20).

In the early 1930s (the Showa era), Kikkoman adopted two strategies for improving sales: diversification and internationalization.

The diversification strategy was "an attempt to develop and sell other kinds of products if the sales of soy sauce will not increase" (Mogi, 2007, p. 20). In those days, Kikkoman started to manufacture and sell tomato ketchup and tomato juice and entered the wine business. In addition, they started supplying raw materials for manufacturing of medicines.

On the other hand, its internationalization strategy was an attempt to "expand into overseas markets if the demand of soy sauce in Japan would not increase" (Mogi, 2007, p. 21). Kikkoman had already aggressively expanded overseas before World War II.[2] However, internationalization during this time after World War II was accompanied by "a drastic change of marketing strategy" (Mogi, 1983, p. 35). Although customers before World War II were "Japanese living in foreign countries, Japanese emigrants, and military men" (Mogi, 2007, p. 22), customers after the War were "general American consumers" (p. 22). Kikkoman took notice of the U.S. market not only in response to the political unrest in Asian countries but also to meet the potential demand for soy sauce in the U.S. market, according to the perception gained from Americans who visited Japan.

3.3. Establishment of a local sales company

With the interest in soy sauce growing in the U.S., Kikkoman decided to establish a sales company in the country (Kikkoman, 2000). In 1957, Kikkoman International Inc. (KII) was established in San Francisco. Thereafter, branch offices were opened in Los Angeles, New York, and Atlanta. KII exhibited its soy sauce in U.S. supermarkets and developed aggressive marketing activities (Kikkoman, 2000).

3.4. Initiatives undertaken by lower managers for local manufacturing

After completing graduate school at Columbia University, Mr. Yuzaburo Mogi joined Kikkoman in 1961. After attaining two years of experience in accounting, he moved to the Office of the President (Mogi, 2007). As Chief of Planning in the Administration Division, he participated in long-term management planning (Kikkoman, 2000).[3] While preparing the plan, Mr. Yuzaburo Mogi confirmed the necessity of implementing the strategies of diversification and internationalization, and at the same time, he was keenly aware of "a deficit in the overseas sector being a problem" (Mogi, 2007, p. 35).

---

[2] Before World War II, Kikkoman exported its products to many countries, centering around China and the U.S., and their manufacturing factories were located in Asian countries.

[3] In Kikkoman, long-term management planning was positioned as a "general plan that incorporates innovative ambitions of top management and guides the basic direction of progress of the company" (Kikkoman, 2000, p. 330).

This period was marked by impressive events. First, Mr. Keizaburo Mogi the Second, then President, who was asked to diversify Kikkoman's business, insisted that the company retain the characters depicting soy sauce in its name, and their company name was changed to "Kikkoman Shoyu Co., Ltd." Second, he unveiled a very important guideline for Kikkoman's employees in his speech on the anniversary of the company's establishment. He insisted on the necessity of expanding soy sauce business. One reason for this is because Kikkoman certainly increased their market share in spite of slowing of the shipping amounts of soy sauce since the late 1950s. Moreover, Kikkoman's diversified businesses were not expected to recover their investments in the short term (Kikkoman, 2000).

Mr. Yuzaburo Mogi believed that Kikkoman "must change its policy" to overcome the deficits in its overseas businesses (Mogi, 2007, p. 76). He told his immediate supervisor, Mr. Nemoto, the then acting Chief in the Administration Division, "we need to construct a local factory in the U.S. and start local production to be a truly international company" (Mogi, 2007, p. 78).

Mr. Yuzaburo Mogi's initiative reflected his experience in the U.S.; at one point, he noted, "looking back now, it might have been the turning point" (Mogi, 2012a). While exhibiting their soy sauce at American supermarkets, he remarked, "(I) thought of seeing their expressions that soy sauce is an international seasoning" (Mogi, 2012a). He felt the company had a crisis even though "people in the company do not have a feeling of crisis about the diversification and internationalization, even though the deficit in the overseas sector in terms of soy sauce sales is quite large" (interview with Mr. Yuzaburo Mogi).

However, it was very risky for Kikkoman to construct local factories in the U.S. at that time,[4] because no Japanese enterprise had a full-scale local production facility in the U.S., and thus, Kikkoman had no prior experiences to refer to (Mogi, 2007). In addition, the foreign exchange rate stood at 1 U.S. dollar = 360 yen, and Kikkoman needed an amount equivalent to its capital stock to construct a factory in the U.S. at that time (Mogi, 2007).

---

[4] Yamasa Corporation, the second biggest soy sauce manufacturer at the time, built a factory outside Japan in the 1990s, while Sanjirushi Co., Ltd. started producing "tamari" soy sauce in the U.S. in 1978.

Mr. Yuzaburo Mogi described the reaction of Mr. Nemoto, who was the first to receive his proposal, as follows: "He was surprised with my proposal but understood its true meaning well. He said, 'It is important. Shall we discuss it with the Executive Secretary?'" (Mogi, 2007, p. 78). Mr. Yuzaburo Mogi and Mr. Nemoto approached Mr. Saheiji Mogi, the then Chief of the Office of the President. Mr. Saheiji Mogi responded that, "It is worth discussing this topic. We should speak to the President about it" (Mogi, 2007, p. 79). In 1965, Kikkoman established the American Plant Committee (AP Committee) to discuss the production of Kikkoman products in the U.S. The President assumed that the Chairman of AP Committee and its other members were Board Members of Kikkoman. This committee included the Secretariat Committee as its Working Committee. Mr. Yuzaburo Mogi participated in this Committee as a regular member.

The Secretariat Committee discussed every detail of the proposal for local production in the U.S. The shared understanding among the members of the AP Committee was that, "a brewery for soy sauce is a process industry and without sufficient demand, the business would not make enough money to survive" (Mogi, 2007, p. 80). The "minimum demand" was thought to be 9,000 kiloliters per year (Kikkoman, 2000). Kikkoman "expanded their sales well, but the annual sales amount was less than half this amount" (Kikkoman, 2000, p. 313). The AP Committee concluded that constructing a local factory in the U.S. was premature. (see Fig. 2).

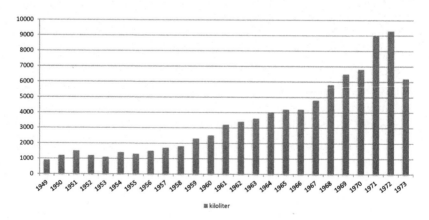

Fig. 2.   Export amounts of soy sauce of Kikkoman
Source: Created by the author using data from Kikkoman (2000, p. 187, 251, 312).

3.5. *"Trial" bottling at the local American factory*

While arguing about the local production in the U.S., the AP Committee also recognized that there were problems with the current soy sauce export mechanism. Kikkoman imported soybeans and wheat as raw materials for soy sauce production from the U.S. and Canada, processed them into soy sauce, and "again shipped it to the U.S. after bottling" (Mogi, 1983, p. 83). Mr. Yuzaburo Mogi examined ways to do away with this "double fare" and proposed that the process of bottling be done locally. After considering the proposal's profitability, Kikkoman "decided to start bottling the soy sauce provisionally in the U.S., looking forward to the future" (Mogi, 2007, p. 36).

Kikkoman signed an agreement to the effect with Leslie Salt Company in Oakland, California (Kikkoman, 2000) and started bottling operations in 1968. During this period, "raw material processing equipment and compressors were improved and modified, and the equipment could be handled by foreign workers" (p. 321). In addition, Kikkoman successfully experimented with "brewing soy sauce with the same taste as that prepared in Noda, albeit outside its traditional manufacturing base" (p. 321).

Kikkoman's business in the U.S. improved, and it broke even by reducing bottling costs by bottling the product locally and by expanding its sales, because its product was recognized as a "Product of America" under the Buy American Policy prevailing at that time (Mogi, 2012a).

3.6. *Reexamining local production in the U. S.*

Mr. Yuzaburo Mogi felt that soy sauce had been gradually accepted by American consumers and thought that "we have to advance to full-scale local production" (Mogi, 2012a). The AP Committee resumed its examination of the feasibility of local production in the U.S.

This time also saw some changes in Kikkoman's organizational structure. In 1969, the erstwhile Export Department was rechristened as the Overseas Business Division, which consisted of two departments: the Overseas Department and the Export Department. The first Overseas Business Division Manager was Mr. Saheiji Mogi (Kikkoman, 2000, p. 322). This organizational change came about as Kikkoman's overseas business could not remain restricted to exports and the KII expanded accordingly (Kikkoman, 2000, p. 322). Mr. Yuzaburo Mogi moved to the Overseas Business Division and was assigned the post of Vice Section Chief. He took charge as a coordinator of the factory construction project.

In September 1970, a preliminary investigation for local production was conducted. Its result indicated that the company could eliminate its cumulative loss if it constructed a factory with a production capacity of 9,000 kiloliters per year (Mogi, 1983). In December, Kikkoman sent the team to the U.S. for further investigation, in order to decide upon the following three problems. "First, do we need to have a production facility in the U.S.? Second, if we construct a production facility there, when should we start operations? Third, which is the best location for such a facility (the western, central, or eastern area) in the U.S." (Mogi, 1983, p. 93).

The proposal concerning the construction of the American factory was submitted to the Board of Directors on March 10, 1971. The total investment needed to construct a manufacturing facility for 9,000 kiloliters per year of sauce was more than two-thirds of the company's capital at that time (Kikkoman, 2000). The approval documentation emphasized the possibility that the "cumulative loss will be eliminated in five years" (2007, p. 94). However, this proposal was put on hold after a discussion held at a meeting of the Board of Directors, where opinions for or against the proposal were not openly expressed (Mogi, 2012b). According to Kikkoman (2000), Mr. Katsumi Mogi, the then Managing Director, remarked that, "we understood that local production had some merits, but there were problems in that we needed a vast amount of money for the investment and we faced the technological problem of brewing soy sauce with the same taste as that in Noda. None of the Board Members openly supported the proposal with confidence" (p. 316).

Again, the proposal documentation was placed before the Board for its approval after half a month. This time, one Board Member suggested that they ask the bank for its opinion. The bank asked Mr. Yuzaburo Mogi to provide the materials because the bank would need them to judge the appropriateness of foreign direct investment (Mogi, 2007). Although the bank recommended reducing the planned equipment capacity at the proposed U.S. factory to 40 thousand *koku*,[5] Mr. Yuzaburo Mogi insisted that Mr. Ishikawa, the then Overseas Division Manager, submit the original proposal because the reduction in the production capacity proposed by the bank

---

[5] 1 koku is approximately 180 liters.

did not significantly reduce the amount of money required for the investment. Mr. Ishikawa "promised to support the original proposal at the meeting of the Board of Directors" (Mogi, 2007, p. 96). Although the approval documentation was submitted for a third time, the Board of Directors did not seem keen to discuss the matter further.

Finally, the then President, Mr. Keizaburo Mogi, consented to the proposal. According to Kikkoman (2000), Mr. Keizaburo Mogi sanctioned the proposal for constructing the factory in the U.S., noting that, "this is a difficult business but we will construct a factory in the U.S."

3.7. Selection of the construction site

Kikkoman decided to construct its factory at Walworth in the State of Wisconsin. After applying for a change in land use in 1972 (as per the prevalent zoning regulations), they started acquiring the ingredients for brewing the soy sauce. The Kikkoman factory in the U.S. had the capacity to brew about 9,000 kiloliters a year of soy sauce and approximately 900 kiloliters a year of teriyaki sauce.

3.8. Operating performance after construction

In 1971, when Kikkoman decided to construct a factory in the U.S., they estimated that the demand for soy sauce would increase to a certain degree. However, the first oil crisis occurred in 1973. The steep rise in oil prices led to increased production and transfer costs, and as a result, the first year's performance recorded huge deficits. The second year also witnessed big deficits (Mogi, 2007, p. 54). However, as the demand for soy sauce continued to expand, Kikkoman planned and implemented a clever pricing policy, and so, surpluses were realized in the third and fourth years. The surpluses actually predated the company's estimates for a profit by one year, and the cumulative deficit was eliminated beforehand.

4. Discussion

The strategically important initiative to "change their [Kikkoman's] policy" (Mogi, 2007, p. 76) and to establish a local production site in the U.S. was proposed by a lower manager, Mr. Yuzaburo Mogi. Of course, we should remember that while he was one of the members of the founding families, he was not the only person from the founding families because Kikkoman was established by merging eight families.

4.1. Why did Mr. Y. Mogi foresee the need to build the factory in the U.S.?

Why did Mr. Yuzaburo Mogi propose that local production in the U.S. was indispensable for Kikkoman to become a truly global firm? The first reason for this concerns the "values" shared by all employees of Kikkoman at that time. As described earlier, Mr. Keizaburo Mogi the Second, then President, was asked to diversify business development, he decided to retain the characters of soy sauce in the company's name. In doing so, he showed the employees that opportunities existed for the soy sauce business and that there was a need to expand it. Marginson (2002) observed that value system in an organization influences strategy formulation through its impact on the strategic atmosphere and employees' attitude toward new initiatives.

The second reason can be traced back to Mr. Yuzaburo Mogi's responsibility at that time, namely, long-term management planning. He was in a position to view the company from a long-term perspective by referring to short-term operational data.

The third, and, perhaps the biggest reason for Mr. Yuzaburo Mogi to propose the factory in the U.S. was his gut feeling about how soy sauce would be accepted in the American market. He called the experience of exhibiting the sauce in American supermarkets as "a turning point" (Mogi, 2012a).

4.2. The role of middle managers in the process of strategy formulation

The role of Kikkoman's middle managers in the process of strategy formulation differs markedly from what was observed in the Burgelman model. Burgelman (1983) posited that middle managers assumed the role of proposing and persuading the top management about promising initiatives from lower managers. However, in the case of Kikkoman, the middle managers did not take on this role. They only communicated their subordinate's promising idea to their superiors and provided the opportunity for discussion. In this sense, their role was that of a "passive supporter" or "provider of the opportunity for discussion." Under these conditions, it is possible that emerging "activities that fall outside the scope of the current concept of strategy" (Burgelman, 1983, p. 61) in the organization may not develop as part of the corporate strategy. However, in the case of Kikkoman at least, the proposal initiated by a lower manager developed into a corporate strategy. I believe that the identity of the middle manager played a vital role in this case. It is quite clear that the time that lapsed between the proposal of the strategy by Mr. Yuzaburo Mogi and its actual implementation was too long. During this duration, the position assumed by Mr. Yuzaburo Mogi in the company changed dramatically. In the beginning, when he proposed his idea, he was just one of the lower managers. However, in time, Mr. Yuzaburo Mogi was gradually promoted to a position that involved overseeing the construction of the factory proposed by him in the U.S. When the agenda about local production in the U.S. was discussed at the meeting of the Board of Directors, Mr. Yuzaburo Mogi occupied the position of Group Manager of the Overseas Business Division, a middle manager position. We can compare this argument with the Burgelman model as follows (see Fig. 3).

4.3. Criteria used for decision-making about the investment at Kikkoman

The proposal for local production in the U.S. was examined in detail at the AP Committee Meeting. Thus, this meeting can be positioned as the "systems (needed) to facilitate information exchange so that promising ideas are identified and supported" (Davila, 2005, p. 54). The meeting set a clear standard for investment decisions. The criteria for the investment decision were the current and potential demand for soy sauce in the U.S. compared to the capacity of the production equipment. These criteria had important implications for subsequent development, as they addressed potential changes in the external environment, similar to the criterion used for making decisions about investments at Intel, as described by Burgelman (2002).[6] In reality,

---

[6] According to Burgelman (1991), "The effectiveness of internal selection processes may depend on how closely they correspond to the selection pressures exerted by the current external environment, while simultaneously allowing new environments to be sought out" (p. 250).

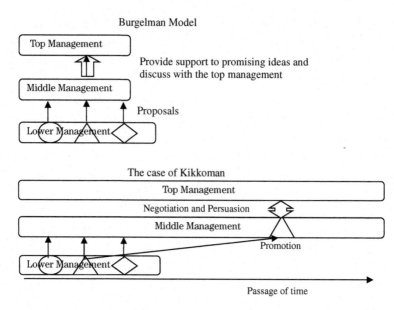

Fig. 3.   Comparison between the Burgelman Model and Kikkoman's Case
Source: Created by the author based on the discussion in Burgelman (1983).

Mr. Yuzaburo Mogi believed it was necessary to table his proposal for local production again after he confirmed the increase in demand for soy sauce in the U.S.

4.4. *Strategic decision-making as organizational learning*

Although the AP Committee concluded that the idea for the construction of a local soy sauce factory was initially premature, they simultaneously decided that there was some merit in bottling soy sauce locally. The decision-making in this regard was postponed as they wondered whether a direct investment in the U.S. was justified. This opinion of the Committee may be interpreted as the company's postponement of the final decision until they could judge with certainty whether the market demand exceeded their criteria. Kikkoman could continue bottling soy sauce locally only if the demand in the U.S. met their criteria. However, if the local demand exceeded their criteria, they could reconsider whether a direct investment was justified. Additionally, although only a part of the production was completed in the U.S., it helped Kikkoman obtain experience in local production and gave the company ample time to refine its production techniques for authentic Japanese soy sauce in America.

4.5. The "decision to put off the decision"

Kikkoman's Board of Directors, who held the final say in the decision, thrice opted to postpone taking a decision about the proposal for direct investment in the U.S. Of course, these postponements were a reflection of not just the problems faced by the company but also the necessity for new production techniques. The meetings, therefore, did not function as avenues for final decision-making. This means the Board decided that it was prudent "not to decide," thus causing the President to determine the final course of action independently.

5. Summary and Future Developments

In this paper, I chose to analyze a strategic decision-making process at a traditional Japanese enterprise to establish a local production base in the U.S. I detected differences between the case study and the Burgelman model, which is based on observations at western enterprises.

The first difference concerns the role of the middle manager in the strategic decision-making process. Burgelman showed that middle managers assume an important role in the evaluation and selection of strategic initiatives "that fall outside the scope of the current concept of corporate strategy" (Burgelman, 1983, p. 61). In the case of Kikkoman, however, the role of middle managers was very much restricted, in that they only communicated the proposal initiated by lower managers to their superiors.

The second difference pertains to the identity of the middle manager. In the Burgelman model, middle managers differed from lower managers. However, in the case of Kikkoman, the employee who initiated the proposal for local production in the U.S. actually played a middle manager's role by promotion because the duration between the time the strategy was proposed to when it was implemented, was long. As the discussion about the proposal continued to develop, the proposer, who was a lower manager at that time, was promoted to the post of a middle manager, and he assumed the important role of developing the proposal into a corporate strategy.

The third difference concerns the role of the meetings of the Board of Directors. Originally, major decisions would be taken at such meetings. However, the Board opted to put off the decision in this case, leaving the President of Kikkoman to make the final decision. Thus, instead of approving the decision, the President assumed the role of decision maker.

These differences imply that the role of middle and top managers in the strategic decision-making process differs among countries.

However, this study also suffers from one limitation. This discussion is based on one case, that of Kikkoman. We need to examine more case studies pertaining to Japanese firms to appreciate whether this discussion is unique to Kikkoman or if it can be generalized to other Japanese firms.

Acknowledgment

I thank Mr. Yuzaburo Mogi, Honorable CEO and Chairman of the Board of Kikkoman Corporation, who granted me the opportunity to interview him. I am also grateful to Prof. Yasuhiro Monden for his helpful comments. This work was supported by JSPS KAKENHI Grant Nos. 26245048 and 15K03789.

References

Abernathy, M. A. and P. Brownell (1999). The role of budgets in organizations facing strategic change: An exploratory study. *Accounting, Organizations and Society*, 24: 189–204.

Anthony, R. N., J. Dearden and R. F. Vancil (1972). *Management Control Systems — Text, Cases, and Readings*. Homewood, IL: Richard D. Irwin, Inc.

Burgelman, R. A. (1983). A model of the interaction of strategic behavior, corporate context, and the concept of strategy. *The Academy of Management Review* 8(1): 61–70.

Burgelman, R. A. (1991). Intraorganizational ecology of strategy making and organizational adaptation: Theory and field research. *Organization Science* 2(3): 239–262.

Burgelman, R. A. (2002). *Strategy is Destiny*. New York: The Free Press.

Davila, T. (2005). The Promise of Management Control Systems for Innovation and Strategic Choice. In Chapman, C. S. (eds.) *Controlling Strategy — Management, Accounting, and Performance Measurement*. New York, NY: Oxford University Press.

Davila, A., G. Foster, and D. Oyon (2009). Accounting and control, entrepreneurship and innovation: venturing into new research opportunities. *European Accounting Review* 18(2): 281–311.

Kikkoman Co., Ltd. (2000). *80 Years' History of Kikkoman*, Kikkoman Co., Ltd. (In Japanese).

Kikkoman. (2015). Annual Security Report. Available at http://www.kikkoman.co.jp/library/ir/library/yuho/pdf/2801_2014yhyh.pdf

Kober R., J. Ng, and B. J. Paul (2007). The interrelationship between management control mechanisms and strategy. *Management Accounting Research* 18: 425–452.

Marginson, D. E. W. (2002). Management control systems and their effects on strategy formulation at middle-management levels: Evidence from a U.K. organization. *Strategic Management Journal* 23: 1019–1031.

Mintzberg, H. (1978). Patterns in strategy formulation. *Management Science* 24(9).

Mintzberg, H., B. Ahlstrand and J. Lampel (1998). *Strategy Safari — A Guided Tour through the Wilds of Strategic Management*. Upper Saddle River, NJ: Prentice-Hall.

Mogi, Y. (1983). Soy Sauce Hits the Mainstream in the U.S — The Strategy for Exporting Food Culture. Tosyoinsatsu-kabushikikaisya (In Japanese).

Mogi, Y. (2007). The Global Business of Kikkoman — Exporting Japanese Food Culture to the World. Japan Productivity Center (In Japanese).

Mogi, Y. (2012a, b). My Resume. *Nihon Keizai Shimbun* 7/3, 7/4. (In Japanese).

Naranjo-Gil, D. and F. Hartmann (2007). How top management teams use management accounting systems to implement strategy. *Journal of Management Accounting Research* 18: 21–53.

Simons, R. (1995). *Levers of Control — How Managers Use Innovative Control Systems to Drive Strategic Renewal*. Boston, Massachusetts. Harvard Business School Press.

Management Control Systems and Innovation: The Case of Micro-Profit Centers

Yuichi Kubota

Professor, Graduate School of Business Administration,
Nanzan University, Japan

1. Introduction

This study investigates how management control systems (MCS) affect creativity or innovation. Although creativity or innovation ensures that a company accumulates and uses strategic intangibles, it is still unclear how MCS, including Simons' (1995) interactive control systems, foster or repress innovation activities. In addition, a set of several control systems as a control package could encourage innovation.

Innovation has various types, and we predict that MCS modes differ depending on the type of innovation. Innovation is a management process, where it is important to select and implement appropriate ideas (Davila *et al.*, 2006). As innovation carries process uncertainty and consumes limited resources, those looking to innovate must show legitimate reasons for mobilizing these precious resources (Takeishi *et al.*, 2010). MCS can assist in creating accountability and legitimizing resource allocation.

Thus, we analyze a case of micro-profit centers (MPC) and discuss the legitimization of resource allocation, types of innovation, and control packages.

Japanese Management and International Studies Vol. 13:
Management of Innovation Strategy in Japanese Companies
World Scientific Publishing Company, September 2016

2. Literature Review

2.1. MCS and innovation

The traditional view of MCS holds that managers cannot effectively cope with innovation, as it is accompanied by uncertainty about the future. MCS are instead mainly used to improve operational efficiency, and therefore has no impact on innovation efforts. However, recent studies indicate that MCS help managers stimulate creativity and innovation under certain conditions (e.g. Simons, 1995, 2005).

Studies investigating the relationship between MCS and innovation and strategy have recently increased, with many researchers discussing this relationship by focusing on the interactive use of MCS (e.g. Abernethy and Brownell, 1999; Bisbe and Otley, 2004; Bisbe and Malagueño, 2009; Henri, 2006; Naranjo-Gil and Hartmann, 2007; Revellino and Mouritsen, 2009). According to Simons, "interactive control systems are the information systems that managers use to involve themselves regularly and personally in the decision activities of subordinates" (Simons, 1995, p. 95). Managers focus on strategic uncertainties to implement specific strategies, and use MCS interactively to create positive dialogue under uncertainty, which in turn generates new ideas and innovation.

Some studies indicate that MCS contribute to effective product innovation (e.g. Cardinal, 2001; Davila, 2000). However, Bisbe and Otley's (2004) findings contradict the idea that using MCS interactively fosters innovation, finding instead that the impact of innovation on performance is moderated by the interactive use of MCS. Bisbe and Malagueño (2009) pointed out that the choice to use MCS interactively varies according to a firm's innovation management mode and suggested that the choice of MCS may create a dysfunctional effect through innovation momentum. In high-innovating firms, excessive and inappropriate innovation could reduce returns. Thus, the earlier research provides contradictory findings.

The MCS requirements may differ according to the type of innovation, be it radical vs. incremental, exploratory vs. exploitative, and sustaining vs. disruptive (e.g. Christensen and Bower, 1996; Davila, 2005; Davila et al., 2009; Jansen et al., 2006). However, there are varying results from survey-based research on the relationship between MCS and type of innovation (Cardinal, 2001; Jansen et al., 2006; Ylinen and Gullkvist, 2014). These findings indicate the necessity of balancing the different innovation efforts.

2.2. *Realizing innovation and managing tension*

Innovation requires a careful consideration of uncertainty and resource allocation (Takeishi *et al.*, 2010). Under high uncertainty, decision makers require valid reasoning or legitimacy. MCS can legitimize resource mobilization for innovation. For example, Mouritsen *et al.* (2009) pointed out that management accounting calculations justify innovation in two categories. In the short translation, management accounting calculations help extend or reduce innovation activities. In the long translation, it develops competing contexts for innovation and impacts firms' innovation strategies and sourcing arrangements.

Another view on the relationship between innovation and MCS highlights tension: efficiency vs. flexibility; standardization vs. differentiation; centralization vs. decentralization; creativity vs. stability (e.g. Ahrens and Chapman, 2004; Davila, 2000; Simons, 1995). MCS do not operate in isolation, but rather as a package (e.g. Malmi and Brown, 2008; Otley, 1980). Innovation requires creativity, but there is an inherent tension between creativity and stability, and MCS impact the degree of creativity.

Simons (1995) proposes four levers of control: belief systems, boundary systems, diagnostic control systems, and interactive control systems. These controls adjust the tension between stability and creativity, wherein belief systems and interactive control systems create positive and inspirational forces, corresponding to the yang in Chinese philosophy. Davila *et al.* (2009) points out that interactive control systems contribute to strategic innovation (radical innovation from the top management) and suggest that corporate entrepreneurship is related to autonomous strategic action (radical innovation from the bottom of the organization). The role of MCS changes according to the type of innovation or organizational context. Therefore, an MCS package is necessary to manage tensions and extend or reduce innovation activities.

This study uses Simons' (1995) framework and investigates the relationship between innovation and various controls with a case study of a highly innovative company to consider the role of MCS in innovation.

3. Hamamatsu Photonics

Hamamatsu Photonics, which manufactures various products related to photon technology, was established in 1953. In 2014, the company employed approximately 4,400 people, and had sales of ¥112 billion and operating income of ¥22 billion. It has three divisions, one development center, and two laboratories. Hamamatsu holds more than 90% of the photomultiplier market, and its technology is highly regarded worldwide. The characteristics of the company's management are philosophy and MPC (Kubota, 2015).

3.1. *Management philosophy*

The management philosophy is the pursuit of absolute truth and "to challenge what mankind does not yet know and has not yet achieved". Hamamatsu Photonics follows the ideas of Kenjiro Takayanagi, who was a university professor and also known as "the Father of Japanese television". Heihachiro Horiuchi, the founder, was his student. Takayanagi let all members of his laboratory to participate in research and challenged them to find something new. He often advised them to "grasp fortune by the forelock, for she has no hair behind". This saying means "if you want to take advantage of the opportunity, you have to prepare for it". Following Takayanagi's teachings, all employees, regardless of educational background, conduct their own research and development (R&D). Therefore, field workers in the manufacturing process also work on R&D. Hamamatsu achieves sustainable growth by predicting and providing for the future.

Teruo Hiruma, Chairman, who attended the same university and adopted Takayanagi's philosophy of challenging mankind, maintains the original management philosophy. Hamamatsu created products through trial and error, even when the customer requirements entailed a high level of difficulty in the technology. The company pursues sustainable growth through innovation in science and technology, and considers itself an R&D company.

All employees understand the vision and share the value. Top management frequently asks employees questions based on the management philosophy, which they keep in mind when answering the questions. However, if the employees conducted their own R&D without considering commercial concerns, the company will not profit. Therefore, Hamamatsu introduced the MPC system to make employees conscious of revenues and costs.

3.2. *MPC*

The MPC system consists of three tools: in-house paper money, in-house promissory notes for borrowing, and a profit and loss report. MPC are organized throughout the company, and promote all employees' participation in management.

This study focuses on the details of the MPC in the production department. At the end of September 2014, there were 45 production departments in the company, each with 7–60 members and a chief manager (*Bumoncho* in Japanese), manager (*Syunin*), section chief (*Sennin*), and other members. The production group is organized according to the production process, led by a section chief. A production department manager is responsible for managing the profit in a specific product line.

3.2.1. *In-house paper money*

The in-house paper money, Hamamatsu Photonics K. K. paper money (HPK money), was introduced in 1975 to give each employee a strong sense of responsibility for their work that ensures cost reductions and cash flow. HPK money provides employees with an awareness of money as a manager and improves managerial awareness. This clarifies the business conditions because they can visualize their group's management as HPK money increases and decreases.

HPK money is printed in thirteen denominations, from ¥100 to ¥100 million. The *in-house paper money center* at the head office plays the role of a central bank by printing and controlling HPK money. All bills, which are payments for personnel expenses, material costs, and expendable supplies, etc., were paid in HPK money. For example, using HPK money, each group in a production department pays for raw materials and receives it for finished goods.

Money is deducted to pay for services and administrative costs and the headquarters' fees (i.e. company income) from the previous month's company sales for each division. To cover manufacturing costs, the money equivalent to the cost of sales in the current week is distributed to the production departments of each business division. The production department obtains HPK money for their gross production in the previous week from the general manager of each division. Gross production is calculated by multiplying the predetermined cost by the actual warehouse quantity. The general manager determines production volume. If the inventory quantity increases, the division's HPK money decreases, creating a severe cash flow problem for the general manager.

In the production department, if actual costs are below the predetermined costs, the group leaders can save up HPK money. In contrast, if actual costs exceed predetermined costs, they lose money. Because the company's product uses the latest technology, the production yields tend to be low. Employees can exercise their originality and ingenuity to generate HPK money by improving production yields through innovation. A production department with a favorable variance has the next predetermined costs cut to match the actual costs by the general manager of the *business management and control division*. Predetermined costs are reviewed every six months. In addition, when the group does not finish the goods on time, this increases goods in process, and the group does not receive HPK money, though they must pay for the materials consumed. This decreases their revenues, and they receive less money. This encourages the groups to follow their production schedule.

Production department managers receive HPK paper money as the product line's income. They also obtain information about market trends (sales prices and volumes, etc.), as well as their section's gross production. Generally, the sales price tends to gradually decrease, while employee salaries tend to increase annually. If the group does not improve anything, their production costs increase. Managers are given a tight target profit rate. Each group must therefore always work to reduce costs enough to offset a fall in sales prices and a rise in labor costs.

Moreover, each department frequently carries out both internal (in-house sales and purchases) and external transactions. The internal transfer price is decided by negotiations between group leaders. The price is not based on costs but on the market price, and includes each department's added value.

3.2.2. *In-house promissory notes for borrowing*

When a department falls into a deficit or must purchase new equipment, general managers can borrow HPK money from the *in-house paper money center* at head office using an in-house promissory note. In the division, each leader can borrow money from the general manager if they issue a note. They must also submit a request that has a joint signature of the surety, an applicant's superior, and to pay interest on the borrowed money.

Borrowers provide the purpose for borrowing (operating funds, equipment purchase, deficit filling, etc.) and the repayment plan in an application form. For example, when the purpose is to purchase new equipment, the applicant must estimate the forecasted sales of the goods that require the equipment and the depreciation plan.

The application form also clarifies the person responsible for borrowing and repaying HPK money. The borrower is thus very conscious of the debt repayment and think seriously about the cash flow. The superiors, as guarantors, monitor the repayment progress and advise subordinates appropriately about the repayment.

3.2.3. *Profit and loss report*

Leaders autonomously manage their group using HPK money and a profit and loss report (see Table 1). The MPC system allows leaders to create their own plans and run their own group. The reports are consolidated from the bottom up. General Managers are accountable for the actual profit "D" as the final profit. A production department manager is responsible for the actual profit "C," which is the profit before paying the headquarters' fees. The target "C" profit rate is set considerably high, and the leaders aim to achieve this target while remaining conscious of sales trends.

With a strong motivation to achieve the target, leaders grasp problems or opportunities (plan), put their plan into action (do), measure the effect (check), and take appropriate action (act). The plan-do-check-act (PDCA) cycle is a methodology for continuous improvement, which is often used in Japanese companies like Toyota (Sobek and Smally, 2008). As all employees think that "our job is in R&D," they find ways to improve the product or equipment by measuring cost reductions at the production sites.

The *business management and control division* collects, analyzes, and reports all profit and loss reports. Based on the aggregated data collected from all MPC managers, the actual profit is monitored at monthly board meetings, executive meetings, and budget committee meetings. Top management can find and solve problems quickly by drilling down from summary data to more detailed data from each MPC. These meetings discuss and approve the applications for expenses related to exceptional events or capital investment.

Table 1. Profit and loss report

		Target	Actual
Sales	I		
Fixed expenses	II		
Personnel			
Depreciation			
Expense transfer from other processes			
....			
Variable expenses	III		
Material cost			
Amount paid to subcontractors			
Improvement expenses			
....			
Total expenses	IV = II + III		
Profit result A	V = I – IV		
Inventory difference expenses	VI		
Profit result B	VII = V – VI		
Overhead expenses	VIII		
Sales commission expenses			
Quality control expenses			
....			
Profit result C	IX = VII – VIII		
Headquarters fees	X		
Profit result D	XI = IX – X		

Finally, the top management communicates the company's performance and market trends at a monthly meeting attended by leaders above section chiefs, about 200–300 employees. Top management provides information about important agenda items to the leaders. This meeting also serves as a place to educate and continuously teach about thinking and work attitudes. The leaders learn about their products' sales trends and the reasons behind this during these meetings or in discussions with the sales staff.

3.3. *Strategy and MCS*

Hamamatsu's strategy is to remain an R&D company, aiming to advance photonic technologies more than anyone else. Not only researchers, but all members in a production department have research areas and daily experimentation. To implement this strategy, group leaders balance R&D and profitability. The leaders strive to meet this requirement, even when it is rather difficult, using their creativity and inventiveness to solve problems. In keeping with the management philosophy, employees must work on R&D to advance the technology.

The MPC system encourages productivity improvements and cost reduction to achieve the profit target determined by the profit and loss report. Group leaders share information about the entire company in a monthly meeting, and act by forecasting their own group's profit. If they miss the target profit, they work to reduce expenses, such as procuring cheaper materials or improving the production process or product design, ahead of R&D activities. They use the technical know-how accumulated from prior research within the entire company to develop and improve their product or production equipment by attending information workshops provided by researchers and engineers from the development division or research laboratories.

The challenges include not only new radical technology, but also improvements to existing technology. The R&D results, such as direct improvements to equipment, could raise productivity and reduce costs, thus boosting profitability. In comparison, it takes a long time to obtain an outcome from new technology, so they must first assess its usefulness. The company carries on professor Takayanagi's spirit and prepares for the future.

4. Discussion

This case confirms the connection between belief systems and interactive control systems. The belief system was a management philosophy that inherited the founder's spirit, affecting the employees' values and shaping the organizational culture. On the other hand, the MPC system, using in-house money, promissory notes, and profit and loss reports as a tool, functioned as the interactive control system. The group leaders estimated the revenue and costs and worked to meet the profit target.

The control package of belief system and interactive control system could contribute legitimacy for mobilizing a firm's resources in the innovation process. The belief system supported resource allocations to meet the challenge of developing new technology under uncertainty by acting as a form of cognitive legitimacy based on clarity and taking things for granted (Suchman, 1995). The management philosophy allowed all employees to conduct their own R&D independently, and this company seemed to mobilize resources to pursue creative ideas.

The MPC system enabled leaders to determine whether to extend or reduce R&D activities. Resources were allocated based on an economic rationale, providing pragmatic legitimacy (Suchman, 1995; Takeishi *et al.* 2010). Top management could evaluate the situation and act immediately, because they could check the profit and loss reports from all groups, and questioned leaders about strategy and offered the firm's information about business conditions. The group leaders could focus on strategic uncertainties and manage their operations, with the MPC system working to maintain or enhance profitability. Leaders who missed the profit target had to determine the cause and respond appropriately, and any R&D investments required an economic justification.

The company managed the tension between economic rationality (stability, efficiency) and uncertainty (creativity, flexibility) (see Table 2). Employees were challenged to meet both higher profit targets based on economics while carrying out R&D activities under uncertainty. The belief system and interactive control system encouraged group leaders to manage the tension. This case showed that an interactive MPC system tends to foster incremental (exploitative) innovation activities, but repressed radical (exploratory) innovation activities.

A group that met the profit goal and saved HPK money as retained earnings, could invest in R&D activities for new business, with an emphasis on the long-term perspective, as this type of R&D could be a source of future revenue. Companies face a constantly changing environment, and strategic change is required to maintain competitiveness. The case illustrated the necessity to reconfigure capabilities or intangible and tangible assets. To cope, managers must accumulate resources, such as intellectual assets related to technological innovation. Management can then allow individuals to learn

Table 2.   Tension and innovation type

	Good condition	Hard condition
Perspective tension	Long-term oriented	Short-term oriented
	Creativity	Stability
	Challenge: New technology	Challenge: Performance improvement
Types of innovation	Radical, exploratory	Incremental, exploitative

by trial and error and stimulate creativity, though success is uncertain, and thereby promote radical and exploratory innovation activities. However, there is a possibility that "superfluous innovation" or "innovation momentum" decreases the returns (Bisbe and Malagueño, 2009).

Groups missing the profit target would have a shortage of HPK money, forcing group leaders to improve short-term profits. They would first find ways to reduce R&D expenses and enhance profitability, such as through kaizen activities including improving equipment and manufacturing processes. Otherwise, they would try to develop a market using the existing technology. In this situation, they would prioritize the profit target and performance improvement, which translates into stable plans with lower uncertainty and higher economic rationality. Managers would emphasize efficiency more than creativity, and would repress radical innovation activities by focusing on incremental and exploitative innovation. Furthermore, to increase profit, they would develop new applications of existing technology by using intangible assets.

The case showed both strategic innovation and autonomous strategic actions because the company interactively used profit and loss reports in the MPC system. The system also led to incremental innovation. The company thus recognized and solved problems caused by the balance of various elements between the long- and short-terms, and between creativity and stability, using tools such as in-house paper money and promissory notes. Group leaders always pursued new ideas to solve problems. The management philosophy and MPC system encouraged employees to manage the tension. These efforts foster creativity, inventiveness, and problem-solving; while also promoting the accumulation and utilization of intangibles that include both technology and human or structural assets.

5. Conclusion

The study obtained the following three main results.

The results clearly show that MCS affect various types of innovation, especially the belief system and interactive control system, which Simons called positive control systems, either promoting or repressing innovation activities. These systems played an important role in legitimizing resource allocations for innovation. The belief system provided cognitive legitimacy, and the interactive control system provided pragmatic legitimacy, such as economic rationality.

Second, a control package can manage the tensions between the types and the impact of innovation. In this interactive MPC system, group leaders who may miss their section's profit target would emphasize stability and efficiency at the expense of radical innovation activities, by mainly pursuing incremental and exploitative innovation. On the other hand, groups achieving the target profit had a belief system that would allow them to conduct R&D activities and exercise their creative potential by prioritizing radical (exploratory) innovation. Thus, an effective control package can balance between types of innovation and coordinate innovation activities depending on the situation. However, the control package in this case was designed in a peculiar organizational context. For example, the management philosophy includes a technology-oriented spirit, which explains why the belief system affected creativity and radical innovation.

Third, the case suggests that an interactive MPC system stimulates autonomous strategic actions that encourage or discourage innovation activities. Each leader could autonomously make decisions using the MPC's tools, which provided an enabling control function. In the concept of enabling control, MCS can simultaneously support the objectives of efficiency and flexibility (Ahrens and Chapman, 2004; Wouters and Wilderom, 2008).

To conclude, MCS can contribute to creativity and innovation. The innovation activities accumulate and make use of the intangible assets, which are not only technological, but also are strategic resources. Future research is necessary to clarify the relationships among innovation, intangibles, and management control.

Acknowledgments

I gratefully acknowledge all Hamamatsu Photonics employees and managers who assisted with this research. I am grateful for the financial assistance provided by JSPS KAKENHI Grant No. 15K03795 and Nanzan University Pache Research Subsidy I-A-2 for the 2015 academic year.

References

Abernethy, M. A. and P. Brownell (1999). The role of budgets in organizations facing strategic change: An exploratory study. *Accounting, Organizations and Society* 24(3): 189–204.

Ahrens, T. and C. S. Chapman (2004). Accounting for flexibility and efficiency: A field study of management control systems in a restaurant chain. *Contemporary Accounting Research* 21(2): 271–301.

Bisbe, J. and D. Otley (2004). The effects of the interactive use of management control systems on product innovation. *Accounting, Organizations and Society* 29(8): 709–737.

Bisbe, J. and R. Malagueño (2009). The choice of interactive control systems under different innovation management modes. *European Accounting Review* 18(2): 371–405.

Cardinal, L. (2001). Technological innovation in the pharmaceutical industry: The use of organisational control in managing research and development. *Organization Science* 12(1): 19–36.

Christensen, C. M. and J. L. Bower (1996). Customer power, strategic investment, and the failure of leading firms. *Strategic Management Journal* 17(3): 197–218.

Davila, A. (2000). An empirical study on the drivers of management control systems' design in new product development. *Accounting, Organizations and Society* 25(4–5): 383–409.

Davila, A. (2005). The promise of management control systems for innovation and strategic change. In Chapman, C. S. (Ed.), *Controlling Strategy: Management, Accounting, and Performance Measurement*, pp. 37–61, Oxford: Oxford University Press.

Davila, A., M. J. Epstein, and R. Shelton (2006). *Making Innovation Work: How to Manage It, Measure It, and Profit from It.* Upper Saddle River, NJ: Wharton School Publishing.

Davila, A., G. Foster, and D. Oyon (2009). Accounting and control, entrepreneurship and innovation: venturing into new research opportunities. *European Accounting Review* 18(2): 281–311.

Henri, J. (2006). Management control systems and strategy: a resource-based perspective. *Accounting, Organizations and Society* 31(6): 529–558.

Jansen, J. J. P., F. A. J. van den Bosch, and H. W. Volberda (2006). Exploratory innovation, exploitative innovation, and performance: effects of organizational antecedents and environmental moderators. *Management Science* 52(11): 1661–1674.

Kubota, Y. (2015). Management control and proactive behavior: the case of Hamamatsu Photonics. *Kigyo Kaikei* 67(2): 56–64 (in Japanese).

Malmi, T. and D. A. Brown (2008). Management control systems as a package: opportunities, challenges and research directions. *Management Accounting Research* 19(4): 287–300.

Mouritsen, J., A. Hansen, and C. Ø. Hansen (2009). Short and long translations: management accounting calculations and innovation management. *Accounting, Organizations and Society* 34(6–7): 738–754.

Naranjo-Gil, D. and F. Hartmann (2007). Management accounting systems, top management team heterogeneity and strategic change. *Accounting, Organizations and Society* 32(7–8): 735–756.

Otley, D. T. (1980). The contingency theory of management accounting: Achievement and prognosis. *Accounting, Organizations and Society* 5(4): 413–428.

Revellino, S. and J. A. N. Mouritsen (2009). The multiplicity of controls and the making of innovation. *European Accounting Review* 18(2): 341–369.

Simons, R. (1995). *Levers of Control: How Managers Use Innovative Control Systems to Drive Strategic Renewal.* Boston, Mass: Harvard Business School Press.

Simons, R. (2005). *Levers of Organization Design: How Managers Use Accountability Systems for Greater Performance and Commitment.* Boston, Mass: Harvard Business School Press

Sobek, D. K. and A. Smalley (2008). *Understanding A3 Thinking: A Critical Component of Toyota's PDCA Management System.* New York: Productivity Press.

Suchman, M. C. (1995). Managing legitimacy: strategic and institutional approaches. *Academy of Management Review* 20(3): 571–610.

Takeishi, A., Y. Aoshima and M. Karube (2010). Reasons for innovation: legitimizing resource mobilization for innovation in the cases of the Okoichi memorial prize winners. In Itami, H., Kusunoki, K., Numagami, T., and Takeishi, A. (Eds.), *Dynamics of Knowledge, Corporate Systems and Innovation*, pp. 165–189, Heidelberg: Springer.

Wouters, M. and C. Wilderom (2008). Developing performance-measurement systems and enabling formalization: a longitudinal field study of a logistics department. *Accounting, Organizations and Society* 33(4–5): 488–516.

Ylinen, M. and B. Gullkvist (2014). The effects of organic and mechanistic control in exploratory and exploitative innovations. *Management Accounting Research* 25(1): 93–112.

Part 3
Related Topics in Business Administration and Management Accounting

Intrinsic and Extrinsic Motivation Viewed from HRM: Based on a Questionnaire Survey of Regular Employees in Middle-Ranking Companies in the Tokyo Area

Eiji Okamoto

Former Professor, Faculty of Business Administration,
Mejiro University, Japan

1. Introduction

In 1995, when the Japanese economy experienced low growth because of the collapse of the economic bubble at the beginning of the 1990s, the Japan Federation of Employers' Associations announced an employment form model titled "a future ideal method of 'Japan Management Systems' of the new times." This model comprised three groups: "a long-term accumulation ability-type group," "a specialist group" to solve a company's problems, and "an employment flexibility-type group" (The Japan Federation of Employers' Associations, 1995, p. 33). Of the three groups, each company seeks promotion of a "company-type employment portfolio" (*Ibid.*, p. 33). This, coupled with a change in employees' working consciousness, was necessary to develop ability based on personal consideration. Furthermore, Lepak and Snell (1999) showed four modes, including "training internally," "procurement from outside," "taking advantage of outsourcing with the

Japanese Management and International Studies Vol. 13:
Management of Innovation Strategy in Japanese Companies
World Scientific Publishing Company, September 2016

contract", and "alliance with the external". Most companies raised weight from long-term to short-term employment, and as a result of trying to achieve employment flexibility, working patterns diversified remarkably (Labour Economic White Paper, 2006, Chapter 2).

Such influence was also seen in the company's reasons for new employee selection. "The future of the company" was the utmost reason in 1971, but since then, aspects related to employees' conscious improvement of work — "I can apply my personality and ability" and "can learn a technique" — gradually rose in rank (Japan Productivity Center, 2009). In addition, The Japan Institute for Labor Policy and Training (JILPT) has investigated the reasons for selecting the current employment form by surveying 1,793 people, regular employees nationwide, aged 20–65 years. The results depicted "stability of income" as the primary reason, followed by "[the employee] wants to work full-time," and "[the employee] wants to work for a specialist" as the response order to the question (Investigation Series No. 15, 2006, p. 20). This implies a rise in employees' aggressive work consciousness, showing the same trend as the Japan Productivity Center's investigation as described above.

This paper clarifies the concept of work consciousness among Japanese employees, and the factors affecting it. Therefore, factors in the investigation are carefully selected through the research of several variables, and human resource management (HRM) points are submitted for Japanese companies to consider.

2. Literature Review and Research Framework

2.1. *Beginning of business administration and motivation theory*

Study of motivation theory began approximately 100 years before business administration was acknowledged as a science. The founder of the American Business Administration, Taylor (1911) insisted that the first objective in management is to unite high wages with a low labor cost, and a person is considered willing to work if he is provided with even wages (p. 63). Mayo (1933) and Roethlisberger and Dickson (1939) and Roethlisberger (1941) argued that informal human relationships at the workplace motivate people to work. Maslow (1954) postulated the theory of human motivation, describing people's hierarchy of needs. He suggested that a person feels happiest or most satisfied when maximizing his or her own sense of self-ability, or self-actualization. Fayol (1916) argued that a person designs a plan, and when its success is reliable, an intellectual person is set to get the best satisfaction (e.g. Okamoto, 2000, p. 30). Likert (1961) solved the authority handover decisions in order to increase high productivity. Herzberg (1966) argued that a person can achieve high satisfaction from motivational factors including a sense of work accomplishment, performance evaluation, and personal growth. Assuming the above assertions, we focus on the research of job satisfaction.

2.2. Research focused on job satisfaction

Regarding "the employee requests investigation," Masato and Otagaki (1958) had said that human beings are organisms that attempt to satisfy their spiritual desire after achieving the minimum economic necessities of life (pp. 209–215). At the same time, Maier (1955) provides evidence from the United States regarding employees' wants or desires in their jobs (p. 412). The study by Masato, Otagaki, and Maier highlighted a tendency similar to Maslow's hierarchy theory (1954), which states that human desire rises to the highest level of self-actualization after achieving lower-level desires, such as physiological and safety needs. Herzberg (1966), influenced by Maslow, undertook an investigation from the hypothesis that a human being had a desire of the pain evasion animal and the mental growth desire.

As a result, he named a motivation factor as a job satisfaction factor, and a hygiene factor as an unsatisfactory factor. He claimed that both factors, the two factors theory of motivation and the hygiene factor, have different dimensions. Some authors have questioned the inclusion of "human relations in the workplace" in the classification of hygiene factors in the Japanese context of Herzberg's two factors theory (Sakuragi, 2006, p. 40). Some Japanese refer to good human relations as "friendly motivation," positioned in between extrinsic and intrinsic motivation (Nakahara, 2006, p. 118). Further, with respect to salary, if the amount affects the employee's motivation and development, some view it as a motivational factor rather than a hygiene factor. Therefore, job satisfaction or dissatisfaction is unitary, and a problem of each degree is not a dimensionally different concept (Hashimoto and Wakabayashi, 1974; Kanai and Takahashi, 2004; Graen, 1968). Thus, it cannot be said unconditionally that "human relations" and "wages" are hygiene factors. If human relations are smooth and an employee is motivated intrinsically, human relations cannot be excluded as a motivating factor.

2.3. Process theory and research theme

Studies related to job satisfaction are primarily classified into two categories by reviewing conventional studies. The first is the contents theory, which is a study of the workplace's job satisfaction component and implies employees' satisfaction levels (Maslow, 1954; Maier, (2nd edition, 1955 and 3rd edition, 1965); Argyris, 1957; Masato and Otagaki, 1958; Herzberg *et al.*, 1959; McGregor, 1960; Herzberg, 1966). Regarding the factors leading to job satisfaction, these investigators explain that the variable factor is not singular, but constructed from many complicated variables. The second category of study is the process theory, which explains the reason that influences job satisfaction factors based on consciousness and actions of employees. Two representative process theories are the Expectation Theory (Vroom, 1964; Porter and Lawler, 1968) and the Goal-Setting Theory (Locke and Latham, 1984), the latter implies that goal setting is an important motivation for work. Research methods described in the following section correspond to the process theory.

From the study described above, job satisfaction is the degree of an employee's satisfaction or dissatisfaction based on his or her perception of the work contents or the neighboring workplace environment, such as work conditions, human relations, wage, and position. The concept of job satisfaction has an influence on employees' consciousness and their actions to work in their organization (Sakuragi, 2006, p. 37). As this study emphasizes a degree of overall satisfaction, from a study perspective, we adopted an interval scale of five phases for the questionnaire survey. Therefore, we use the concept of intrinsic and extrinsic motivation to classify job satisfaction factors in detail. The intrinsic motivation factors are also referred to as personal factors, or a state in which an employee's mind is moved by a rewarding feeling, creative work, sense of competence, and fun in work itself (Deci, 1975; Kanai, 2006). The extrinsic motivation factor is an outside motivational reward, monetary or otherwise, and is the figure or action that an employee tries to work for to receive these rewards (Kanai, 2006, pp. 136–137). Discussions in this paper focus on intrinsic motivation factors.

Recently, the term "human resource management," or "HRM," is increasingly used. This includes not only the facilitation of employees' growth as "human resources," but also the development of company strategy

(Morishima, 2004, pp. 15–16). However, companies prefer to achieve labor costs reduction and increase the ratio of non-regular workers committed to profit rather than "fostering human resources" (Labour Economic White Paper, 2014). Thus, the paper considers that employees' job satisfaction is affected by intrinsic or extrinsic motivation, identifies these characteristics through a survey, and suggests a single direction to HRM.

2.4. Framework on research — questions

For our research, we sought to understand their influence on awareness and employee behavior rather than the constituent elements of job satisfaction factors. Therefore, this paper clarifies HRM's direction with an example of the job satisfaction of regular employees working for 23 wards of Tokyo and Middle-Ranking Companies listed on the Tokyo Stock Exchange's first section. In this procedure, (1) we identified the items considered as main job satisfaction factors by a preceding investigation; (2) we carefully selected and investigated these items in reference to the Minnesota Satisfaction Questionnaire (MSQ) short version (1967) by Weiss and others from the University of Minnesota, who have developed a model for the job satisfaction standard to prevent partiality of extraction items; and (3) subsequently, we administered a questionnaire and studied the employees' work consciousness and actions.

3. Method of Investigation in Actual Conditions

3.1. Development of the questionnaire structure

As the question items, or variables are not biased, the necessary items have to be added or modified. For example, the items added related to organizational commitment (Meyer and Allen, 1997) and work-life balance (Hall, 2002), and the resulting questionnaire comprises 33 items. The MSQ is the form for assessing the intrinsic and the extrinsic satisfaction of employees (Lartham, 2007 (Japanese version 2009, p. 406)). According to the definition of job satisfaction in this paper, we do not consider only the objectivity of job content and its surrounding environment in order to understand job satisfaction, but the employees' consciousness and behavior is also important. Therefore, to study employees' work and environment, we conduct a quantitative analysis to grasp the degree of satisfaction or dissatisfaction. For this, we combined the five-step interval scale and question choice methods to provide answers for the variables as shown in Table 1.

3.2. Contents of investigation

(1) Research purposes: To grasp the factors of job satisfaction or dissatisfaction of regular employees' workplace.
(2) Breakdown of regular employees as research subjects ($n = 474$): (1) company size and its range: Tokyo's 23 wards and its surrounding prefectures (Kanagawa, Saitama, and Chiba), Tokyo Stock Exchange' first section listed companies (5,000 around from 500 people before and after an employee scale); (2) age and gender: men and women, 474 people aged 20–59 years (323 men, 151 women. Average age: 39.8 years; (3) regular employees' occupational status: 234 general employees, 94 chiefs and assistant managers, 98 managers, and 48 directors.
(3) Research methodology: (1) conducted by online distribution and recovery of questionnaire survey forms; (2) Number of samples: 691 forms distributed, 474 valid responses, recovery rate 73.2%; (3) study period: February 18–22, 2011.

4. Results of the Investigation

4.1. Factors and reasons for their adoption

The objectives of this factor analysis are: (1) to find an immeasurable potential variable (factor) from a measurable variable, (2) to name the whole considering from a variable and quantity of load constituting each factor (factor name), and (3) to examine the correlation between each factor (inter-factor correlations); by doing so, we can understand the actual situation of employees' job satisfaction.

A factor pattern line of Table 1 is a line of the factor loading after an oblique rotation, or a promax rotation. Four factors having an eigenvalue of one or more were extracted, and the cumulative proportion of variance explained was 58.96%. The question variable at the time of the survey had 33 items, but the factor loading of the variable is 0.3 or less, and items over

Table 1.   Factor pattern (factor loading)

Variable	Factor 1	Factor 2	Factor 3	Factor 4
03. There is a sense of accomplishment in my current job.	0.8873	−0.0210	−0.0007	−0.0029
07. I can now demonstrate the ability and creativity to work.	0.8361	0.0125	−0.0201	0.0726
01. I am able to do desired job now in the workplace.	0.8331	−0.0078	0.0665	−0.0173
04. With the current work, I feel like I have a life worth living.	0.8185	−0.0089	−0.0033	0.0442
08. Now the work is right for me.	0.8177	0.0660	−0.0554	−0.0105
06. I feel my work is meaningful and I have a sense of mission.	0.76694	0.0511	−0.0049	−0.0057
09. I have grown through work.	0.6100	0.1171	0.0413	0.0968
12. The current joy is highly discretionary for me.	0.4735	−0.0229	0.00958	0.2283
13. The current work has been assigned in my hope.	0.4434	0.0737	0.0696	0.1193
16. Currently, I have been entrusted with a responsible work.	0.4288	0.1336	0.0536	0.1623
22. I think that my workplace communication skills are high.	−0.10093	0.8178	−0.1026	0.1425
19. Currently, the relationships between colleagues are good.	0.0997	0.7735	0.0278	−0.1383
23. I now have a coordination integer in the workplace.	−0.0046	0.7707	−0.0649	0.0775
20. Currently, the human relationship with the boss is good.	0.2239	0.6609	0.0628	−0.1670
21. I have a good evaluation of the workplace surroundings.	−0.0110	0.6519	0.1541	0.0654
25. I have an emotional attachment with the current company.	0.2551	0.4126	0.1619	0.0163
18. I enhance both work and leisure.	0.2401	0.3730	0.0208	0.1274
30. I'm convinced of the evaluation of the current company.	−0.0363	0.0310	0.9327	0.0154
31. I feel I have received appropriate treatment from the company.	0.0581	−0.0185	0.9130	−0.0335
27. My wages are more than the world average.	0.0080	−0.0433	0.5203	0.1252
29. Currently, I feel stable and have a sense of job security.	0.0683	0.0611	0.4678	−0.0313

(Continued)

Table 1.   (*Continued*)

Variable	Factor name			
	Factor 1	Factor 2	Factor 3	Factor 4
14. I have a joy that has not been experienced as much at any time.	0.0697	−0.0093	0.0380	0.7840
15. I actively undertake the job that can have various experiences.	0.1641	0.0665	−0.0191	0.7709
17. I make a self-investment for technology and capacity development.	0.1965	−0.0257	0.0349	0.3916
Factor correlation matrix by oblique rotation:				
Factor 2	0.5976			
Factor 3	0.5329	0.4599		
Factor 4	0.5486	0.4018	0.2934	
Eigenvalue	10.8918	1.8421	1.7197	1.1754

Note: (1) Question number of the item (variable) is not especially mean in reference number; (2) The statistics software used was Excel statistics 2012 ("Social Survey Research Information Co., Ltd.") for Microsoft Excel, 2010.

two factors more than 0.3 or more were also deleted. We conducted the factor analysis four times and deleted nine items. The result comprises the variables as shown in Table 1. In addition, we performed an exploratory factor analysis because this study did not provide a clear hypothesis about the behavior of the factor.

4.2. *Naming of factors and reasons*

A variable and load quantity to constitute each factor is important for naming it. The variable components in factor 1 are: "sense of accomplishment of work," "work that can demonstrate ability and creativity," "be able to do the desired work now," "to feel a life worth living to the current work," "to feel that the work is right for me," "to feel my work is meaningful and has a sense of mission," and "to feel that I have grown through work." These seven items have a positive load quantity, and have a response of "I think so" corresponding to the question variable. Further, employees' intrinsic motivation factors to work have a property that cannot be an incentive for other extrinsic monetary rewards. The other three items, or explanation variables, are: "work discretion is high," "the current work has been assigned in my hope," and "I have been entrusted with a responsible job." These items have a positive load quantity and are the origin of the previous seven items. From this, we named factor 1 as "sense of accomplishment by discretion characteristics."

Factor 2 comprises five items including "communicative competence of the workplace is high," "human relations with co-workers are good," "the workplace is cooperative," "human relations with bosses are good," and "I think that the neighboring evaluations are good." These items are the mild environmental elements of the need for affiliation, by McClellant (1961), such as the workplace that surrounds an employee, and has a positive load quantity. Such an environmental element enables the feelings of "I have attachment toward the company," and "I have to balance work and leisure." From this, we named factor 2 as "a feeling of affinity toward the workplace." Furthermore, factor 3 has two variables, including "I can understand the evaluation of the company," and "I am appropriately treated by the company," and have a positive load quantity. The factors that guarantee these are "an ordinary wage" and "employment stability." Therefore, we named factor 3 as "suitable treatment by the company." Finally, the variables of factor 4 include "I have a job that I have never experienced" and "I have to actively work for the experience," and have a positive load quantity. Employees who perform such actions intend to do a self-investment, and therefore we named factor 4 as "self-development."

5. Discussions on the Investigation

From the above four factors, we can consider the following characteristics of job satisfaction.

5.1. *Correlation among the four factors and characteristics of each factor*

(1) The analysis of this paper adopted the promax rotation, and the correlation of the four factors is shown in Table 1. As a result, the correlation of factor 3 and factor 4 is low (see Table 1).

(2) Factor 1

Keywords of explanatory variables for this factor are: "a sense of accomplishment, demonstrate ability, and creativity, having joy now in the workplace, life worth living, work that suits oneself, meaning and sense of mission, growth, discretion, hopeful arrangement, and job responsibility." As a result, employees feel "interest and meaning" in their jobs, and achieve high satisfaction from their work. Because of this fact, many employees obtain a sense of accomplishment when they feel growth occurs by being entrusted with a hopeful job rather than task obligation. This is referred to as "discretion characteristics" as indicated by McClelland (1961), and implies that employees obtain job satisfaction by doing the work they decide upon. This is the case that, "when we can act with the conquest of optimal challenge, for the first time we feel competent and self-decisive" (Deci, 1975; Japanese version, 1980, p. 69). Therefore, subordinates have the rights to select any means with respect to the target as the boss has instructed. We consider that "the fun of the challenge of work is to be able to determine on its own." (Okamoto, 2000, p. 4). This will be ascertained in the data from the study questionnaire (February 18–22, 2011).

First, regarding the efforts method and job attitude, the respondents answered that "it is possible to determine on their own regardless of the boss (rank 1), and it is possible to determine on their own after the boss' instructions (rank 2)." Further, the questionnaire allowed respondents to select one of the four choices, and 291 people or 61.4% responded "very satisfied + somewhat satisfied." As a result, the primary reason is "challenging for [the employee] because they will leave after boss' instructions," followed by "a challenging job because the boss will leave for me." The second rank is the same for men and women. Thus, to enhance job enrichment by employees "determining on their own," such an environment motivates employees intrinsically by providing work challenges as pointed out in factor 1, and the environment allows the employee to be immersed in their work.

(3) Factor 2

Employees were the serious consideration of "human relations in the workplace" in the preceding investigation. However, "a feeling of affinity" implies a wide sense of concepts, such as cooperation in the workplace and an evaluation of neighboring people, which are new discoveries made by the questionnaire survey. This "workplace environment is easy to work"[1] (Morishima, 2004, pp. 162–163). This workplace environment is nurtured by the desire of position and love (Maslow, 1954) and good human relations (Mayo, 1933; Roethlisberger and Dickson, 1939; Roethlisberger, 1941). The study's analysis of "behavior of human relations at the workplace" is a reference for this. According to this research, it is the employee's "human relationship to focus on work" and to emphasize most the workplace's human relations. He considers "human relations are useful in their work." However, employees also emphasize a "relationship as friends, regardless of the work." In addition, this "drive to bond" leads to the corporate culture of respecting teamwork and the underlying trust and friendship in the organization (Lawrence and Nohria, 2002). It is necessary to specially consider this in the management of Japanese companies for "a feeling of affinity" in the workplace.

(4) Factor 3

High load quantity was recognized for "consent for the evaluation of the company" and "appropriate treatment from the company" in a question related to fact-finding in this paper. However, "the world average wages," and "stability and sense of security of employment" had a load quantity lower than expected. It is considered that the subjects of the survey are regular employees of stable service companies. A similar tendency was seen in the comparative study between small, medium, and large factories by Masato. A high desire was observed, especially in the large factory setting, in "evaluating the company for the rewarding feeling and personal work rather than wages" as "factors close to the higher-order self-realization desire to say the spiritual needs or status requests" (Masato and Otagaki, 1958, pp. 203–215).

From this case, it can be asserted that if the employee receives a world average wage, they should develop a growing desire to work, which would be an intrinsic motivation factor. According to the questions choice method of survey, "wages" were, for both men and women,

---

[1] As an employee's social work environment, Morishima (2004) has pointed out the importance of the workplace without bullying and sexual harassment (p. 163).

primarily "wages corresponding to the work," followed by "world average wages," and "wages being due to the type and degree of difficulty of the work," consecutively. However, there were few "wages by age and years of service" in traditional Japanese companies. Further, the second and third positions are ranked differently by men and women, where women ranked the "world average wage" higher, and men focused on "work of the type and degree of difficulty." Lawrence and Nohria (2002) have proposed a reward system to differentiate between the outcomes of the organization, called "drive to acquire," in the four drives from several surveys.

(5) Factor 4

The self-development approach is the "opportunity to use your ideas" noted by Maier in previous studies (Maier, 3rd edition, 1965, pp. 472–473; Table 14.3). This is a new concept as factors that indicate intellectual curiosity and autonomy were not included in the prior study. This creates an internal and external network. The fact that employees may hope to participate actively in their work, even for self-investment, is a new discovery that was not seen in the prior survey. In this manner, Argyris (1957) said, the human always wants to grow, but the organization's environment persuades subordinates to be dependent and passive by the mechanism of power hierarchy, as noted in "Task (Work) Specialization" (p. 59) and the "Chain of Command" (p. 60). This continues to halt employees' growth (p. 60). Argyris suggested increasing opportunities for job ability to expand to affect the direction of conflicts between employees and the organization. He says that there is a need to improve the organization to achieve self-realization by exerting leadership.

In Japan, self-certification and in-house staff recruitment systems exist as concrete measures to exert such autonomous ability. The author questioned 94 people, who replied that they underwent a fact-finding[2]

---

[2] The research scope is full-time employees working at the First Section of the Tokyo Stock Exchange locations in Kanto, Kinki, Tohoku, and Chugoku. The target audience is men and women aged 18–65, of which 177 are general permanent employees and 57 managers. Across the company, the number of employees is more than 2,000 and the company notes annual sales of over 100 billion yen (Okamoto, 2010, p. 157, p. 219).

self-assessment system (February 3–4, 2010). The results, based on possible answers from five choices were: (1) Employees were "hopeful to receive work they wanted to do" (92.6%); (2) "Management by individuals' objectives" (75.5%); (3) "Report of the qualifications acquired" (59.6%); and (4) "Promotion" (33.0%). From these results, a strong action is indicated by employees' position on autonomous work.

5.2. Characteristics of job satisfaction factors

In this way, the job satisfaction characteristics indicated by this study's employees combines the four concepts of "sense of accomplishment at the discretion" with respect to work, "a sense of affinity to the workplace," "suitable treatment from a company," and "self-development."

However, in the recently added questionnaires, the load amounts for the items that "heartily love the company," "work hard to obtain revenue," and "want career advancement" were low. Therefore, these were not considered factors necessary to increase recent employees' job satisfaction. This almost agrees with employees' consciousness to choose suitable work by themselves rather than to choose the future of a company for the new employees that we considered in Section 1. This tendency has been noted as a common feature, from high school students to adults. In other words, it is intrinsically motivated.

6. Conclusion

6.1. Intrinsic motivation and human resource management (HRM)

Based on the results of factor analysis, the following conclusions are derived from Section 5.1(2)–(5).

(1) From Section 5.1(2), employees are driven by a strong motivation to obtain a "sense of accomplishment" and recognition that "is determined by myself" about work. Therefore, management's seedling of awareness regarding the employee is because of a desire to incite work motivation. Among the four factors, factor 1 showed the highest load with a "sense of accomplishment by decision." Further, in an option method study that was conducted simultaneously, the first choice, for both men and

women, was "possible to determine on their own regardless of the boss (42.2%)," followed by "possible to determine on their own after the boss' instructions (39.7%)."

As discussed earlier, the factor items that are the most highly motivational in young people were "discretion rewarding" and "interesting work itself," rather than "the company." It is understood that the intrinsic motivation from the discussion above is strong. Providing the freedom of choice to employees increases their confidence and autonomy, thus making it possible to promote interest in problem solving. As a result, they are able to tackle problems with full responsibility, and the sense of accomplishment at that time will lead to higher satisfaction than when they are allocated from others [self-determination theory: Deci and Ryan, 1990; Ryan and Deci, 2000; Latham, 2007 (Japanese Version, 2009, Supervisor of translation); Kanai, p. 220)].

(2) From Section 5.1(3), employees are motivated by the workplace atmosphere and environment as well as the "work itself." Factor 2, an "affinity, desire, or sense of affinity" is said to have mainly human relations in the workplace, and is indicative of the workplace atmosphere. Since this has the highest load among the four factors, we cannot exclude this hygiene factor.

The survey by Nohria, *et al.* (2002) led to four drives, and found that the "drive to bond" is intended to foster a corporate culture that develops from respect for teamwork by the organization. This requires special consideration in the management of Japanese companies with respect to the "feeling of affinity for the workplace" found in factor 2.

(3) From Section 5.1(4), employees are motivated to be treated according to the outcomes of their own hard work. However, this treatment is not necessarily wages, or an extrinsic reward, but is also motivated by intrinsic rewards. Employees become highly motivated in some cases of appropriate company evaluation. The desires for "the rewarding feeling of work" and "evaluation of the company for individual work rather than wages" were also seen in the case studies by Masato (1958) and Maier (1955, 1965).

According to the survey regarding wages using the question choice method, for both men and women, first place was the "wage appropriate to their work styles," followed by the "world average wage," "wages by the type and degree of difficulty of the job," and "wages by age and length of service," consecutively. This implies that employees want to gain more than the world's average wages, but this is not absolute (see question factor No. 27 of factor 3).

However, employees desire evaluations and treatments commensurate with their performance, and thus do their best to accomplish results (factors 1 and 3). This wage counteracts the "opinion that extrinsic motivation factors of money, etc. reduce the intrinsic motivation" (Deci, 1975). In Japan, some researchers noted that the deleterious effects of reward on intrinsic motivation occur only in very limited conditions[3] (Okochi *et al.*, 2006, p. 119).

(4) From Section 5.1(5), employees have the desire of "I want to grow," but the organization has the property to be passive, or dependent upon, the behavior of subordinates by the mechanism of power hierarchy, or the bureaucracy's organization. Hence, the organization is required to devise management strategies to help employees who push the company's subordinates. The self-development approach is equivalent to the opportunity to take advantage of the self-idea (creative) by Maier (1965). The fact that employees want to join actively in work, even by self-investment, is a new discovery that was not shown in the preceding survey.

For this reason, the organization needs to increase the opportunity for employees to demonstrate their abilities, and to improve the organization to achieve self-realization by exercising leadership (Argyris, 1957). In Japan, there are self-reporting and internal recruitment systems. According to the results of this study (February 3–4, 2010), this research indicates that employees prefer self-declaration of (1) "the hope of work we want" (92.6%); (2) "to be related to the management by objectives of the individual" (75.5%); (3) "declaration of the acquired qualification" (59.6%); and (4) "matters relating to promotion" (33.0%) (multiple answers possible from five choices). This commitment to employees' autonomous work shows its strength comes from above.

6.2. Perspectives of HRM

The results are summarized in the following four points: (1) Organizations can incite a sense of accomplishment by employees having a sense of "to

---

[3]The use of remuneration impacts how this is determined (Okochi *et al.*, 2006, p. 120).

decide this by oneself." (2) Organizations can motivate employees not only by work, but also by building a workplace atmosphere that cherishes the people. (3) Organizations can incite work motivation by intrinsic rewards to reward employees' hard work, and not just wages. (4) Organizations support opportunities for employees' self-development, and can increase their motivation by designing the job for employees to "feel oneself growing."

7. Future Research

(1) All men and women surveyed, indicated "we want to decide on our own" as to how to proceed with the work. Such a trend is considered a manifestation of western-type emphasis on the individual seen recently in Japanese employees, as previously described in Section 2.1. Western researchers have said that "to emphasize the importance of individual choice is a peculiar western cultural phenomenon" [d'Ailly, 2004; Latham, 2007 (Japanese Version, 2009, Supervisor of translation); Kanai, p. 222]. The role of HRM needs to be reexamined as it pertains to the conventional group mentality in Japan.

(2) In this paper, the "feeling of affinity to the workplace" centered on human relationships was revealed to have a significant effect on employee motivation (as previously described in Section 5.1(3)). It is assumed that the results of some studies were between extrinsic and intrinsic motivation. Hence, we cannot say categorically that the factor of human relations is the hygiene factor, and not the motivation factor. A more detailed survey and study is required.

(3) Wage is not an absolute factor necessary for job satisfaction, as suggested by previous studies and this research. Researchers tended to focus on intrinsic motivation factors rather than "wage (but at least the world average wage required)," as previously described in Section 5.1(4). More detailed research is required to address this issue thoroughly.

(4) Some researchers suggest that "If you strengthen the extrinsic motivation (especially economic rewards), the intrinsic motivation is weakened" (Deci, 1975). Another researcher argues that the adverse effect of reward occurs only in very limited conditions, as noted in the above Section 6.1(3).

We were not able to issue an answer to this problem in light of the survey's purpose. Therefore, it is necessary to develop a related future demonstration case.

References

Argyris, C. (1957). *Personality and Organization: The Conflict Between System and the Individual.* New York: Harper & Brothers.

d'Ailly, H. (2004). The role of choice in children's leaning: A distinctive cultural and gender difference in efficacy, interest and effort. *Canadian Journal of Behavioural Science* 36: 17–29.

Deci, E. L. (1975). *Intrinsic Motivation.* New York, NY: Plenum. [Japanese Version: translator; Ando N. and Ishida U. (1980), Seishin Syobou (in Japanese)].

Deci, E. L. and R. M. Ryan (1990). A Motivational Approach to Self: Integration in Personality, In R. Dienstbier (Ed.), *Nebrasca Symposium on Motivation*, Vol. 38, pp. 237–288. Lincoln: University of Nebrasca Press.

Fayol, H. (1916). *Administration Industrielle et Générale.*

Graen, G. B. (1968). Testing traditional and two-factor hypotheses concerning job satisfaction. *Journal of Applied Psychology* 52: 366–371.

Hall, D. T. (2002). *Careers In and Out of Organizations.* Sage Publications, Inc.

Hashimoto, M. and M. Wakabayashi (1974). Some Problems on Herzberg's "Two-Factor Theory of Job Satisfaction": A Review. *Keio University Sociology Graduate School Bulletin*, No. 14, pp. 19–30 (in Japanese).

Herzberg, F., B. Mausner, and B. Snyderman (1959). *The Motivation to Work.* New York: John Wiley & Sons.

Herzberg, F. (1966). Work and the Nature of Man. World Publishing.

Japan Productivity Center and Economic Youth Council (2009). *Research Report in relation to New Employees and Awareness of working* (in Japanese).

Japan Federation of Employers' Associations (1995). *'Japan Management Systems' of the new times* (in Japanese).

JILPT Investigation Series No. 15 (March 2006). *Working Styles of the Japanese in the Diversification of Employment: Survey* (1st) (in Japanese). Available at : http://www.jil.go.jp/institute/research/documents/015/research015_00.pdf; Accessed July 19, 2016.

Kanai, T. (2006). *Motivation for all people to work.* NTT Publisher. (in Japanese).

Kanai, T. and K. Takahashi (2004). *How to think of Organizational Behavior*, Toyokeizai Shinpousha (in Japanese).

Labour Economic White Paper (2006) (in Japanese).

Labour Economic White Paper (2014) (in Japanese).

Labor force survey by the Ministry of Internal Affairs and Communications Statistics Bureau (2015).

Lartham, G. P. (2007). *Work Motivation: History, Theory, Research, and Practice.* Sage Publications. [Japanese Version, 2009, Supervisor of translation; Kanai, T., Translator; Yoda, T., NTT Publisher (in Japanese)].

Lawrence, P. R. and N. Nohria (2002). *Driven: How Human Nature Shapers Our Choices.* Jossey-Bass.

Lepak, D. P. and S. A. Snell (1999). The human resource architecture: Toward a theory of human capital allocation and development. *Academy of management Review* 24(1): 31–48.

Likert, R. (1961). *New Patterns of Management.* New York: McGraw-Hill.

Locke, E. A. and G. P. Latham (1984). *Goal setting: A motivational technique that works!* Englewood Cliffs, NJ: Prentice Hall.

Masato, S. and M. Otagaki (1958). *Safety labor and labor psychology* (business management Zensho 82 volumes) Nihon Keizai-shinbunsha (in Japanese).

Maier, N. R. F. (1955/1965). *Psychology in Industry* (2nd ed./3rd ed.). Houghton Mifflin Co.

Maslow, A. H. (1954). *Motivation and Personality.* New York: Harper & Row.

Mayo, G. E. (1933). *The Human Problems of an Industrial Civilization.* The Macmillan Company.

McClellant, D. C. (1961). *The Achieving Society.* New York: Free Press.

McGregor, D. (1960). *The Human Side of Enterprise.* New York: MaGraw-Hill.

Meyer, J. P. and N. J. Allen (1997). Commitment in the Workplace, Sage Publication.

Morishima, M. (2004). *Introduction to Human Resource Management.* Nikkeishinbun Publisher (in Japanese).

Nakahara, J. (ed.) (2006). *Corporate Human Resource Development Introductory.* Diamond-Sha (in Japanese).

Okamoto, E. (2000). *Human sides on organization and information: from sightseeing of management.* Hakuto-shobo(in Japanese).

Okamoto, E. (2010). *From an organizational management to autonomous management.* Hakuto-shobo (in Japanese).

Okochi, H. *et al.* (2006). Does reward weaken intrinsic motivation? *Osaka kyoiku University Bulletin,* No. IV department, 54(2): 115–123 (in Japanese).

Porter, L. W. and E. E. Lawler (1968). *Managerial attitudes and performance.* Homewood, IL: Irwin.

Roethlisberger, F. J. (1941). *Management and Morale.* Harvard University Press.

Roethlisberger, F. J. and W. J. Dickson (1939). *Management and the Worker*. Harvard University Press.

Ryan, R. M. and E. L. Deci (2000). Self-determination theory and the facilitation of intrinsic motivation, social development, and well-being. *American Psychologist* 55: 68–78.

Sakuragi, A. (2006). Structure of job satisfaction concept and function. *Toyohashi Sozo University* 10: 37–47 (in Japanese).

Taylor, F. W. (1911). *The Principles of Scientific Management*. Harper & Brothers Publishers.

Vroom, V. H. (1964). *Work and Motivation*. New York: John Wiley & Sons.

Weiss, D. J., Dawis, R. V., England, G. W., and Lofquist, L. H., (1967). *Manual for the Minnesota Satisfaction Questionnaire*. Minnesota Studies in Vocational Rehabilitation, 22.

Japanese Multinational Enterprises' Preventive Actions Against Transfer Pricing Taxation

Koji Umeda

Researcher, Graduate School of Economics,
Nagoya City University, Japan

1. Introduction

This paper investigates the actions taken by Japanese multinational enterprises (JMNEs) against the transfer pricing taxation (TPT) using survey data and the management accounting perspective.[1] As business globalization intensifies, intra-group transactions within multinational enterprise groups[2] (MNEgrps) increase. The JMNEs' main concern is constructing their management control systems (MCS) as MNEgrps and remaining compliant with the TPT.

The TPT is a tax system requiring multinational enterprises (MNEs) to determine their corporate income tax on the assumption that they trade with their foreign affiliates (FAs) at a theoretical transfer price, the "arm's length price (ALP)". For example, an MNE that exports goods to its FAs at an international transfer price (ITP: an actual price given for each transaction)

---

[1] This paper's discussion of JMNEs' actions against the TPT is based on Umeda (2012, 2013).

[2] A multinational enterprise group (MNEgrp) is a business group consisting of a parent company and foreign affiliates. A multinational enterprise (MNE) is the parent company of a multinational enterprise group. A Japanese multinational enterprise (JMNE) is the Japanese parent company of a multinational enterprise group.

Japanese Management and International Studies Vol. 13:
Management of Innovation Strategy in Japanese Companies
World Scientific Publishing Company, September 2016

lower than the ALP, must determine its income tax by adding the income transfer overseas (ITO), calculated from the variance between the ITP and ALP, to its book income. This tax calculation process is called a "tax adjustment." Back taxes are usually charged to MNEs that neglect to perform a tax adjustment, even if an ITO is generated. The TPT was designed to ensure that MNEs calculated their income tax correctly rather than to interfere with ITP settings among MNEgrps. However, an MNE will likely set its ITP with reference to the TPT and its application by tax authorities (Kaneko, 1996).

Thus, excessive responses to the TPT may be an obstacle to an international pricing strategy or a performance evaluation system that uses MNEgrps' profit indexes. Therefore, exploring the actions that JMNEs take to comply with the TPT is important. The literature has identified the environmental factors that JMNEs consider important when setting their ITP but does not provide rich information on this paper's main concern.

The transfer pricing issue should be discussed in terms of both international tax law and management accounting, but these dimensions have been treated separately so far. This study contributes to the literature by showing that a discussion of international transfer pricing needs an interdisciplinary approach.

This paper consists of six sections. Section 2 explains the TPT and the calculation of the ALP. Section 3 reviews the literature, presents two research questions, and proposes a research framework and a hypothesis. Section 4 explains this study's research method. Section 5 presents the results and discusses the actions that JMNEs have taken. Finally, Section 6 concludes this paper.

2. The Method of Calculating the ALP and Issues with the TPT

2.1. Traditional transaction methods

The TPT is a tax system developed in the U.S. Its substantial beginning was the 1968 revisions of the Department of the Treasury regulations, specifically section 482 of the Internal Revenue Code (IRC482; Mochizuki, 2007). The result was three transfer pricing methods (called the "traditional transaction methods"): Comparable Uncontrolled Pricing (CUP), Cost Plus (CP), and Resale Price method (RP). An OECD tax committee regulates the traditional transaction methods under the 1979 OECD transfer pricing guidelines (OECD, 1979) through Japan's Special Measures concerning Taxation, section 66.4.2, enacted in 2004 (Mochizuki, 2007).

By this method, an MNE calculates its ITO to FAs based on the price variance between its ITP and the ALP. For export transactions, the ITO amount is calculated as the volume of transactions × (ALP–ITP). The method to be used depends on the comparability between a "controlled" (i.e. intra-group) transaction and an "uncontrolled" transaction (i.e. with an independent company). Significantly, however, MNEs often cannot apply these methods because they lack the comparable uncontrolled transactions used to determine the ALP.

2.2. *Transactional Net Margin Method*

The OECD introduced the Transactional Net Margin Method (TNMM) in 1995 guidelines; it was enacted in 2004 in Japan by the Order for Enforcement of Act 39.12.8 under section 66.4 of the Special Measures concerning Taxation (OECD, 1995; Yanai, 1999; Mochizuki, 2007). Initially, the TNMM was a revision of the RP or CP method. Its purpose was to make it easy for MNEs to find uncontrolled transactions. The TNMM eased the strictness of the comparability between controlled and uncontrolled transactions by using an operating income ratio indicator instead of a gross profit ratio indicator. As Iimori (2010) pointed out, however, though the examining indicator changed, the difficulty of finding comparable uncontrolled transactions remained.

Finally, the tax authorities increased the TNMM's applicability by expanding the examination targets from limited transactions to business units and whole companies, thus turning the TNMM into a method similar to the Comparable Profit Method (CPM) introduced in the U.S. through the 1993 Regulations and the 1994 Regulations under IRC482.

In the TNMM and CPM, the ITO is calculated without comparable uncontrolled transactions, but by comparing the operating income ratios to its FA sales and those of some independent companies.[3] For example, if the FA's operating income ratios exceed the arm's length income ratio range

---

[3] The CPM requests that, between MNEs and FAs, the operating income ratios of the one without significant intangible assets be used for the calculation. The FAs are always more likely to lack significant intangible assets.

(composed of the operating income ratios of several independent companies), it would be concluded that ITO from the MNE to the FA was generated. The ITO amount is calculated as Sales amount of the FA × (operating income ratios to the sales of the FA — averaged operating income ratios of the some independent companies).

Mori *et al.* (2008) stated that the TNMM is a compromise with the CPM, but both methods risk charging tax that includes more than just transfer pricing factors, such as FA efforts or unordinary market environments, because operating income is usually affected by such factors.

2.3. Issues with the TPT

We described the issues with the TPT by discussing the ALP calculation method; however, the TPT has another, more basic, issue — the "international double taxation" or "economical double taxation" issue. Tax adjustments according to the TPT force MNEs to impose double taxation on the MNEgrp because the FAs are not allowed to deduct the same amount of ITO, calculated by MNEs, from their book income, even when the ALP of the import goods from the MNE is higher than the actual ITP. The easiest way for MNEs to avoid double taxation is to adjust the ITP so that an ITO will not be generated. However, excessive price adjustments are likely to reduce the FAs' profits.

3. Literature Review and Research Framework

3.1. Literature

Several research surveys have focused on JMNEs' international transfer pricing policies (Shimizu, 1994, 1999; Shiiba, 2007; Lee and Kazusa, 2009). They investigated the environmental factors that JMNEs considered when setting the ITP. These surveys show that the "maximization of profit in MNE group" and "compliance with each nation's tax legislation" are always highly ranked and that "performance evaluation of foreign subsidiaries" is falling in the rankings[4] (see Table 1). However, the literature has not determined the actions JMNEs have taken to handle their ITP under the TPT.

---

[4] The same tendency can be seen in Tang's continuous surveys on U.S. MNEs (Tang, 1979, 1992, 2002).

Table 1. Ranking of importance of environmental variables

Environmental variables	Shimizu (1994)	Shimizu (1999)	Shiiba (2007)	Lee and Kazusa (2009)
Maximization of overall profit to the MNE group	2,3	2	2	1
Compliance with each nation's tax and other legislation			1	2
The competitiveness of foreign subsidiaries	1	1	3	3
Fluctuation of foreign exchange rates in foreign countries				4
Difference in income tax rates and tax legislation among countries	6	5	6	5
Maintaining good relationships with business partner in foreign country			5	6
Cash flows in foreign subsidiaries			4	6
Rate of customs duties and customs legislation where the subsidiary operates				8
Performance evaluation of foreign subsidiaries	4		5	9
Restrictions on repartriation of profits of dividends	5	4	9	
Maintaining good relationships with host governments			8	
Easiness			7	
Maximization of foreign subsidiary's profit		3		
Maximization of parent company's profit	7	6		
Overall group tax amount		7		
Tax amount of parent company		8		

Note: This table is the same as Table 5 in Umeda (2012).
Sources: Shimizu (1994, p. 131), Shimizu (1999, p. 106), Shiiba (2007, p. 16) and Lee and Kazusa (2009, p. 118).

3.2. Research framework

3.2.1. Actions taken when JMNEs recognize the ITO

Describing the actions that JMNEs takes to handle their ITP under the TPT requires information about how they resolve the ITO after intra-group transactions begin as well as how they set their ITP policy. There is always a risk of an ITO, even when MNEs set their initial ITP to be compliant with the ALP because the ALP is likely to change according to changes in the price of transactions with independent companies or in the methods of calculating the ALP. Therefore, this study poses the following research question:

Research Question 1: What actions have JMNEs taken when they recognize the ITO?

Mori (2000) presents a typology of the actions taken against the TPT. The "non-aligned type" of MNE resolves the ITO through tax adjustments. The TPT was designed for this type (Kaneko, 1996). The problem with the non-aligned type is the double taxation issue, as mentioned in Section 2. The "aligned type" of MNE resolves the ITO by adjusting the ITP; the disadvantage is the likelihood of the reduced FAs' profits. Therefore, identifying the actions JMNEs have taken against the TPT requires that we know which method — tax adjustment or ITP adjustment — has been used when they recognize the ITO.

3.2.2. The actions of JMNEs applying the TNMM

However, investigating JMNEs' method of resolving the ITO in intra-group transactions is insufficient for identifying the actions JMNEs have taken against the TPT. As stated in Section 2, some MNEs cannot apply the TNMM for lack of uncontrolled comparable transactions (i.e. transactions with independent companies). For an MNE applying the TNMM, the higher the FA's profit, the higher the risk of an ITO. Accordingly, an MNE applying the TNMM is likely to control its FA's profit to keep it within non-taxable range; an ITP adjustment is one method of doing this, but its effect is usually limited. Thus, MNEs applying the TNMM need another method of controlling their FA's profit. Accordingly, this study poses the following research question:

Research Question 2: What actions have JMNEs applying the TNMM taken to reduce the risk of TPT application?

Solomon (1965) argued that decision-making authority over sales and manufacturing must be delegated from headquarters to each business division for the system to be successful. Authority over sales includes determining the timing of new product launches, accepting or rejecting orders from customers, and setting new product prices. Authority over manufacturing includes deciding to make new products or components internally or to outsource them to parties such as other divisions within the company or independent companies. The decision-making authorities over sales and manufacturing affect firm profits.

The above discussion suggests that MNEs applying the TNMM should maintain decision-making authority over the sales and manufacturing of their FAs in order to control their profits. For MNEs applying traditional transaction methods, however, the FAs' profits are not a direct cause of an ITO. This study therefore proposes the following:

Hypothesis: *The MNEs applying the TNMM tend to centralize decision-making authority over sales and manufacturing more than do MNEs applying traditional transaction methods.*

4. Research Method

This study distributed mail-in surveys to Japanese MNEs in order to answer the above research questions. The questionnaires were delivered in May 2011, and all responses were received by the end of July 2011. The sample consists of 1,069 Japanese manufacturing firms listed, and 269 manufacturing firms not listed, on the Tokyo Stock Exchange. Of the 1,069 questionnaires sent, 55 were usable; of the 269 questionnaires sent, 15 were usable (see Table 2). The overall usable response rate was 5.5%.

The questionnaires contained 20 questions. Table 3 shows the questions and their answer categories. The survey asked MNEs to select a representative FA from each of two regional groups. The first region comprises North and South America ("The Americas") and Europe. The second comprises Asia, including Australia and excluding Japan. The survey asked JMNEs to answer questions about their controlled transactions with their FAs in each region.

The questions concerned (1) their method of resolving the ITO, (2) their method of calculating the ALP, and (3) their pattern of decision-making authority over sales and manufacturing. For questions (1) and (2), the JMNEs were asked to answer questions about exported finished goods and components, respectively. Question (1) was intended to produce answers

Table 2.   Industrial classification of the respondent firms

Industry	Listed on the Tokyo Stock Exchange		Not listed		Total	
	Number of firms	Percent of total	Number of firms	Percent of total	Number of firms	Percent of total
Food	3	5.1	1	6.7	4	5.4
Apparel, Textile	1	1.7	1	6.7	2	2.7
Chemicals	6	10.2	0	0.0	6	8.1
Pharmaceuticals	2	3.4	0	0.0	2	2.7
Rubber Products	1	1.7	0	0.0	1	1.4
Iron and Steel	2	3.4	1	6.7	3	4.1
Non-ferrous Metal	4	6.8	0	0.0	4	5.4
Metal Products	4	6.8	0	0.0	4	5.4
Machinery and Equipments	5	8.5	3	20.0	8	10.8
Electronics, Appliances	14	23.7	2	13.3	16	21.6
Transportation	11	18.6	3	20.0	14	18.9
Precision Equipment	2	3.4	3	20.0	5	6.8
Other Products	4	6.8	1	6.7	5	6.8
Total	59	100.0	15	100.0	74	100.0

Note: This table is the same as Table 7 in Umeda (2012) and Table 2 in Umeda (2013).

Table 3.   Variables and answer category in questionnaires

Variables (Question)	Answer category (single answer method)
(1) The method of resolving ITO	1: Gradual adjustment of ITP
	2: Lump sum ITP adjustment at the year end
	3: Adjustment by Advanced Pricing Arrangement
	4: Tax adjustment (No adjustment of ITP)
	5: Other
(2) The method of calculating the ALP	1: CUP method, 2: RP method, 3: CP method, 4: TNMM, 5: RPSM, 6: Profit split method
(3) The pattern of decision-making authority over sales and manufacturing functions	1: Parent company (MNE) decides sales and manufacturing matters
	2: Foreign affiliate (FA) decides sales matters and parent decides manufacturing matters
	3: Foreign affiliate (FA) decides sales and manufacturing matters

Note: This table is the same as Table 3 in Umeda (2013). RPSM means the Residual Profit Split Method.

to research question 1, while questions (2) and (3) were intended to address the hypothesis and research question 2. The JMNEs were required to select one appropriate answer category from each question.

5. Results and Discussion

5.1. Results

Tables 4 and 5 show how the respondent JMNEs resolve their ITO for "Finished Goods" and "Components" transactions. The method used most frequently was the "gradual adjustment of ITP" in both regions for both transactions. Including "Lump sum adjustment at year end," more than 56% of the respondents adjusted their ITPs. On the other hand, the number of JMNEs that used "tax adjustment (No adjustment of ITP)" was less than 17%, while less than 22% used "adjustment by Advanced Pricing Arrangement."[5]

Table 4. The methods of resolving ITO

The method of resolving ITO	The Americas and Europe		Asia	
	Number of firms	Percent of total	Number of firms	Percent of total
Finished Goods				
Gradual adjustment of ITP	27	52.9	37	64.9
Lump sum ITP adjustment at the year end	2	3.9	3	5.3
Adjustment by advance pricing arrangement (APA)	11	21.6	4	7.0
Tax adjustment (no adjustment of ITP)	7	13.7	8	14.0
Other	4	7.8	5	8.8
Total	51	100.0	57	100.0

Note: Twenty-three responses in the Americas and Europe, and 17 responses in Asia are missing because they were not applicable. This table is the same as Table 12 in Umeda (2012).

---

[5] Advanced Pricing Arrangement (APA) is a system developed by Japanese tax authorities, which more than 30 countries have adopted. Under the APA, companies and tax authorities determine the method of ALP calculation and the adjustment method when ITO is generated during some future period. The main advantage of the APA is that a MNE group can avoid double taxation.

Table 5.   The methods of resolving ITO

The method of resolving ITO	The Americas and Europe		Asia	
	Number of firms	Percent of total	Number of firms	Percent of total
Components				
Gradual adjustment of ITP	26	53.1	36	60.0
Lump sum ITP adjustment at the year end	4	8.2	5	8.3
Adjustment by APA	6	12.2	3	5.0
Tax adjustment (No adjustment of ITP)	7	14.3	9	15.0
Other	6	12.2	7	11.7
Total	49	100.0	60	100.0

Note: Twenty-five responses in the Americas and Europe, and 14 responses in Asia are missing because they were not applicable. This table is the same as Table 12 in Umeda (2012).

Tables 6 and 7 illustrate the results of the test of the hypothesis, verified using the chi-square test. For both "Finished Goods" and "Components" transactions, the relationship between the two variables was significant at less than a 5% level in both regions. Therefore, the hypothesis is supported.

5.2. Discussion

As described in Section 1, the TPT was not designed to affect MNEgrps' ITP policies. However, this survey finds that more than 56% of JMNEs resolve their ITO by adjusting their ITP rather than through tax adjustments, implying that JMNEs intend to prevent double taxation and that the ITP-controlling policy of many JMNEs is affected by the TPT.

The results of the hypothesis tests for "Finished Goods" and "Components" supported the hypothesis: MNEs applying the TNMM tend to centralize decision-making authority over sales and manufacturing more than do MNEs applying traditional transaction methods, and they do so to control their FAs' profits.

When a too-profitable FA receives a new profitable business, the MNE may direct the FA to control only sales and put another non-profitable FA in charge of manufacturing. If the MNE directs the non-profitable FA to export its products with a high manufacturing margin and the profitable FA to resell

Table 6.   The pattern of decision-making authority and transfer pricing methods finished goods

Decision-making authority over sales and manufacturing	Finished Goods		
	Transfer pricing methods		
	Traditional transaction methods	TNMM	Total
The Americas and Europe			
Parent company (MNE) decides sales and manufacturing matters	7	15	22
Foreign affiliates (FA) decide sales matters and parent decides manufacturing matters	5	11	16
Foreign affiliates (FA) decide sales and manufacturing matters	11	3	14
Total	23	29	52

Twenty-two responses are missing because they were not applicable. Chi-square value is 9.2. The degree of freedom is 2. *P*-value is 0.010. **The relationship is significant at 1% level.**

Asia			
Parent company (MNE) decides sales and manufacturing matters	11	17	28
Foreign affiliates (FA) decide sales matters and parent decides manufacturing matters	11	10	21
Foreign affiliates (FA) decide sales and manufacturing matters	10	2	12
Total	32	29	61

Thirteen responses are missing because they were not applicable. Chi-square value is 6.5. The degree of freedom is 2. *P*-value is 0.038. **The relationship is significant at 5% level.**

Note: This table is the same as Table 7 in Umeda (2013).

Table 7. The pattern of decision-making authority and transfer pricing methods components

	Components		
	Transfer pricing methods		
Decision-making authority over sales and manufacturing	Traditional transaction methods	TNMM	Total
The Americas and Europe			
Parent company (MNE) decides sales and manufacturing matters	9	14	23
Foreign affiliates (FA) decide sales matters and parent decides manufacturing matters	5	10	15
Foreign affiliates (FA) decide sales and manufacturing matters	11	1	12
Total	25	25	50

Twenty-four responses are missing because they were not applicable.
Chi-square value is 11.1. The degree of freedom is 2. *P*-value is 0.003.
The relationship is significant at 1% level.

Asia			
Parent company (MNE) decides sales and manufacturing matters	13	16	29
Foreign affiliates (FA) decide sales matters and parent decides manufacturing matters	11	9	20
Foreign affiliates (FA) decide sales and manufacturing matters 11	11	1	12
Total	35	26	61

Thirteen responses are missing because they were not applicable.
Chi-square value is 7.7. The degree of freedom is 2. *P*-value is 0.021.
The relationship is significant at 2.5% level.

Note: This table is the same as Table 8 in Umeda (2013).

the products with a low sales margin, the profitable FA's profits will decrease, as will the risk of an ITO.

Therefore, JMNEs tend to take preventive actions against TPT application to avoid double taxation or minimize the imposition of back taxes.

6. Conclusion

This paper investigated the actions JMNEs have taken against the TPT and produced two main empirical findings. First, many JMNEs adjust their transaction ITPs to resolve their ITO. Second, MNEs applying the TNMM are likely to centralize decision-making over sales and manufacturing to contain their FAs' profits within a non-taxable range. Thus, many JMNEs have taken preventive action against TPT application to avoid back taxes and double taxation.

The results imply that, though the TPT was not intended to interfere with ITP practices nor performance evaluation systems based on an FA's profit index, it does seem to interfere considerably: the more an MNE strengthens its preventive actions against TPT application, the more it depresses its FAs' profits.

However, this study is limited by its relatively small sample. Additional surveys and testing are needed. Moreover, future studies should investigate what types of MCS have been introduced by JMNEs to manage their FAs if the TPT has interfered with performance evaluation systems based on FAs' profit indexes. Answers to these questions will advance the global management accounting research.

References

Iimori, K. (2010) (in Japanese). Nihon ni okeru dokuritsu kigyokan kakaku no genjō to mondaiten. Honjo, Tasku (ed.), Iten kakaku zeisei sikkō no riron to jitsumu, *Ookura Zaimu Kyokai*, pp. 541–554.

Kaneko, H. (1996) (in Japanese). *Shyotoku kazei no hō to seisaku ;Syotoku kazei no kiso riron (2/2)*, Yuhikaku Publishing Co., Ltd.

Lee, K. and Y. Kazusa (2009) (in Japanese). Nihon kigyo no kokusai iten kakau no settei no kansuru jittai chōsa. *Melco Journal of Management Accounting Research* 2: 111–126.

Mochizuki, F. (2007) (in Japanese). *Nichibei iten kakaku no seido to tekiyō; Mukei shisan torihiki wo chushin ni*, Okura Zaimu Kyokai.

Mori, N. (2000) (in Japanese). Keiei kōdō to shiteno iten kakaku wo meguru kadai to taiō. *International Taxation* 20(1): 57–60.

Mori, N., K. Suzuki, Y. Suzuki, M. Iketani, and K. Maeda (2008) (in Japanese). National Economic Research Associates (ed.), *Iten kakaku no keizai bunseki; Chōka rieki no kizoku to sangyo betsu mukei shisan no kachi hyōka*, Chuokeizai-sha, Inc.

OECD (1979). *Transfer Pricing and Multinational Enterprises; Report of the OECD Committee on Fiscal Affairs 1979*, Paris: OECD.

OECD (1995). *OECD Transfer Pricing Guidelines for Multinational Enterprises and Tax Administrations 1995*, Paris: OECD.

Shiiba, A. (2007) (in Japanese). Takokuseki kigyo ni okeru kokusai iten kakaku no yakuwari; Nikkei takokuseki kigyo no jitsumu. Ueno Susumu (ed.), *Nihon no takokuseki kigyo no kanri kaikei jitsumu; Yuso shitsumon hyo chosa karano chiken*, Zeimu Keiri Kyokai, pp. 39–52.

Shimizu, T. (1994) (in Japanese). Management accounting practices among Japanese Mnes: Findings from a mail Questionnaire survey. *Asahi Business Review* 9(1): 129–140.

Shimizu, T. (1999) (in Japanese). The investigation of performance evaluation and transfer pricing in multinational enterprises. *The Waseda Commercial Review* 381: 93–117.

Solomons, D. (1965). *Divisional Performance: Measurement and Control*, New York: Financial Executives Research Foundations, Inc; Reprinted, 1983, New York: Markus Wiener Publishing.

Tang, R. Y. W. (1979). *Transfer Pricing Practices in the United States and Japan*. New York: Praeger Publishers.

Tang, R. Y. W. (1990). Transfer pricing in the 1990s. *Management Accounting* 50(1): 22–26.

Tang, R. Y. W. (2002). *Current Trends and Corporate Cases in Transfer Pricing*, Westport: Quorum Books.

Umeda, K. (2012) (in Japanese). Research on international transfer pricing practices in Japanese multinational enterprises. *The Journal of Management Accounting* 20(2): 63–77. Japan Cost Accounting Association.

Umeda, K. (2013) (in Japanese). The effect of transfer pricing taxation on foreign subsidiaries decentralization. *The Journal of Cost Accounting Research* 37(2): 170–181. The Japanese Association of Management Accounting.

Yanai, K. (1999) (in Japanese). *The Theory of Transfer Pricing Legislation*, Chuokeizai-Sha, Inc.

Economic Analysis of Strategy Risk and Transaction Cost: The Case of an Air Transportation Company

Chiungfeng Ko

Associate Professor, Department of Accounting, Business School
Soochow University, Taiwan

1. Introduction

The Organisation for Economic Cooperation and Development (OECD) classifies the Aviation Industry as a high-technology sector producing high-technology products, based on the high level of investment in R&D in the industry (OECD, 2011).

The Airline Industry is part of the aviation industry, and is a system of transportation that provides scheduled flights for passengers or goods. The aviation industry is a labor-intensive, technology-intensive, and capital-intensive industry. However, to cope with the huge capital expenditure, most airline companies use credit, resulting in a high debt ratio. Chang *et al.* (2010) concluded that the average debt ratio in the airline industry is higher than that of domestic listed companies.

The airline industry not only has the characteristics of high investment and slow return, but also has high operating expenses. In addition, air fares are not determined by the market; the price is limited by government regulation. This results in thin profit margins that do not fully reflect the cost of inputs.

Japanese Management and International Studies Vol. 13:
Management of Innovation Strategy in Japanese Companies
World Scientific Publishing Company, September 2016

Moreover, the aviation industry is very sensitive to fluctuations in the economic cycle, and vulnerable to external international events, such as the 9/11 terrorist attacks, the war in Iraq, SARS, H1N1, and financial crises. In other words, the aviation industry has high investment, high debt, a high level of regulation, and is vulnerable to the global economic environment.

Accordingly, the aviation industry faces a high level of risk, including strategy risk, financial risk, supply chain risk, and operational risk. Ko and Sha's (2010) analysis of financial data of the aviation industry found that indices of efficiency, safety, and liquidity can be used as indicators for the management of financial risk.

Airline companies typically possess the following features: first, demand is influenced by external factors. Second, fixed cost, rigid underlying cost structures account for a major percentage of total costs. Thirdly, there is strong price competition. Under liberalization and deregulation in Asia and the Middle East, the air transport industry faces downward pressure on revenue growth. Moreover, the increase of low-cost airlines (LCC) has also greatly affected the earnings of existing airlines.

Accordingly, airlines must revise their competitive strategies. Jeng and Su (2013) suggest airlines should consider adopting a low-cost carrier business model as well as focusing on flights to regions not served by High Speed Rail (HSR), and incorporate its services into their networks as hubs to complement and substitute for short-distance aircraft services.

In this paper, I will discuss the causes for the failure of innovation projects in the air transportation company. The reasons for failure will be analyzed in accordance with transaction cost theory, and the appropriateness and efficiency of organizational governance and investment decision processes will also be discussed. The study is expected to expand the breadth of aviation industry research, and also to extend the fields of organizational behavior and financial management so that market participants can fully understand the industry's operating and financial position. Finally, the study will investigate other innovations and reforms in the industry, how bankruptcy may be eliminated, and how to make the industry competitive once again.

Hobcraft (2012) concluded that the three main reasons for failure are (1) unrealistic prospects from top management regarding resources and the time really required in reaching innovation, (2) the lack of resources allocated in terms of budget, people, and infrastructure, and (3) far too much effort on products and technology, and ignoring the other alternatives within innovation, such as service, business model, platform collaborations, etc.

2. Literature review

2.1. *Transaction cost economics*

Transaction cost economics (TCE) has become one of the most influential and controversial theoretical perspectives in organizational and strategy research (Coase, 1937; Williamson, 1975, 1985). Williamson (1975, 1985) examines directly the question of how firms efficiently develop capability. Transaction cost logic argues that the activities are internalized when the cost of governing the activity through the market exceeds the cost of governing it within the internal hierarchy of the firm.

Coase (1937) indicates that within a firm, market transactions are eliminated, and in place of the varied market structure with exchange transactions is substituted with the entrepreneur, who directs production.

The determinants of transaction cost are frequency, specificity, uncertainty, bounded rationality, and opportunistic behavior.

The key characteristics of TCE are as follows: (1) the transaction is the basic economic activity; (2) for transactions within the market or alternative organization, the important factors include transaction frequency, transaction uncertainty, asset specificity, etc.; (3) transaction costs differ according to individual structural differences of the various forms of organization; (4) different organizations have different contractual forms, but the transactions cost carried out by the internal organization are relatively low compared to those of market mechanism; (5) with changes in the institutional environment, the transaction costs will also change (Koyama and Tezuka, 2003).

Transaction costs include costs that arise with respect to searching cost, information cost, negotiating cost, contracting cost, monitoring cost, and enforcement cost.

According to Williamson (2009), the transaction is made the basic unit of analysis and is thereafter divided into different dimensions with emphasis on asset specificity, contractual disturbances (uncertainty), and frequency. Asset specificity is one source of transaction costs, and is defined as the extent to which the investments made to support a particular transaction have a higher value to that transaction than they would have if they were redeployed for any other purpose. Williamson (1983) identified four dimensions of asset specificity, i.e. Site specificity, Physical asset specificity, Human asset specificity, and Dedicated asset specificity.

According to the International Civil Aviation Organization (ICAO) analysis, the costs of aviation are divided into direct operating costs and indirect operating costs.

In addition, according to the analysis of Taipei Airlines Association, the domestic air transport operating costs are divided into four categories, namely: direct variable costs, direct fixed costs, indirect operating costs, and financial charges. Direct variable costs can be subdivided into flight crew costs, fuel costs, flight attendant costs, direct repair costs, direct service ground station and transport costs, and direct passenger service charges. Direct fixed costs include: aircraft insurance, depreciation, and rentals. Indirect operating costs include indirect repair costs, indirect costs of the ground station and transport services, indirect passenger services costs, operating expenses, and management fees. Financial charges include interest expense, etc. (Chang, 2008).

2.2. Review of aviation industry risks

Airline operators are faced with diverse and challenging risks that can affect daily operation. These include strategic risks such as supply volatility, fuel prices, and factors influencing public image, and also operational risks such as health and safety, dangerous goods handling, environmental hazard management, and security and disaster recovery planning. Zea (2002) divides the aviation industry risks into four categories, these being strategic risks, operational risks, hazard risks, and financial risks. Zea (2002) showed that the strategic risk to the company caused the greatest loss, followed by the financial risk. The Finnair Executive Committee (2013) conducted its own risk assessment and concluded that risk factors include business environment risk, process risk, and information risk. Some of these processes are also security-related risks, such as human resources, namely, personnel recruitment, training, and management.

Beaver (1966) and Altman (1968) constructed an enterprise financial crisis model in the 1960s. Related research methods principally utilize financial variables, including single variable, multivariate analysis, logit model, probit model, and other methods (Beaver, 1966; Altman, 1983; Zea, 2002).

In contrast, Argyres and Zenger (2008) contend that capabilities and transaction cost determinants interact with each other dynamically, and that the two theories of the firm cannot be conceptually separated.

3. Case Study

The Aviation Industry has become increasingly complex with advances in technology, training, and safety. Following the implementation of the open skies policy in 1987, Taiwan civil aviation grew at an average rate of 20% for the first decade. However, since highway and intercity traffic systems become better developed, especially after the HSR started operation in January 2007, Taiwan's civil aviation industry has faced a severe competitive environment.

The domestic air travel market fell as the Taiwan HSR absorbed demand, and oil price rose to a record high. The market scale declined from approximately 3 billion NT dollars a year to 1 billion NT Dollars.

The first domestic airline to experience a financial crisis was Far Eastern Air Transport, which will be referred to here as FAT. FAT was established in 1957 and started operations in November 1957. It originally focused on charter flights until the introduction of scheduled services in January 1965. For the next 30 years, this carrier was the No. 1 brand in Taiwanese domestic routes and was granted the right to fly regular international flights in 1996, from Kaohsiung International Airport to Palau and Subic Bay.

In 1997, it accounted for 34.26% of the domestic market. The company began official international scheduled flights in January 1997, and in December 19, 1997 began official OTC stock trading. It started cargo operations in the Asian region in 2004. The airline had 1,220 employees (in March 2007). Beginning in 2004, FAT invested in the Cambodian airline, Angkor Airways.[1] Angkor Airways subsequently shut down flight operations on May 9, 2009.

Due to ever-rising fuel prices and Taiwan High Speed Rail's inauguration, the airline began suffering financial losses from early 2007, and the

---

[1] Angkor Airways Corporation is a now-defunct airline based in Phnom Penh, Cambodia. This carrier started service in 2004 and received substantial investment from Taiwan's Far Eastern Air Transport (FAT) as its subsidiary to make use of the Angkor International Airport in Siem Reap as its hub and as a fast transit station between Taiwan and People's Republic of China (as direct flights between the two locations were previously banned due to the political status of Taiwan). At the same time, it also operated some charter flights in the East Asia and Southeast Asia region. Its entire fleet was wet leased from FAT. Following a chain of financial crises in its parent FAT, on May 9, 2008 Angkor Airways Corporation ceased all operations due to financial issues.

situation was seriously worsened by poor financial management and risky investments. On February 13, 2008, the airline failed to pay the US$848,000 it owed to the International Clearing House, a financial subsidiary of IATA, and IATA cancelled the airline's membership as a result. After a chain of financial crises broke out in early 2008, the airline publicly announced its bankruptcy and stopped all flights on and beyond May 13, 2008. The airline stopped paying employee salaries, but the staff remained on duty from May 2008 because they wanted to try to save the company. After reorganization, the airline restarted its services on April 18, 2011. It now has a total fleet of seven aircraft, serving 29 cities worldwide.

3.1. Organization structure

Over 50% of the airline shares were acquired by A1 company and A2 holding company in 1995. According to data collected by the end of 1998, the company's major shareholders consisted of A1 Development Company, A7 Bermuda Investment and Development Corporation, A3 Airline, A2 Company, and the family of the founder's holdings. In other words, the patterns of the company's organizational structure did not change much during this period, and the effect of such changes on related transaction costs were not great. However, personnel changes in important managerial positions resulted in changes in decision-making, greatly influencing trading decisions and costs.

The major decision-makers in the company were N2 and N4, who have a venture capital professional background. N2 has served as a general manager of a well-known development company, and chairman of a development bank. In 1995, after joining the board as the legal representative of A1 Company, he was elected as chairman. He immediately made a "financial transformation" plan, set out large purchases of new aircraft and a foreign investment plan. Part of this plan was for FAT to make significant investment in subsidiary companies.

Tables 1–4 present the investment information for subsidiaries. As we can see, S2–S10 were founded during 1996–1998. As the parent company, FAT holds a 99.99% stake in most subsidiaries, except for S8 and S11. In contrast, each subsidiary's holdings of the parent company's shares amount to only 0.62–3% for a total of 11.75%. This cross-holding situation allowed

Table 1. Table of personnel changes for the airline company

Company name, representative code	Share holding ratio (%) 1997	Board position changes by year					Share holding ratio (%) 2005
		1997	2000	2001	2004	2005	
S6 investing co.	1.35	Chairman N1	Director	Director	—	—	—
A1 company; Representative N2 N3	13.14		Director and Supervisor				13.14
A2 company; Representative N4	4.66	Vice Chairman	Chairman	—	—	—	—
Individual stockholder N4	—	—	—	Chairman	Chairman	Chairman	0.03
A3	9.32	Director	Director	—	Director	Director	7.61
S5 investing co.; Representative N5	1.53	Director	Vice Chairman	Vice Chairman	Vice Chairman	Vice Chairman	11.79
A4 company; Representative N6	1.29	Supervisor	Supervisor	Director	Supervisor	Supervisor	1.29
A5 company; Representative N7	0.41	Supervisor	—	—	—	—	—
A6 company; Representative N7	—	—	—	Supervisor	Supervisor	Supervisor	0.41
A7 Bermuda Investment and Development Co.	12.43	Large stockholder	Large stockholder	Director	Director	Director	12.42

Source: Footnotes and supplement tables of annual financial reports, 1997–2005.

the unchallenged rotation of board members, which took effect upon approval at a board meeting.

3.2. *Aircraft capital expenditures*

The first innovation strategy used was to target the opportunity of direct cross-Taiwan Straits flights. To cope with the robust growth in domestic and international scheduled flights, as well as to replace old aircraft, on October 29, 1997, the company signed a contract with Boeing for five new 757-200 aircraft, which would be delivered in December 1998, July 1999, December 1999, and January 2000, respectively. The total amount for the purchase was US$331 million, of which the total cost of the first two aircraft was US$105 million. Besides, the company signed another agreement with the

Table 2.   Details of aircrafts purchases (in thousands of US dollars)

No.	Date	Type	Manufacturer	Amount	Note
P1	1997/10/29	757-200	Boeing	104,707	Delivered on 1998/12/24
P2	1997/10/29	757-200	Boeing		Delivered on 1998/12/24
P3	1997/10/29	757-200	Boeing	200,451	Delivered on 1999/7/8
P4	1997/10/29	757-200	Boeing		Delivered on 1999/12/22
P5	1997/10/29	757-200	Boeing	43,994	Delivered on 2000/1/27
P6	1997/10/29	757-200	Boeing	Option	Option premium was US$350,000 per
P7	1997/10/29	757-200	Boeing	Aircraft	aircraft, with rights given up in 2000
P8	1997/10/29	757-200	Boeing		
P9	1997/10/29	757-200	Boeing		Delivered in 2003/1
P10	1997/12/1	MD-83	McDonnell Douglas	57,235	Delivered in 1998/1
P11	1997/12/1	MD-83	McDonnell Douglas		Delivered in 1998/2
P12	1999/12	757-200	ERA AVIATION	53,660	Down payment US$11.58 million, the remainder divided into 48 payments of US$877,000 each
P13	2000/1/27	757-200	ERA AVIATION	43,994	Down payment US$2.152 million, the remainder divided into 48 payments of US$877,000 each

Source: Footnotes and supplement tables of annual financial reports, 1997–2000.

Boeing company for four purchase options on 757-200 (Option Aircraft), with US$350,000 for each right, and the planes to be delivered between January 2001 and January 2003. However, three of the four rights were given up in 2000, resulting in a total loss to the company of US$1.05 million. In addition, FAT also bought two MD-83 aircraft from Macdonald Douglas on December 1, 1997, worth US$57 million, to expand its fleet. In short, including the purchase option, the company signed up to buy 11 aircraft in 1997, of which seven planes were ordered and the remaining four were optioned.

The Board's decision to expand the fleet by leveraged financing may have been the underlying cause of the company's financial crisis. The orders, collectively the biggest in FAT's history, came as the airline aimed to expand its international presence. The company had to pay for the order of over US$323 million in three years. In response to the above-mentioned major capital expenditures, the company traded off 15 aircraft to other operators between 1996 and 1999. For example, FAT sold six Boeing 737 aircraft to EASCO in 1996, six MD to Grand Capital Intl 'Ltd., Meridiana Airlines and Worldwide Leasing Enterprises Inc. respectively in 1998, and three Boeing 737 to PT Airfast Indonesia and Boeing Capital Corporation in 1999.

Table 3.   Details of aircrafts proposal (in thousands of NT dollars)

No.	Year	Type	Trading partners	Gain/Loss	Note
SP1	1998	MD-28007	Grand Capital Intl' Ltd.	503,677	Sale and leaseback 24 months
SP2	1998	MD-28011	Grand Capital Intl' Ltd.		
SP3	1998	MD	Meridiana Airline	114,732	Delivered in 1998/5
SP4	1998	MD	Spirit Airline	148,391	Delivered in 1998/7
SP5	1998	MD	Worldwide Leasing Enterprises Inc.	430,456	Delivered in 1998/8
SP6	1998	MD	Worldwide Leasing Enterprises Inc.		Delivered in 1998/9
SP7	1996	Boeing 737	EASCO	8,755	Delivered in 1996
SP8	1996	Boeing 737	EASCO		
SP9	1996	Boeing 737	EASCO		
SP10	1996	Boeing 737	EASCO		
SP11	1996	Boeing 737	EASCO	18,341	Delivered in 1997/4
SP12	1996	Boeing 737	EASCO		Delivered in 1997/10
SP13	1999	Boeing 737	PT AIRFAST INDONESIA	101,502	
SP14	1999	Boeing 737	PT AIRFAST INDONESIA		
SP15	1999	Boeing 737	WEL 27203 INC	29,872	
SP16	2000	Boeing 737	Boeing Capital Corporation	162,724	Sale and leaseback 60 months

Source: Footnotes and supplement tables of annual financial reports, 1997–2000.

3.3. Long-term Investments

Dazzled by the prospects offered by investments outside the core business, the company invested significant assets in this area, which subsequently resulted in the rapid deterioration of their financial position. According to information from TEJ (Taiwan Economic Journal, TEJ) database, FAT invested in over 10 entities between 1996 and 1998. Most of its investments in subsidiaries were in equity, and the company exercised significant influence on the investees' operating and financial policy decisions. The total amount of accumulated outflow of investments was equivalent to its issued capital.

The development of cross-holding let the board of director have sufficient control on the investment and finance decisions. However, as investment activities are not part of the aviation business for an air transport

Table 4. Gains and losses for non-operating investments (in thousands of New Taiwan dollars)

Year	Ratio of funds and investments over assets	Long-term investments unrealized losses	Losses on valuation of listed stocks	Gain (losses) on valuation of investments	Losses on sale of investments	Impairment losses	Subtotal
1997	12.92%			10,399			10,399
1998	25.89%	–526,756	–19,132	–224,069			–769,984
1999	22.99%	–896,084	–40,995	–157,867			–1,094,946
2000	25.27%	–937,975	–47,619	272,971			–712,623
2001	19.58%	–1,747,523	–21,807	–273,448			–2,042,778
2002	17.88%	–1,812,528	–20,210	–256,855			–2,089,593
2003	20.21%	–174,144	–13,091	161,958			–25,277
2004	21.81%	–1,767,720	-	–64,356			–1,832,076
2005	18.77%	–1,757,940		–58,592			–1,816,532
2006	12.13%	–1,718,749		–114,394			–1,833,143
2007	4.79%			118,641	–1,881,571	–2,01,7554	–3,780,484
2008	4.92%			28,710	39,499	127,699	–138,488

company, the deviation from the core business resulted in the company suffering major investment losses.

Eager to resume flights, in mid-June FAT asked more than 80 of its staff to report for work, paying them 80% of their salaries until such time as flights were resumed. Many of its staff remained at work for several months, making use of every chance to save the company. Meanwhile, the airline received a court order after three months, allowing it to initiate a restructuring plan.

4. Analysis results

This paper provides a set of results about the common cause of innovation failure. The three main reasons for failure have been given as (1) unrealistic expectations from top management regarding the opportunity of direct cross-Taiwan Strait flights, which resulted in (2) the decisions to expand fleet by leveraged financing, and (3) far too much focus on investments outside the core industry and ignoring other options for innovation. I have no doubt that each of these failures is a high-level management failure. The high-level management of the company did not have a real understanding of the complexity of innovation, and starved it on essential resources. Equally, not to explore all the types of innovation available does not make sound business sense.

4.1. Organization Structure

FAT announced the cessation of all operations beginning May 13, 2008, just before the financial tsunami, when the global economy was in unprecedented prosperity. How can the management be leaders of organizations, claiming they are keen to grow and expand, if they do not get fully involved in providing the appropriate framework for innovation to thrive? This is a failure of strategic leadership.

In the first decade of the 21st century, due to ongoing privatization and the liberalization of air services, the local airline industry entered a new era of competitiveness. The airline intended to fly into some emerging markets such as China, because of their rapid economic growth and strong potential. This was a significant opportunity, and could have had a lasting impact. From the viewpoint of organization theory, the high density of the airlines eager to launch cross-strait flights and routes, which may have produced a load factor increase and contributed to higher passenger revenue for FAT.

From the perspective of resource dependence, the organization's survival depends on whether the operation can muster the necessary resources. For FAT, aircraft were an essential resource for charter passenger and cargo flights. However, with the increase in the number of aircraft, the direct operating costs such as flight costs, repair parts costs, depreciation costs, and debt servicing costs increase dramatically.

However, with an expansion of the business scale, if the increased frequency does not produce a sufficient increase in load factor, this could lead to overcapacity. Coupled with this, the result of competition in terms of airfares would compress profit margins. The average load factor of FAT was 59.44% from 1998 to 2001, slightly higher than the industry average of 59.15% at the same period. In other words, though FAT was committed to improving service quality by converting old aircraft into freight-carriers and replacing them with new aircraft, the outcome was only the maintenance of its market share, and it did not bring the expected significant benefits.

4.2. Aircraft Capital expenditures

Asset specificity is an important factor affecting transaction costs. When the transactions concern goods or personnel with a specific purpose, such assets are difficult to replace with other assets. Thus, the value of assets other than the specific assets will be forced to decrease. The change of operating revenue from 1996 to 2008 is detailed in Table 5. On average, during these years, its operating costs increased slightly, but net income decreased sharply. In addition, the increase in operating expenses and non-operating losses grew by 14.95% and 67.33%, respectively, due to higher loss assessments of financial assets.

Frequent fluctuations in fuel prices and the global economic situation also significantly increased operating risks for the company. The company's strategy was to increase revenues, so it began to operate international services to Southeast Asia, South Korea, and Palau. In order to make up international scheduled routes, the company upgraded its internet reservation system to cope with demand for international passengers, thus increasing FAT's costs. As the introduction of the HSR system caused the air transport market to shrink, the company struggled to increase load factor, but finally it could not maintain its passenger numbers, nor could it avoid downward trend in fare price.

Table 5. Percentage change of operating revenue and expenses (1996–2008)

	1996	1997	1998	1999	2000	2002	2004	2006	2007	2008	Average	Standard deviation
Operating revenue	−6.34	2.81	−5.96	5.48	16.40	4.50	20.95	10.13	−7.71	−77.52	−4.16	24.02
Operating cost	15.76	5.03	7.14	−1.37	11.98	8.96	12.17	6.62	7.59	−50.86	1.62	16.87
Gross profit	−49.83	−7.29	−73.39	147.51	52.87	−37.84	622.09	108.70	−227.34	245.85	46.72	209.65
Operating expenses	7.04	−0.77	6.98	−3.64	−11.54	−21.37	14.61	−3.54	212.79	−8.65	14.95	60.46
Operating income	−78.78	−24.04	−343.09	−75.71	−324.44	308.53	−131.40	−80.87	3521.26	58.63	191.62	1020.67
Non-operating income	79.51	12.39	92.88	−79.73	80.72	3.90	−48.76	−2.03	96.70	−55.41	13.11	60.46
Non-operating loss	−35.61	−3.87	113.12	14.71	−4.29	−57.51	0.78	41.88	838.00	−81.95	67.33	238.28
Net income	−42.85	0.74	−67.25	−352.56	−117.83	−61.71	−115.32	−28.18	1579.65	−29.95	−198.25	793.78

Source: Footnotes and supplement tables of annual financial reports, 1996–2008.

4.3. Long-term Investments

Since 1996, more than a dozen of subsidiaries were set up by FAT. Most of these focused on investing-oriented activities. This was closely related to the professional background of the top managers and the board members, and this shows that the core members of the organization had common conceptions in running operation for the company, conceptions which were often not directly related to the airline's core business. It also shows that a small number of key people on the board had taken strong control of the enterprise, and expanded investment to fully utilize the resources of the company in areas not related to the core business of the company. As a result of this, cross-holding and overinvestment resulted in transaction uncertainty.

From a business strategy perspective, the merger may be able to alleviate the short-term financial problems of the company, but those issues such as market complementarity, strategy schemes, dispersed ownership, aviation fleet, claims processing, etc. may have increased transaction cost at each step. In response to rocketing fuel prices and the threat of the HSR, other domestic airlines strived to enhance their quality and improve cost control. In contrast to FAT, CAL (China Airlines) has unveiled a long-term "Commitment to Excellence and Reliability," during the past few years. To fulfill this vision, nine strategies were implemented, and innovative management was achieved by carefully examining and executing their annual operational plans.

4.4. Reviving Innovation

FAT resumed operations on April 4, 2011, following its reorganization. On October 31, the carrier launched 10 new routes to China with McDonnell Douglas DC-9-83s. Since being allowed to resume services, the carrier has been approved by the aviation authorities to provide a total of 19 cross-strait flights using the six airplanes in its fleet that have been certified safe by the authorities.

In addition to the cross-strait flights, FAT provides regular flights to Angkor in Cambodia, while offering charter flights to Cebu in the Philippines and Da Nang in Vietnam. The carrier also provides domestic flights to the outlying Taiwan-controlled islands of Kinmen and Penghu.

The general manager and chairman, Kang-Wei Chang, participates in the company's various planning decisions and plans all operating details of the company. Chang is known for his involvement in the construction business, and looks at the company from a different perspective to the previous leadership. In a short time, he has mastered the aviation business know-how, and then combined this with his cross-industry experience. The airline has drawn up a "model flight attendants" service strategy, and has selected kind, friendly, service-oriented flight attendants to place an emphasis on service quality. This strategy has proved popular among passengers.

Chang continues the operating philosophy of the airline as a "Tour Factory," expanding the scale of operations, aiming at passengers traveling around the Asian regional routes of under six hours. This involves combining the group's resources to construct hotels and other tourist facilities to establish the so called "one-stop shop" for tours (Kuo, 2013).

The company has begun to purchase new aircraft, rather than leasing, and has simplified operations by using one type of aircraft to control the maintenance operating costs. Meanwhile, FAT has also become quite well known in the domestic aircraft maintenance business. Not only does it have many seasoned veterans in maintenance, the company itself also has a variety of domestic and international service licenses, and all of these are important intangible assets.

As this carrier was the No. 1 brand in Taiwanese domestic routes for many years, and has continued to support residents of outlying islands with its services, passenger domestic load factor has been maintained at an average of 70–80%.

5. Conclusions

After analysis, this study makes the following conclusions.

(1) The consequences of cross-holdings not only result in the lack of a clear separation of corporate operation and ownership, they also encourage the tendency for the board to become more internalized and insular, resulting in an increased tendency to engage in risky investments, increased transaction uncertainty, and increasing the risk of financial crisis.

(2) Business that devotes a large amount of capital expenditure to replacing older aircraft may only achieve the maintenance of current market share, and can expect few other benefits.

(3) In the face of intense competition, enterprises that try to use a cash flow-increase strategy may actually increase their costs. In contrast, cost control is a more effective viable strategy.

(4) The perils of the traditional airline business model in recent decades have been short-term thinking, destructive decision-making, and poor employee relations. Over the years, the airline industry has been eager to pursue revenue and business growth, tending to ignore the assessment and control of investment strategy, which could result in innovation failure.

(5) The company has learned from experience and realized that, with the right culture and values and the right people, including directors with diverse expertise who can form effective strategies, it can break away from his competitors.

References

Altman, E. I. (1968). Financial ratios, discriminant analysis and the prediction of corporate bankruptcy. *Journal of Finance* 23(4): 589–609.

Altman, E. I. (1983). *Corporate Financial Distress: A Complete Guide to Predicting, Avoiding and Dealing with Bankruptcy*. John Wiley & Sons, New York.

Argyres, N. and T. Zenger (2008). Capabilities, Transaction Costs, and Firm Boundaries: A Dynamic Perspective and Integration. *Working Paper*. School of Management, Boston University.

Beaver, W. H. (1966). Financial ratios as predictors of failure. *Journal of Accounting Research* 4: 71–111.

Chang, D. C., C. F. Ko, and Y. C. Chuang (2010). Research on financial supervision mechanism of national airlines, Civil Aeronautics Administration, Ministry of Transportation and Communications (in Chinese).

Chang, Y. H. (2008). Management and administration for aviation. 2nd edition, Hwa Tai Publishing (in Chinese).

Coase, R. H. (1937), The Nature of the Firm. *Economica* (New Series) 4(16): 386–405.

Hobcraft, P. (2012). Innovation failure starts at the top. Available from http://paul4 innovating.com/2012/12/07/innovation-failure-starts-at-the-top/. Accessed June 5, 2015.

Jeng, C. R. and C. H. Su (2013). The predicament of domestic airline service after the introduction of Taiwan high-speed rail. *Transportation Journal* 52(1): 134–143, Published by: Penn State University Press, Stable URL: http://www.jstor.org/stable/10.5325/transportationj.52.1.0134

Ko, C. F. and Y. C. Sha (2010). Discussion on financial risk indicators for aviation industry. 2010 Conference on Cross-Strait and East Asia Finance and Economics, Taipei (in Chinese).

Koyama, A. and K. Tezuka (2003). Economic analysis of the Allfinanzstrategie (2) — from the point of view of the economics of organizations. Research Paper of the Japan Securities Scholarship Foundation (in Japanese).

Kuo, M. (2013). From "Chang boldly" of the construction industry to the "savior" of the Far Eastern, Airway, No. 193 (in Chinese). Available from http://124.9.6.242/Press/newsshow.aspx?id=469. Accessed June 1, 2015.

OECD, Directorate for Science, Technology and Industry (2011). ISIC REV. 3 Technology Intensity Definition, OECD Economic Analysis and Statistics Division.

Williamson, Oliver E. (1975). Markets and hierarchies: Analysis and antitrust implications. New York: Free Press.

Williamson, Oliver E. (1983). Credible commitments: Using hostages to support exchange. *American Economic Review* 73(4): 519–538.

Williamson, Oliver E. (1985). The economic institutions of capitalism: Firms, markets, relational contracting. *Administrative Science Quarterly* 32(4): 602–605.

Williamson, Oliver E. (2009). Transaction cost economics: An overview. Available from https://organizationsandmarkets.files.wordpress.com/2009/09/williamson-o-transaction-cost-economics-an-overview.pdf. Accessed June 5, 2015.

Zea, M. (2002). Is airline risk manageable? *Airline Business,* pp. 68–70.

Index